# The Military, Militarism, and the Polity

# The Military, Militarism, and the Polity

## Essays in Honor of Morris Janowitz

EDITED BY

Michel Louis Martin
and
Ellen Stern McCrate

THE FREE PRESS
*A Division of Macmillan, Inc.*
NEW YORK

Collier Macmillan Publishers
LONDON

The Free Press
A Division of Macmillan, Inc.
866 Third Avenue, New York, N.Y. 10022

Collier Macmillan Canada, Inc.

Printed in the United States of America

printing number

1    2    3    4    5    6    7    8    9    10

**Library of Congress Cataloging in Publication Data**

Main Entry under title:

The Military, militarism, and the polity.

Bibliography: p.
Includes index.
1. Sociology, Military—Addresses, essays, lectures.
2. Janowitz, Morris—Addresses, essays, lectures.
I. Martin, Michel L.   II. McCrate, Ellen Stern.
III. Janowitz, Morris.
U21.5.M498   1984          306'.27          83-48763
ISBN 0-02-920190-X

# Contents

# Preface

The present collection of essays is a tribute to Morris Janowitz for his seminal contribution to the study of the military and more especially to the development and the academic dignity of this area of intellectual pursuit. It is not a *Festschrift* proper but rather marks twenty-five years of scholarship devoted to the analysis of the military as well as a whole era in the institutional history of the Inter-University Seminar on Armed Forces and Society which Morris Janowitz founded, nurtured, and presided over.

This collection was prepared with the collaboration of a few of Morris Janowitz's "old" American and foreign colleagues and friends who partook in this scholarly adventure. These few also performed a symbolic role as they speak for all those who were drawn in increasing number to military studies by the personality and the scholarship of Morris Janowitz.

Though each of the papers seeks to enrich or to explicate existing knowledge in the field, the collection as a whole has no pretense at demonstrating any particular thesis; the plan adopted thence is intended only to facilitate the presentation. The reader, therefore, should not expect any conceptual or thematic unity. Yet the very variety of the essays and the range of questions to which they are addressed reveal something of the breadth of the field, with all of its interdisciplinary implications—a comprehensiveness that Morris Janowitz's own work reflects and which he has always sought to instill in the researcher's mind.

The editors wish to express their gratitude to the various contributors for what has been an enthusiastic collaboration and to express, also, their regrets for not having been able to include the many papers that were offered. The editors also called upon the help of others for which they express their appreciation, in particular to Jeremiah Kaplan, Charles E. Smith, Joyce Seltzer, and Eileen DeWald of Macmillan Publishing Company and The Free Press for their interest in this project, and to the members of the IUS at the University of Chicago for their assistance.

M. L. M. and E. S. M.

# Editors and Contributors

MAURY D. FELD, an early associate of the IUS, is with the Littauer Library of Harvard University. He is the author of many articles on military history and *The Structure of Violence* (1977).

NANCY LORING GOLDMAN is a research sociologist with the Inter-University Seminar on Armed Forces and Society, serves as the Secretary/Treasurer of the IUS, and is the editor of *Female Soldiers: Combatants or Non-Combatants* (1982).

GWYN HARRIES-JENKINS is director of the Department of Adult Education at the University of Hull, England, and is the author of *The Army in Victorian Society* (1977) and the editor of *The Military and the Problem of Legitimacy* (1978). Mr. Harries-Jenkins is an Associate Chairman of the IUS.

KURT LANG, professor of sociology at State University of New York, Stonybrook, is one of the original scholars in the field of military sociology and has authored numerous articles in this field. He is the author of *Military Institutions and the Sociology of War* (1972) and *Military Sociology: 1963–1969* (1971).

MOSHE LISSAK, professor of sociology at Hebrew University, is among the founders of the Inter-University Seminar on Armed Forces and Society with Morris Janowitz in the 1960s and is the author of *Military Roles in Modernization*.

JOHN LOVELL, professor of political science at Indiana University, is the author of *New Civil-Military Relations* (1974) and *Neither Athens Nor Sparta: The*

*United States Military Academy in Transition* (1979) and is one of the early participants in the IUS.

*CHARLES C. MOSKOS, JR.*, is professor of sociology at Northwestern University and is a leading authority on the state of the American army in the post-Vietnam period. He is the author of *Peace Soldiers: The Sociology of a United Nations Military Force* (1976) and *The American Enlisted Man* (1970) and is an Associate Chairman of the IUS.

*SAM C. SARKESIAN*, current Chairman of the IUS, is professor of political science at Loyola University of Chicago and a retired army colonel. He is the editor of *The Military-Industrial Complex* (1972) and author of *The Professional Army Officer in a Changing Society* (1974).

*DAVID R. SEGAL*, a former student of Morris Janowitz at the University of Chicago, teaches sociology and political science at the University of Maryland. He is the editor of *Society and Politics: Diversity, Uniformity, and Modern Democracy* and many articles on military issues. He is the editor of *Armed Forces and Society*, the IUS quarterly.

*JACQUES VAN DOORN*, professor of sociology at Erasmus Universiteit, The Netherlands, is an early contributor to the field of military sociology and is the author of many books and articles in this field, including *The Soldier and Social Change* (1975) and the editor of *Military Profession and Military Regimes* (1969).

*WILFRIED VON BREDOW* is professor of political science at Philipps-Universität, Marburg, West Germany, and the author of many articles on military sciences. He recently completed a book on the redefinition of militarism.

*MICHEL LOUIS MARTIN* is professor of law and political sociology at the Institut d'Etudes Politiques at the University of Toulouse, France, and is a visiting scholar at the University of Chicago. He has written extensively on African politics, the French military, and the development of the sociology of military studies in France and the United States. He is an Associate Chairman of the IUS and with the editorial board of *Armed Forces and Society*.

*ELLEN STERN McCRATE* was Executive Secretary of the IUS from 1974 to 1979 and edited *The Limits of Military Intervention* (1977). She worked with The Free Press in New York City and presently lives in Durham, North Carolina.

# Of Arms and the Man : A Short Intellectual History of Morris Janowitz's Contribution to the Sociology of the Military

MICHEL L. MARTIN

It is a fact, though difficult to appreciate, given its central place in man's history, that only recently has *res militaris* become the object of an orderly and systematic investigation. This was particularly true in America. Until two decades ago the state of scholarship on war, armies, and militarism irresistably reminded one of Borges' *trouvaille*, that Chinese encyclopedia of fauna wherein animals are classified into those belonging to the emperor, those stuffed and tamed, piglets, mermaids, and fabulous beasts. Military studies consisted of scattered writings in which myopic applied research and trivia eclipsed the precious few findings of lasting worth. No conceptual or thematic unity, nor any consistent framework

I wish to record here my appreciation to Mrs. Gayle Janowitz who provided me with many valuable biographical insights and to Mr. Douglas Sharps for his editorial skills.

for comparative analysis had been developed. Particularly striking was the fact that the military reality was conceived—often with little objectivity—as a distinct category removed from its parent social constellation.

The area was dominated by non-academic specialists, military professionals in particular, of whom only a handful made valuable contributions: Colonel Edward L. Munson, with *Management of Men*, and Brig. Gen. S. L. A. Marshall, with *Men Against Fire*, are two cases in point. In the academic world, social scientists who dealt with the military were rare, and rarer still were innovators. William Graham Sumner, Pitirim Sorokin, and Quincy Wright were the exceptions, and they had been attentive mainly to war. About the military *qua* institution, there were few—although distinguished—analyses. Most of these appeared in the area of military psychology, the classic example being *The American Soldier*. The remaining works are noteworthy as harbingers of a comprehensive view of the field: in them military institutions were treated as a part of the entire play of social relations. The writings of Harold D. Lasswell, Alfred Vagts, Hans Speier, and E. Pendleton Herring in the 1930s deserve special praise, not least because they were so atypical of the scientific production in the social sciences. Until 1960 then, most of military studies was a frontier field which had yet to be settled.

The reasons for this particular situation are too well-known to be rehearsed in depth. Briefly: the geo-political situation of the United States—its relative remoteness from the precincts of armed conflict—and the antagonistic relationship of American values to military norms shaped the initial stages of inquiry. Further, social issues such as industrialization and urbanization which presided over the shaping of emerging social sciences preempted nascent scientific curiosity. What is more, the dominant epistemological postures of sociology at the time—evolutionism and social-Darwinism—assumed that military phenomena were anachronistic residues and dictated their obsolescence in irenic, "modern" society. Adopting the meliorist and liberal amilitary tradition, a secularized version of the humanist persuasion of their forerunners, most social scientists expressed no interest in military affairs and ignored the position of the military in social life. Finally, the military establishment itself saw little advantage in encouraging sociological research (an attitude shared for a long time by the whole federal administration as evidenced by the Bush Report) save in relation to specific applied undertakings, via ad hoc contracts generally struck with in-service or non-academic institutions.

Given this history of neglect, the recent revaluation of the military studies constitutes one remarkable change in the social sciences. And signs of this change are by now quite tangible. One is the growing number of scholars in academic settings who are involved in the study of the military and defense issues; another is the expansion of specialized research centers, the multiplication of journals, and the frequency of intellectual gatherings addressed to these concerns. More decisive, indicative of a genuine academic recognition, is the fact that armies, war, and militarism have been introduced in the teaching syllabi of many universities and even admitted as a legitimate topic of doctoral undertaking.

The growth of the literature is another manifestation of the change. The number and volume of bibliographical material and other research inventories are symptomatic of this affluence, at the quantitative level at least. The increasing monopoly of the scientific mode of inquiry over these issues marks the qualitative dimension of the shift. The fragmented approach has been displaced in favor of a more integrated and inter-displinary outlook. Today, military history is being enriched with socio-political perspectives, while sociological and political analyses draw more heavily on historical, as well as economic and legal material. Most studies now strive for a macroanalytical vision which sees the military reality as a "total phenomenon," in Marcel Mauss's words, inclusive of the parent social configuration. The use of transnational comparisons, without which no genuine knowledge exists, as the late Professor Marc Bloch noted, allows the unveiling of common institutional patterns and the logic of their evolution. All these changes have favored a greater intelligibility of military phenomena, while they have also helped to distinguish the science of military affairs from an intuitive, immediate, and vulgarized military sociology, more or less still in vogue.

Thus, in two decades or so, military phenomena have come to be viewed, within the social scientists' collective *représentations* regarding the content and the boundaries of the discipline, as a set of fundamental categories relevant to the understanding of the nature and dynamic of the society as a whole.

Like any socio-cultural process, this "academic enfranchisement" of the study of the military reality in America is the result of various historical and international circumstances. Because of the ubiquitous threats it poses to human welfare, because of the diffusion and the technological awesomeness involved, because of the subsequent urgency for, as well as the complexity of, its control—in other words, because of its political and social centrality—armed violence has emerged as a paramount issue that the scientific community could not neglect. However, as with any movement of knowledge, this trend is not inexorably determined by materialistic forces alone. Rather, it is also molded by the cognitive undertakings and the will of certain individuals, its "great men," in Jacob Burckhardt's sense, who break away from conventions

and vogues governing movements of knowledge, and fight for the legitimation, academic as well as scientific, of the new object of analysis.

Among these, few have been more widely influential than Morris
Janowitz, now the Lawrence A. Kimpton Distinguished Service Professor
of Sociology at the University of Chicago. His service as a teacher,
intellectual leader, and administrator certainly has played a decisive role
in the institutionalization of what has come to be known today as the
sociology of the military. The extent of his contribution, the creation of
the Inter-University Seminar on Armed Forces and Society, the wide
range of his scholarship and the innovative nature of his approach, are
indeed pivotal.

The purpose of the present introduction is simply to offer a glimpse
into Professor Janowitz's intellectual history, his contribution to military
studies and the rise of that field. These reflections have no pretense to
being exhaustive, much less critical; they certainly will not do sufficient
justice to the richness of his achievements nor to the intricacy of their
logical development. A review of an author's *vita* and work, his bio-
bibliography in other words, is a difficult genre which requires particular
talents and an intimate long-standing knowledge. In the case of Morris
Janowitz, it would be an exasperating exercise given the extent of his
writings and the nature of his personality. He is surely a "mystifying
man" to use the words with which Bruce Lannes Smith qualified Harold
Lasswell who, for that matter, was Morris Janowitz's own mentor. If the
following comments are ventured, it is out of the compelling need to
manifest a disciple's gratitude to a *maître* who greatly influenced and
inspired his own intellectual, if not personal, outlook; after all, he did
turn this Frenchman into a part-time Hyde Parker and a complete "U of
C" sectarian. In any case, others among Morris Janowitz's long-time
colleagues and friends will certainly come along and offer a more rigorous
analysis of his life history and the whole range of his tremendous and still
expanding intellectual undertakings, not only in the area of armed forces
and society, but also and especially, in that of sociological knowledge in
general.

*I*

Morris Janowitz's long-standing awareness of the perennial centrality of
armed violence in the dynamics of society is certainly the primary factor
in the decisiveness of his influence upon the development and orientation of the scholarly study of military affairs. This consciousness itself is
intimately linked with the particulars of his background.

Morris Janowitz was born on 22 October 1919 in Paterson, New Jersey, where he lived until his third year of college. He is the second son of modest income parents who emigrated from Eastern Europe and met in America. His father, Samuel, the youngest son of nine children, came from a poor family of silk-weavers from Lodz. He left for the United States when his older brothers sent for him and their parents, Sarah and Morris Solomon. Samuel Janowitz worked first in one of the crisis-ridden textile factories which made up the rather gloomy decor of Paterson. Morris Janowitz's mother, Rachel Meyerovich, was the daughter of a tailor for the Russian army from Bialystok in Poland. She came to America in 1905, as an escort for a niece, and ended up staying when she realized that the United States would be a safe place for a Jewish mother to raise and educate her children. Changing her name to Rose Meyers, she took a job in a hat design shop for $1.50 per week.

Though seemingly disparate, these pieces of life history are quite instructive for even an amateur biographer. The epoch, the place, and the familial background in which Morris Janowitz grew up are critical and could not but influence the fashioning of his vision of the social world and his perception of its most relevant working variables.

By the 1920s, collective violence had waned compared with what had earlier been, but it had not disappeared. Post-war America entered with "New Era" with a stabilized price level and a booming economy. There was, however, no across-the-board prosperity, and social struggle remained endemic and violent. Editorials in the *American Federationist* and recollections such as Samuel Gompers' *Seventy Years of Life and Labour* are telling in that regard. Recessions struck cyclically, in 1920–22, in 1924, and 1927, before the Great Depression of 1929. Certain sectors of the economy, in addition, were left on the periphery of development, notably agriculture and the coal and textile industries. The number of unemployed workers reached five million in 1920 and afterward fluctuated between half a million and two and a half million. As a result of this situation, and of heightened unionist awareness as well, labor disputes, with their accompanying violence, never ceased. Between 1916 and 1923, for instance, an average of two million workers went on strike, many of which degenerated into clashes with the forces of order. In 1919 alone, 2,665 labor disputes occurred involving more than four million people. Butte, Montana; Bisbee, Arizona; McDowell, Mingo, and Logan counties, West Virginia; Franklin and Poplar Bluff, Missouri; Denver, Colorado, to name a few from a long list, were battlefields of post-war labor history on which men, led by the United Mine Workers of America, the Industrial Workers of the World, and the

National Shopmen's Union confronted the U.S. Army, the National Guard, and local police agencies.

Paterson had a notoriety of its own. With its long legacy of industrial brutality, its vast population of migrant laborers prone to unpredictable outbursts of violence, it contained the social contradictions of American industrial modernization. The general strikes of 1902 and 1913 in the silk mills had been memorable events. The twenty-two-week-long Wobblie-led strike of 1913 spread to Metuchen and Mount Hope, and ended with 2,238 arrests after much bloodshed, prompting John Reed to speak in *Masses* of "War in Paterson?" Though never as severe as those before the Great War, later economic difficulties frequently erupted into sharp crisis, like the furious confrontation that Morris Janowitz, then a boy of seven, witnessed in Passaic where strikebreaking troops were called up to crush a Communist-led demonstration. The Janowitz household was not spared the unmerciful business cycle. Samuel Janowitz eventually acquired his own silk business but was soon bankrupted with the development of synthetic fibers. He and his wife (though a member of a temperance league!) started again with a small liquor store, in which Morris Janowitz lent a hand after school.

As with most East European immigrant groups, which have a strong collective memory of oppression, rebellion, and war, as shown by William I. Thomas and Florian Znaniecki in their masterpiece, *The Polish Peasant in Europe and America,* the experience of violence was an integral part of the Janowitz family's own past. Morris Solomon, the grandfather, had, as a truant officer in a Jewish school, daily witnessed the brutality and corruption of the Russian police—which had to be bribed in order that the school not be shut down. Rachel Meyerovich had an even more active experience of armed rebellion. "My mother was a terrorist," Janowitz likes to banter. She was indeed involved with the Bund, the Polish branch of the Socialist revolution of the early 1900s, carrying messages and perhaps even weapons for the underground; a photograph from a Jewish newspaper showing her with two other women bore the caption "women leaders of the Socialist movement in Bielsk, Poland." Finally, the recurrent repressions against Jews in the Soviet Union—something Morris Janowitz's mother had foreseen in the chauvinism and the latent anti-semitism of the Russian revolutionary leaders—and the German assault on Eastern Europe, continued to feed the memory of violence in the Janowitz household. Many European relatives, close or remote, fell victim to Nazi enormities. The Jewish communities of Lodz and Bialystok were destroyed; in the latter no fewer than forty-six Meyerovich relatives were murdered.

Against this background, the dramatic events which took place on the international scene in the decades following the Versailles Treaty certainly further heightened Janowitz's consciousness of, as well as crystallizing his interest in, the critical importance of armed violence in modern societies. Among these events, the Spanish Civil War and the militarism of German Fascism captured the attention of many American intellectuals. The arrival in New York of escapees of the collapsing Weimar Republic, men like Herbert Marcuse and Theodore Adorno from the expelled Institut für Sozialforschung, as well as Hans Speier, the author of innovative articles on war and militarism whom Morris Janowitz met at the New School for Social Research, brought home tangible signs of the continuous reality of violence.

Nothing in his antecedents predestined Morris Janowitz to an academic career in the social sciences. The education he received in one of those old-fashioned high schools which today have disappeared from the American scene did stimulate his already perceptive and rather mature mind for social questions. His wife, Gayle, confided that "it was while seeking to help in the business reconversion of his parents that he did his first 'community survey.'" He also wrote editorials in the school paper and prepared reports on the impact of technology and labor disputes in Paterson. At the time, the young Morris Janowitz did not have any professional aspirations. He knew only that he did not want to be a medical doctor—his mother's wish, which was to be satisfied by her other son—nor to embrace the liquor or the silk trade. In 1937, he enrolled in Washington Square College, located in that area of New York so well described by Albert Parry in his *History of Bohemianism*. It was indeed a place and time to stir the curiosity of a young articulate undergraduate.

There he took classes in economics, the field in which he received his bachelor degree, in anthropology, philosophy, and sociology. It was not yet a period of high specialization, which undoubtedly accounts for his healthy indifference to rigid boundaries between disciplines. He studied under important scholars who greatly influenced him, including Sidney Hook, a leading philosopher of the pragmatic school. The writings of Charles Pierce and John Dewey, among others, were essential in shaping Morris Janowitz's realism and detachment from the then intellectually fashionable ideologies. He always remained independent of Leftist groups even at a time when pro-Russian feelings were popular; his mother's own disillusion with the Socialist revolution certainly counts for something in this. But he was no less skeptical of the Manchesterian points of view. He ironically confesses sometimes that these influences saved him from the burden of Hegelian idealism and historical materialism. For him they thwart both the development of serious research in social sciences and the effectiveness of democratic institutions.

Morris Janowitz's sociological calling originated with Bruce Lannes Smith, a communication specialist, and with his meeting with two scholars from the University of Chicago, one already a towering figure—Harold D. Lasswell, Professor Charles Merriam's former protégé, who later left Chicago upon President Hutchins's refusal to grant him full professorship. The other, Edward Shils, was a pupil of Professors Robert E. Park and Louis Wirth. In a matter of few years, Morris Janowitz found himself exposed to the best that sociology had then to offer: the Chicago School tradition, particularly the work of William I. Thomas, and the more theory-oriented Europeans. Harold Lasswell was fully familiar with the works of Max Weber, Vilfredo Pareto, Georges Sorel, and Sigmund Freud; Professor Shils was, at the time, immersed in the translation of Karl Mannheim and Weber. Both, together with men like Frank Knight, Talcott Parsons, and Lawrence Henderson, played a key role in introducing European social thought into the American sociological curriculum.

These teachers and students were also men quite aware of the central role of the military in the dynamics of society. Harold Lasswell is the best example, as testified to by his masterpiece, *World Politics and Personal Insecurity*, and his original analytical construction of the garrison state developed as early as 1937 in his "Sino-Japanese Crisis: The Garrison State and the Civilian State," for *China Quarterly*. Bruce Smith, a close associate of Harold Lasswell, worked on war propaganda while Edward Shils would soon write on German and Russian military prisoners of war and, later, on the military and politics in non-Western societies.

The originality of the ground of Morris Janowitz's intellectual growth and deepening academic vocation fed his perceptive conviction of the relevance of armed violence to the study of society. At the same time, it provided him with the framework for the ordering of his interest. His association after 1941, as a research assistant with Lasswell in the War Communications Project on propaganda issues, is not unrelated to Morris Janowitz's institutional as well as developmental approach to military reality, typical of the author of *Politics: Who Gets What, When, How*.


II


After Pearl Harbor and Hitler's declaration of war, America for the second time in the century mobilized its men. At the time, Morris Janowitz was serving as a senior propaganda analyst with the Organization and Propaganda Analysis Section of the Department of Justice, involved in the study of fascist ideologies and activities in the United States. Like many other social scientists, he was called up by the formidable institutional machinery of total war. The experience was a crucial one for him. He came into physical contact with the other face of collective violence and its attendant dramas: the combat, the prisoners, the concentration camps, the inimitable quality of comradeship in arms, the exhilaration of victorious pushes, the courage born out of the presence of friends. As a private first, then as an officer, he got a sense of the various stations of the military establishment. As a member of the most advanced armed forces, he experienced the growing internal tensions between the heroic leaders, the Victorian figures of MacArthur and Patton, and their technocratic peers, the Eisenhowers and the Marshalls.

Because of his expertise, Morris Janowitz, then 23, served as Chief Wehrmacht morale analyst in the Psychological Branch of SHAEF. Among the missions of this service, the evaluation of the allied propaganda effectiveness became particularly crucial after June 1944. Disembarked on the Normandy beaches, the American forces soon saw their advance threatened by the unflinching combativeness of the German troops, and had to find the means to avoid costly last-ditch resistance and arrange for honorably acceptable local ceasefires. Ultimately, the success of the whole operation depended upon deciphering the code of the extraordinary morale of the Wehrmacht, surprisingly unshaken after so many years of setbacks and finally defeat.

This issue was to give birth to one of the most seminal pieces of sociology, "Cohesion and Disintegration in the Wehrmacht in World War II," which Morris Janowitz co-authored with Edward Shils. It is ironic yet instructive that this paper, now translated into many languages and integrated into sociological textbooks, was rejected by several journals before its publication in 1948 in *Public Opinion Quarterly*. This journal had already published an earlier piece written in collaboration with M. I. Gurfein, "Trends in Wehrmacht Morale" (1946). After having collected abundant data from interviews with several hundred German prisoners, the authors demonstrated that anti-Nazi propaganda would meet with little success since, contrary to what was commonly held at the time, cohesion in the Wehrmacht did not depend only on ideological convictions. In the United States, militarism of the Wehrmacht was mistaken for a form of national-socialism; this confusion, let it be said in passing, prevented Americans from playing the military against the regime. The cohesion and the morale of German units resulted from the existence of primary groups, a constellation of informal solidarities, tolerated and actually encouraged by the military leadership, which helped to satisfy the most pressing psychological needs of fighting troops. This process was enhanced by various policies involv-ing manipulation, use of fear, paternalism, as well as by the closeness between junior line officers and their men. In this respect, Morris Jan-owitz likes to say that the heir of the Junker imperial army was in·many ways in wartime more "democratic" than the American armed forces themselves!

Indeed, since the pioneering work of Charles Horton Cooley the primary group had been the object of systematic research, for example, the writings of Elton Mayo and George Homans. Newer was the notion that such modes of organization could exist and operate within formal institutions such as the military; it was confirmed by parallel psycho-sociological surveys, notably *The American Soldier* or *Men Under Stress.* Two ideas were fully original, however. The first treats group cohesion as a dependent variable and demonstrates that its sources rested upon fac-tors such as the psycho-sociological profile of the group, the nature and the prestige of the branch of service, or the proximity to danger. The second was to evaluate the consequences of the existence of such groups, not so much from the standpoint of institutional efficiency as from the point of the interactions between the men, the institution, and the parent social system. By hypothesizing that the internalizing by the sol-dier of political and ideological values was linked to their relationship with the prior satisfaction of elementary needs, Morris Janowitz and Edward Shils unveiled the mediating function, negative or positive, ful-filled by the primary group.

Such an approach which articulates the military to its socio-cultural environment anticipated the domain of sociology of the military, to which "armed forces and society" was to become an appropriate term. It implied, in addition, a comprehensive vision of military phenomena. Such a conception, entirely new, had its roots in a macroanalytical current of thought which began to develop in other research areas, for instance, in industrial sociology. This new and more fundamental type of research aimed at understanding the general principles of the functioning of bureaucratic organization as wholes, and helped compensate for the weaknesses of explanatory models based on narrower systems of variables (often circumscribed to questions of social psychology) suggested by ap-plied styles of research.

## III

Demobilized in 1945 with GI Bill in hand, Morris Janowitz decided to undertake graduate studies. He probably would have gone to Harvard had he not been persuaded by Edward Shils to attend the University of Chicago. After finishing the graduate program, he prepared his doctoral dissertation titled, "Mobility, Subjective Deprivation and Ethnic Hostility," and defended it in 1948. Then he served as an instructor at the College from 1947 to 1948 and as an assistant professor until 1951. He worked closely with Edward Shils and Bruno Bettelheim, the founder of the Orthogenic School, with whom he co-authored *The Dynamic of Prejudice*. By 1950 he had written more than ten articles. These years in Chicago, which had influenced him so much, ended in 1951. The department of sociology, still imbued with the grand vision of the past and still led by a few now aging glories of the past, Louis Wirth, William F. Ogburn, and Ernest Burgess, refused obstinately to tenure young faculty members. So after his marriage to Gayle Shulenberger, an educational specialist, Morris Janowitz accepted a position as associate professor at the University of Michigan. These years in Ann Arbor were extremely active. He occupied various administrative positions with the department of sociology and was associated with the Institutes for Social Research and for Public Administration. He spent a year abroad at the restored Institut für Sozialforschung in Frankfurt (1954–1955) and later got involved in politics, running for election to the state legislature. It was also a time of intense academic productivity. Between 1951 and 1961, when he left Ann Arbor, Morris Janowitz had published no less than six books and twenty articles, edited four collections of essays, and written two book-length monographs, on topics ranging from military questions to communication and community affairs. During that period *The Professional Soldier* was completed and the Inter-University Seminar was launched, two undertakings that were to have a profound bearing upon the development and consolidation of the sociology of the military as an academically and scientifically legitimate discipline.

## IV

The study of trends in knowledge shows that the consolidation and the development of an intellectual activity is not only the result of fundamental works, but also that of its institutionalization. The preeminence of the Chicago School of sociology following the creation of the first department of sociology at the University of Chicago under President William Rainey Harper is a case in point. This illustrious precedent might very well have been in Morris Janowitz's mind when he sought to establish the IUS.

The IUS is truly Morris Janowitz's "lengthened shadow," to use

Emerson's image. He not only created it but chaired it for more than twenty years; today his role still remains decisive. The organization was founded in the mid-1950s while Janowitz was in Ann Arbor. An informal working group, named the Inter-University Seminar on Military Organization, it was mainly composed of a handful of former schoolmates at the department of sociology at Chicago and colleagues from various universities. Renamed the Inter-University Seminar on Armed Forces and Society in 1960, the group moved to Chicago when Morris Janowitz was appointed there. It was conceived as an academic institution independent from the military and the government, a collegial meeting place for scholars, financed with private funds, such as the Russell Sage and Ford Foundations. Today, with more than a thousand members, including military professionals, civilian experts, and academics of various disciplines, with its own journal, newsletter, biennial conferences, and regional organizations, the IUS is one of the largest and most important networks of specialists in military affairs. It fulfills important functions among which three deserve to be examined briefly, given their relevance to institutionalization of this field of study.

The first of these concerns the delimitation of the discipline's thematical boundaries. This operation was undertaken in a relatively expansionist fashion and included three areas of research: civil-military relations, the institutional (i.e., professional and organizational) parameters, and armed conflicts. Moreover, this conception of the subject matter of the field was accompanied by the desire to separate the latter from its intellectual neighbors, military history, strategy, and international relations.

The second function was to insure an efficient and systematic exploitation of the theme as it had been defined. This action began with a review and ordering of original issues. It was followed by the establishment of an interdisciplinary conceptual framework and a methodological protocol derived from the canons of the scientific inquiries. This gave scientific legitimacy to a research operating in a field hitherto dominated by non-academic specialists.

The third function, finally, could be defined as one of promotion. Its purpose was to accredit the new discipline on the academic market. This policy developed in two directions. It materialized first in the establishment of scientific forums for intellectual exchanges (a role played by the IUS biennial conference, and the regional meetings) and by the participation (often via an institutional representation such as with the ad hoc Committee of Armed Forces and Society of the International Sociological Association) in national and international social science societies. Second, this policy incited scholarly production on military affairs and its dissemination within an appropriate editorial structure. The *Series on Armed Forces and Society* (with more than twelve volumes since 1971), the annuals of the *Series on War, Revolution, and Peacekeeping*, and above all *Armed Forces and Society*, a quarterly journal, constitute the main components of this structure. To this should be added collective works regrouping communications presented for the ad hoc Committee sessions, as those of London (1964 and 1967), Evian (1966), Varna (1970), and Toronto (1974).

*Armed Forces and Society* is without any doubt the key instrument of the strategy for the development and scientific legitimacy of the discipline as it was conceived by Morris Janowitz. In that regard, its logic reminds us of that which presided over the creation of the *Archiv für Sozialwissenschaft* by Weber, Sombart, and Jaffé, or of the *Année Sociologique* by Durkheim. Launched in the mid-1970s, it has appeared on a quarterly basis since October 1974; it is the first academic journal entirely devoted to the social science analysis of the military. From its inception, it was conceived as a purely scientific review. It is no coincidence that the members of the editorial and advisory boards are all academics, some quite renowned. The articles, structured on the scholarly mode of erudition common to all social science journals, have essentially a theoretical nature. They are based on research which relies on the classic means of the scientific approach and ethics, at the methodological level (participant observation, statistical analysis, comparativism) as well as at the theoretical level (causal model). By distinguishing the sociology of the military from all other analyses published in the popular and professional press, and by reinforcing the position of the scientific discourse in the study of military affairs, this effort has undoutedly favored the academic acceptability and scientific status of the study of the military. It also has contributed to the creation of a consensus around the identity of this subject matter and has forced a greater orderliness in its production.

There are obviously other functions which, without being as essential as those just described, are nonetheless important. The IUS functions to encourage its members; it aims to develop their sense of corporate pride, as well as the feeling of relevance of research undertaken in a domain too often considered by academic opinion as marginal and as the refuge of the less bright scholars.

Though the complete history of the IUS remains to be written, it can be seen from these brief remarks that far from being only an organizational epiphenomenon, a learned society, the establishment of the IUS had profound repercussions over the nature and the orientation of the discipline. In that it certainly proceeds from a self-conscious strategy of scientific legitimation.


## V


At the same time Janowitz was establishing the IUS, he was working on *The Professional Soldier,* which appeared in 1960. This work was acclaimed by scholars and military professionals alike as crucial for the understanding of the modern military, and it soon became a classic in sociology. It is the first piece in a series of major writings on military affairs which can be regarded as the founding work of the field of armed forces and society, the other dimension of the institutionalization of the discipline.

It took ten years for Morris Janowitz to complete this piece. It had to be conducted in "clandestiness" to use his own word, along with more conventional research on which the professional career of a young American sociologist depended at the time. However, the outlines of this work were elaborated much earlier as evidenced by a mimeographed article titled "The Professional Soldier and Political Power," prepared in 1953 for the Institute for Public Administration of the University of Michigan. The analysis grew more precise with two other articles, "Military Elites and the Study of War," in 1957 and "Changing Patterns of Organizational Authority," in 1959, and finally with a monograph published in 1959, *Sociology and the Military Establishment.* The 1957 article is interesting in another respect since it also offers a typology of civil–military relations which distinguishes between four models. First is the pre-industrial model based on social kinship between military and civilian elites, a model that Mosca in *Elementi di scienza politica* already regarded as a source of the political stability of nineteenth-century Europe. Second is the democratic model based upon a strict differentiation between the two elites. Third is the totalitarian model in which the political elites permeate the military. Last is the garrison-state model, of a Lasswellian inspiration, the military elites dominate the political scene, taking advantage of prolonged international tensions. As for *Sociology and the Military Establishment,* a research inventory prepared for the American Sociological Association, it delineated the major hypotheses which were to be developed in *The Professional Soldier* as a means to proceed to a critical evaluation of the existing literature on military affairs.

*The Professional Soldier* is a study in social change. It is characterized by one main purpose: to highlight the nature and logic of the transformation of the organizational and professional formats of the American military under the impact of post-war changes in the area of military technology, international relations, and strategy. It also weighs the countereffects of such organizational mutations over the civil–military interface and strategic and international relations. Its originality resides in the institutional level of analysis: Karl Demeter's *Das Deutsche Offizierkorps in seinem historisch-soziologischen Grundlagen,* Michael Lewis's *England's Sea Officers: The Study of the Naval Profession,* both published in the 1930s, are, together with the interesting article by Franz Carl Endres which appeared in 1927 in the *Archiv für Sozialwissenschaft und Sozialpolitik,* the only outstanding exceptions which provided precedents for *The Professional Soldier.* Owing to the perennial nature of its structure, the military institution was considered intangible and the analysis tended to focus on the technological change and strategic and tactical issues. By shifing its focus at the institutional level, the analysis showed that the military was affected by changes in its environment and that the modes of adjustment to change had in turn an effect upon this environment. The lesson of such a work lay in the demonstration of the relevance of the institutional approach as an appropriate means for understanding the whole logic of military phenomena.

In the empirical tradition, Morris Janowitz founded his analysis on the basis of rich historical, literary, and biographical material concerning 760 generals and admirals, completed by a questionnaire survey of 576 officers and interviews with 113 staff officers. The observation serving as the point of departure is that the kind of technological development which began in the early twentieth century and expanded after World War II had two important consequences. One, the civil–military dichotomy lost a great part of its relevance because of increasing involvement of the civil community in the military reality and the civilianization of the military world, accentuated by the substitution of deterrence for warmaking. Second, the usefulness of force as a means to influence international relations had lessened considerably, especially in a strategic system based upon the "neither war nor peace" parameter. As a consequence, the role of armed forces is radically altered, resembling an organization whose ideal type is the "constabulary force," a system "continuously prepared to act, committed to the minimum use of force, and [which] seeks viable international relations, rather than victory, because it has incorporated a protective military posture." It is a theme to which the author will return in detail.

The core of the study revolves around the various effects induced in

the military establishment by this evolution. It falls into five propositions, which have become classical hypotheses in the field and there is
hardly any need here to expatiate at length. Each proposition concerns a
particular level of the institution. At the level of internal division of
labor, one observes that "non-military" occupations requiring administrative and technical know-how have multiplied and outnumber combat-related occupations based on martial skills. As a result, the command
structure is shared between traditional heroic leaders and emerging managerial and technical specialists. At the level of organizational control,
styles of authority that are based on persuasion, which calls for initiative
and lateral cooperation, displace those founded on domination. The
complexity of the division of labor and the subsequent complexity of
the decisionmaking process require both a delegation and sharing of the
responsibility which thwarts centralization of power and authority. At
the level of career development, one notices the increasing role and
length of both specialized training and general education. Innovative
behavior, if not non-conformism, opens the upper rungs of the hierarchy
to the so-called adaptive leaders. Military calling and tradition tend to
mix with material motivations and careerism. At the level of the sociological structure, the main feature is the democratization of social
recruitment, notably in the officer corps, which becomes more representative of the regional, racial, and cultural organization of the parent
social fabric. Finally, at the normative level, absolutism, which characterized the traditional military mind, declines, replaced by a greater
political pluralism and a more pragmatic conception of both the career
and the missions of the institution. It may be noted that in evolving the
hypothesis that a growing ideological sensitivity helps make secure har-
monious civil–military relations, Morris Janowitz rejected the two then
current theses on the question—that developed by C. Wright Mills in his
*Power Elite* and the one that Samuel P. Huntington had proposed in *The
Soldier and the State*. For Morris Janowitz neither Mills's claim that the
military is a powerful and anti-democratic force nor Huntington's asser-
tion that the military can achieve its objectives and maintain its professional integrity only if a clearcut distinction exists between the civil and
the military realm, successfully capture the full complexity of the political–military articulation.

These changes reflect a long-term trend by which the military institution loses its martial particularism and comes to resemble any complex
organization, civilianized and integrated in the parent community. What
must be emphasized is that, in Morris Janowitz's analysis, trend does not
mean destiny on the one hand, and does not, on the other, imply

imminent isomorphism between the military and the civilian universes. The residues of the traditional model are not bound to disappear. Morris Janowitz, for that matter, stresses their functionality, all the more so in the contemporary international context, where the effectiveness of nuclear deterrence remains based on combat readiness and, in any case, does not preclude the eventualities of limited conventional confrontations. The author, therefore, was aware of the counterforce limiting convergence and at the same time was able to unveil the major dilemma faced by modern military establishments whose success rests in their ability to prevent the outbreak of war while always being prepared to fight.

## VI

During the following years, Morris Janowitz continued to develop and test the hypotheses elaborated in *The Professional Soldier*. In "Military Organization and Disorganization," which appeared in 1961, he examined the consequences of the multiplication of role conflicts generated by the convergence process and the subsequent organizational adjustments, e.g., the expansion of the welfare function of the military. In "Organizing Multiple Goals: War and Arms Control," which introduces a collective study published in 1964 under his direction, *The New Military*, he underlined the growing importance of preventive missions of a peacekeeping nature (a trend which he highlights by an analogy with that undergone by the modern medical profession—preventive medicine) as well as the multiplication of non-military tasks. Both types increasingly compete, in organization, training, etc., with the combat functions still required by the paradox of deterrence. The overall convergence tendency hence does not exclude the existence of an internal heterogeneity. And therefore, the so-called pluralistic hypothesis, developed later on by Charles C. Moskos and others as an alternative to the convergence model, is simply another reading—with a different level of emphasis—of a phenomenon explicitly established in the Janowitzian paradigm.

Janowitz, however, was not content with exploring the American case study alone. He was also concerned with the comparative dimension to the field of military analysis. Such an emphasis, which offers, as Weber and Durkheim among others had argued, a substitute to direct experimentation in the social sciences, can be interpreted in connection with the continuing effort to enhance the scientific legitimacy of this area of research. So, he pressed within the IUS for a greater commitment to the comparative investigation of military institutions, while enlisting the participation and enrollment of foreign scholars in the Seminar. In his own research, he extended his reflections on the American case to the Western world, as in his "Armed Forces in Western Europe: Uniformity and Diversity" (1965), and, more important, toward the non-industrialized world. The latter was intriguing because it sheltered unstable forms of civil–military relations whose dynamics had not yet been satisfactorily explained.

The freshness of Janowitz's discussion of the issue, proposed in 1964 in a small penetrating book—*The Military in the Political Development of New Nations*—covering some fifty third-world countries, derived from his focusing upon institutional factors as the main sources for the collapse of the civilian control of the military. He never pretended to reject or even minimize the validity of all non-military factors, generally given priority by most third-world specialists, Marxists, and developmentalists alike. He only conferred, in the chain of causal priorities, greater precedence to professional and organizational variables. Praetorianism in non-industrial societies, under the form of civil–military coalitions or direct military rule (the most common types of the five models of third-world political–military relations) is, for Janowitz, linked primarily to the state of local military institutions.

For various reasons, which include a lower exposure to technology and industrialism, the armed forces of the new nations exhibited most traits associated with traditional "non-civilized" military institutions. Such characteristics, particularly in the context of underdevelopment, both economic and political, and in the absence of a viable tradition of civilian control, have drawn soldiers into political affairs; militarism in these cases is more an unanticipated action than one designed or conspired. The phenomenon would have only secondary importance, had the praetorians become the efficient agents of social and economic change they declared themselves to be; actually their claims were a means to render their unconstitutional usurpation of power legitimate. These pretenses, let us note in passing, are often taken for granted in the literature, which, for example, saw in the recruitment from the middle class of the officers, in their nationalism or their sense of order the guarantees of a modernizing spirit and the will to implement it. But, in general, nothing of that sort took place and, in most instances, the military rulers proved to be mediocre actors. At that level, too, the causes of the praetorians' failure are structural. The traditional style of authority or the ascetic and heroic sense of professionalism, to choose two traits among others, tended to generate an absolutist as well as unitary conception of power, incompatible with the pragmatism and pluralism required for the management of the polity. The disdain for the *res politica* and the distrust of ideologies also prevented the uniformed governors from mobilizing sufficient popular support to undertake any viable modernizing policy. Janowitz's book thus shows clearly the dilemma of praetorianism in the third-world by pointing out that the institutional parameters which induce the interventionist phase are by nature antithetic to political and modernizing objectives.

For the purpose at hand here, the argument was quite simplified. Morris Janowitz is fully aware that there are cases in which, for reasons linked to local specificities, to the nature of the social structure of the military, or to the process of professional socialization, the military is able to supply energetic cadres or partners to the political class. He is equally aware that military even may have beneficial effects. This issue was to be more fully investigated in subsequent regional analyses. For instance, in "The Comparative Analysis of Middle Eastern Military Institutions" (1970), Janowitz discusses the factors that have made the structural-military restraints less operative and he draws particular attention to the Kemalist experiment as a model of effective assumption of power followed by a successful return to the civilian normality.

In 1977, the University of Chicago Press published a second edition of the 1964 book under the title of *Military Institutions and Coercion in the Developing Nations*, with a new introduction. This introduction is important because it focuses on a variable which had not been discussed previously in this type of research, namely the paramilitary forces whose visibility has continued to increase in the last few years. Morris Janowitz shows how their role has become relevant to the stabilization of military regimes whose dynamic—and this is the other original aspect of the study—follows what seems to be the "natural history" of revolutions, with its moderate, radical, and thermidorian phases. In addition, he notices that the role of the paramilitary forces is not confined to the maintenance of order but also encompasses a function of political patronage which serves to compensate for the absence or deflation of national consensus.

With the issue of paramilitary forces, Morris Janowitz has enlarged the domain of the sociology of the institutions which monopolize legitimate coercion, restricted heretofore to the military. Other formations, in their role as agencies of social change, seem at least as important as military organizations. It can be remarked here that it was not his first attempt in that direction: as early as 1968, he grappled with the issue in a controversial, yet often misunderstood monograph entitled *Social Control of Escalated Riots,* in which he discussed the redefinition of the police's roles in the changing context of racial unrest.

It is not possible here to mention, less to review, all the other works that Janowitz published throughout the 1960s. What can be said, however, is that they illustrate his continuous concern for a macrosociological and comparative analysis of the military reality. A few examples will serve. "Armed Forces and Society: A World Perspective" (1968) is a synthesis of the main themes in the field of military sociology, notably the process of professionalization, social recruitment, the changing military roles in international relations, and militarism. Collections such as *On Military Ideology* and *On Military Intervention,* edited in 1971 in collaboration with Jacques Van Doorn, point to a concern for stimulating research in order to highlight regional patterns of military organizations and civil–military relations. Though his thinking soon extended toward other aspects of the military reality, Janowitz has not ceased to deal with this comparative perspective. In *Civil-Military Relations: Regional Perspective,* edited in 1981, he uses a regional approach to account for the effects of socio-cultural variables in order to identify patterns of military influence in the world and their political and economic consequences.

By the early 1970s, Janowitz had left a profound imprint on the study of military affairs and was recognized as the leading scholar in the area. This rather intense intellectual production, all the more impressive in that it also covered a wide range of non-military topics, was paralleled by other activities. He acted as consultant for several agencies, such as the U.S. Senate Committee on Armed Services, the National Advisory Commission on Selective Service, and the National Commission on the Causes and Prevention of Violence. He served as a member of the board of the National Research Council and of the National Academy of Science, and as chairman of the National Seminar on Sociological Theory and Survey Research. He also participated in the Executive Committee of the *International Encyclopedia of the Social Sciences.*

Locally, in Hyde Park, that once fashionably intellectual and bohemian part of the near South Side of Chicago, he was continuously involved in community actions and politics and contributed much to its renewal. Staver's, Powell's, and O'Gara's bookshops, which count among the best in the country, owe him a great deal in this regard. The habitués of Jimmy's, particularly Reid Michener, the endearing gentleman of the evening shifts at O'Gara's and the neighborhood's living memory, are never short of anecdotes which implicate Janowitz. It is no coincidence that he has been acknowledged, even by Hanna Gray, the University President, "the mayor of 57th street!"

At the University of Chicago, his presence was no less influential. He worked with the Committee on New Nations, organized by his friends Edward Shils and the late Lloyd Fallers, the reputed anthropologist. He set up and for twelve years directed the Center for Social Organization Studies. More important, he chaired, between 1967 and 1973, the department of sociology. This was no meager task given the ongoing state of crisis created by the sharp opposition between the quantitative ahistorical school and the old humanistic and "civility-oriented" tradition. In this regard, his role as chairman has been decisive for it restored the strength of that once prestigious department.

## VII

In 1972, Janowitz left with his family for England where he had been invited as the Pitt Professor at Cambridge and Fellow of Peterhouse, the oldest College of the university. It was a time, well deserved, without administrative pressures, a time also of stimulating intellectual exchanges with his European peers. This period actually marks the beginning of a new phase in his reflections on military affairs. Though not a break with all his preceding work, Janowitz's area of interest spread toward the analysis of international relations. Moreover, and this must be stressed, it merged more intimately into a general theorization concerning social change in the Western world.

Though it is limited to a small number of articles, Janowitz's contribution to the understanding of international relations and strategy (which systematizes a number of ideas outlined in his earlier work) is important. "Toward a Redefinition of Military Strategy in International Relations," published in 1974, revised later in 1977 in "Beyond Deterrence: Alternative Conceptual Dimensions," questioned the validity of current antithetic concepts such as War and Peace, Defense and Offensive, Strategic and Tactical. Its purpose was to shed a new light on the nature of the contemporary international environment and how it affects the roles of the armed forces. For him, international relations are characterized today by a high degree of complexity and fragility. This situation results from two factors. First, the acceleration of the process of political emancipationism within the international arena has destabilized the former world order by multiplying the number of power-centers while creating zones of high concentration of military strength. Here Janowitz applies to the international realm Karl Mannheim's principle of "fundamental democratization." Hence, tensions and crises, formerly episodic, have become enduring fixtures of the modern world.

The second factor is linked to the recent revolution which has affected the conduct of diplomacy. Because of deterrence, and especially because of the increasing functional interdependence within the world network, hence because of the expansion of areas of common interests, negotiation can no longer separate force from persuasion but seeks to integrate them constantly. In such a context, the traditional parameters of military strategy have been upset and the operational usefulness of armed force has been reduced considerably. Reduced also was its legitimacy, economic as well as psychological (a point which had already been touched on by Lasswell). "The Limits of Military Intervention," published in 1978 in collaboration with Ellen Stern, demonstrates moreover the existence of technological obstacles to the use of armed force. Consequently, the role of military institutions—and at this point Janowitz comes back to his idea of the "Constabulary Force" sketched out fifteen years earlier—is bound to change radically. The call to force is no longer capable of insuring peace; the stabilization of international relations can only be handled preventively by the establishment of communications, the inhibition of tensions, and arms control. Thus, the role of the military is not geared toward periodic warmaking, but instead toward the ongoing tasks of crisis-management.

But it is essentially the institutional analysis of the military universe proper that Janowitz addressed during this last decade. The reissue of *The Professional Soldier* in 1971 afforded him an occasion to expand, in a new introduction, his observations on the dynamic of military institutions, using the case of the American forces as they emerged from the 1960s. The main idea, soon to be explicated in a series of articles, among which are "The Decline of the Mass Army," and "Toward an All-Volunteer Force," both published in 1972, is that Western military establishments are undergoing profound mutations similar in scale to those that occurred during the fifteenth century with the disappearance of the feudal modes of military organization and during the nineteenth century with the rise of the mass armies. This pattern of organization, derived from the revolutionary concept of the nation in arms based on conscription and mobilization, was displaced by a new form of organization that Morris Janowitz named "force in being," defined as "a smaller establishment recruited permanently on an all-volunteer basis and organized predominantly on a force-in-being basis, with a de-emphasis of the older tradition of cadre for mobilization." The causes of such a mutation were essentially born from the build-up of atomic technology and the corollary priority given to nuclear deterrence in strategic planning, from the decline of traditional modes of imperial hegemony, the extension and civilianization of the concept of national security, and from the obsolescence of participation in the military as a means for accession to full citizenship.

This evolution, which was completed in the United States in 1973 (the Korean War and to some extent the Vietnam War, fought along, when all is said, a rather classic pattern) had important repercussions upon the organization and the professional profile of the military. They were discussed in various articles such as "The U.S. Forces and the Zero Draft" (1973) or "The All-Volunteer Force as a Socio-Political Problem" (1975), in which Janowitz analyzes the questions of personnel recruitment and retention, of cost/effectiveness, of racial and social representativeness, and the tensions created in the moral and professional self-image by the dilemmas of deterrence and crisis-management. A good synthesis of these issues, prepared in collaboration with Charles C. Moskos, appeared in 1979 under the title "Five Years of the All-Volunteer Force: 1973–1978." It must be pointed out here, contrary to what is often argued, that in Janowitz's interpretation, most of the institutional consequences of that transformation do not necessarily constitute a rupture in previous trends. Reversals can be observed in, for example, the social and racial-cultural composition or in the accentuation of boundaries' distinction. In general, however, there was either a continuity with the past—at the level of the hierarchical and vertical structure, of civilian and female employment—or simply a slowing down of previous trends, such as at the level of the skill and occupational organization. What has actually occurred and which was confused with a reversal (of the divergence hypotheses) is not so much a break in the convergence movement as a "disarticulation," Janowitz's neologism designating a normative divergence between the value system of the military and that of the civilian community. Organically, the convergence still persists.

In addition, the importance of the phenomenon must not be exaggerated, and Janowitz rightly stresses that the ideal of the citizen-soldier, the most appropriate political-military formula in a democratic system, has never ceased to operate in the all-volunteer force. In his 1977 criticism, "From Institutional to Occupational," of Charles Moskos's widely publicized formulation of a shift from profession to occupation, he emphasizes that cleavages, discontent, strain in cohesion or weakened performance are not normally distributed characteristics and in any case cannot be equated with an undermined professional identity which continues to be at work in the current setting. In "Citizen-Soldier and National Service," published in 1979, he shows that the flow of personnel in and out of the military, in other words, the exchange between the society and its armed forces, is as important today as it was at the time of the draft. Despite increases in salaries and material gratification, there is no significant trace of *mercenarisation*, as was feared, and the service to the state and nation remains one of the dominant aspects of career motivations and image.

Morris Janowitz sees these trends as positive signs of the viability of the all-volunteer force. Though personally disposed toward a conscription-oriented system, he does not consider the experiment introduced in 1973 a failure, despite problems yet unsolved. In any case, to pronounce the all-volunteer force a failure is at least premature. Recent data show that the racial imbalance is no longer deteriorating and that the educational level has been improving. In 1982, two men out of three had a high school education against only one out of three in the late 1970s, though the shift is in part attributable to the economic recession. Morris Janowitz argues, however, that the success of the reforms depends upon a social and humanistic vision of the realities of the military and not, as is often the case, a conception limited to an economic or systemic modeling of the issue. Thus, among the measures susceptible to building up the efficiency of the all-volunteer force, to reforming its morale and esprit de corps, and to redefining more harmoniously its role in the parent community and the international world, one appears far more crucial to Janowitz than a policy exclusively based on financial incentives. In "Civic Consciousness and Military Performance," written in 1981, and "Patriotism and the U.S. All-Volunteer Military," published in 1982, he points out the advantages, besides the cosmetic boon of reducing disruptive personnel rotation, that there would be in encouraging a sense of civic responsibility in the military. This is not meant as a return to a simplistic form of crude nationalism, but a self-critical version of patriotism resting on education rather than on indoctrination. In this regard, he proposes to develop the cadres' political and diplomatic training (by instituting regular civilian–military contacts) and to increase their participation in a national civic education program. At the domestic level, this type of reform would give a new meaning to the military's participation in the national community and lessen civilian indifference toward their defense institutions. At the international level, it would be especially useful for crisis-management and arms control dialogues.

It remains that for Janowitz, such a type of military organization, the all volunteer force, is nothing other than a transition toward a more complex system which integrates a professional military and a national service (that is, civil and military services, linked by an "exchange rate" insuring a reciprocal parity at the level of the obligations entailed) thereby answering both the military and the social demands which advanced industrial liberal societies pose. The institution of national service, which had in the past drawn his attention, e.g., "the Logic of National Service," in 1967 and "National Service: A Third Alternative" in 1971, appears to him crucial. It first would offer military advantages such as an enlargement of the recruitment pool, an improvement of the general level of qualification, and an attenuation of the feeling of alienation among career personnel. But the main purpose of the institution is not solely military, it is also social and political. In this regard, it could be said that Morris Janowitz's analysis of the *res militaris* is actually a genuine macro political-sociological theory.

Like many of his colleagues, he has sought to understand the nature of the crisis affecting Western contemporary societies. *The Social Control of the Welfare State* published in 1977 and, above all, the impressive Laing Award winning *The Last Half Century: Societal Change and Politics in America* (1979) witness this effort. For Janowitz, the crisis results from the corruption of the sense of citizenship from which democratic forms of social control derive. This corruption, which is an unanticipated perversion of the expansion of the welfare state and the failure of the traditional educational systems, arises out of the distortion of the balance between rights and obligations which constitutes the essence of public citizenship in a democracy. This was detailed in his "Observations on the Sociology of Citizenship: Obligations and Rights," published in 1980. National service, being founded on the principle of service to the state, would contribute to the proper balancing of rights and duties, the condition in which citizenship might again become operative in the survival and the functioning of democratic systems. Such too is the theme at the center of the thesis developed in the book Janowitz has just completed, *The Reconstruction of Patriotism.* "Military Institutions and Citizenship in Western Societies," written in 1975, had already, for that matter, highlighted the historical importance of a popular military participation in the French and the American Revolutions as the capital factor for the sense of citizenship and, by way of consequence, for the emergence of democratic political institutions during the nineteenth century.

It is manifest at this juncture that Janowitz's "military contribution," while central to the understanding of the world of arms proper, is not an end in itself, not closed in. It also serves as a pertinent instrument for analyzing the larger issues centered around social-political change and, to be more precise, around the changing pattern of man's participation in the various institutions of modern societies in the West.

## VIII

The strength and the relevance of Morris Janowitz's thought resides not only in its content, but also in its methodology and its philosophy. His techniques and views exhibit all the characteristics of scientific analysis. He is constantly concerned with bridging careful empirical research with a theoretical argument operating at a macrosociological level. This effort is conducted through diachronic and synchronic perspectives in order to enhance the validity of his hypotheses. This is indeed an elementary and expected requisite, but one that deserves to be mentioned since today social science research often falls short of such considerations.

The relevance of Janowitz's paradigms lies in the nature of his approach and the level of analysis at which the theorization unfolds. As we have seen with *The Professional Soldier*, even implicitly in "Cohesion and Disintegration in the Wehrmacht," which were pioneering in this regard, the unit of analysis is the institution itself. In the case of the military reality, such an angle of analysis is the one most appropriate to fathoming the internal structures and dynamics of the armed forces, and also to elucidating those of other relevant phenomena such as war, conflict management, or civil-military relations. Adding interest to this approach of the military reality is Morris Janowitz's concern for situating his argument in a historical perspective, but more especially his readiness to hypothesize patterns of evolution. In an age when social scientists increasingly shy away from social dynamics and comfortably entrench themselves in microscopic social statics—an attitude partly, but only partly, excusable after the excesses of nineteenth-century teleological reductionism—such a posture is laudable. In any case, it would be an error to classify Morris Janowitz in the neo-evolutionist or social-law schools. The axiomatic basis of his approach, which proceeds from the so-called "developmental analysis" rejects all determinism. "Developmental analysis" simply consists of a meaningful reconstruction of past trends, of specifying what is currently taking place and proposing a reasoned assessment of future possible patterns of change. Therefore there is no room for necessitarianism; first, because a developmental construction includes the idea of alternative paths and second, because corrective decisions taken in consideration of those "possible futures" may affect the predicted course of things. The paradigm, in other words, integrates the notion of freedom, precluding the logic of what Jean Piaget called "totalitarian realism." It seeks only to give sense to a succession of facts and phenomena without postulating that such sense is inscribed in a predetermined reality.

These analytical procedures are clearly derived from Lasswell's methodology, as Janowitz himself points out in the introduction of his collected essays, *Military Conflict*. Yet, he cannot be considered Lasswellian; he actually denies that he is, feeling uncomfortable with the "Sorelean-Freudian formulations" of his former mentor. It remains, however, that Lasswell's influence was decisive in initiating Morris Janowitz into two of the greatest traditions of the social sciences, the Weberian and the Chicago Schools.

These legacies have inspired Janowitz beyond mere methodology. They have also shaped the substratum of his intellectual preoccupations, and inspired his sense of his own academic vocation. Weberian, for instance, is his attention to the decline of calling that he observed not only in the military, with the rise of careerism, but also in other areas of the professional world, in medicine, in academia and in the media. The same can be said for his study of the displacement of heroic forms of leadership in the contemporary armed forces, the military equivalent of charismatic leadership, by bureaucratic, managerial, and technical styles of command. Following Lasswell's example, Morris Janowitz seeks to illustrate that aspect of Weber's theory of history which emphasizes the nature and the consequences of the growth of bureaucratic systems following *Rationalisierungdrang*. Equally of the Weberian orthodoxy is Morris Janowitz's dualistic mode of theory-building which incorporates socio-historical models into long-term perspectives, a combination which, as shown by Günther Roth, constitutes the hallmark of the Heidelberg scholar's methodology. The heroic leader, the manager, the technician, the citizen-soldier are unambiguously, with the mass army, the force in being, and the constabulary force, his socio-historical types (ideal-types, one should add); they are the milestones on the course of the history of Western military institutions, the history encapsulated in his developmental construction of the "convergence theory."

Janowitz is above all a product of the grand "Chicago School" tradition (which, actually, has something in common with the Weberian legacy). It is true that in the late 1940s, the department had entered a period of relative eclipse following three decades of extraordinary innovation and leadership—the time of epigones always seems crepuscular. Yet, the spirit of Albion W. Small, William I. Thomas, Robert E. Park, and Herbert Mead endured with Louis Wirth, Ernest Burgess, William Ogburn, and their students, Everett C. Hughes, and Edward Shils. The recent autobiographical piece "Some Academics, Mainly in Chicago," that Edward Shils wrote for the *American Scholar*, conveys a measure of the perennial influence of the founders. But even before arriving at the

University of Chicago, Janowitz was already familiar with most of the school's seminal production. The scope of *The Polish Peasant*, as well as the personality of its main author, quite fascinating actually, particularly impressed him. The intellectual style and outlook of the author of *The Unadjusted Girl* had a profound impact on Morris Janowitz's scholarship. Thomas's fusing of minute empirical material into a macro-sociological formulation is at the origin of Janowitz's procedures of sociological analysis. He later paid homage to William I. Thomas in a long introduction to a collection of Thomas's essays published in the formidable series, *The Heritage of Sociology*, that he edits for the University of Chicago Press.

In addition, Janowitz's noted reluctance to bind himself in the narrow confines of one single discipline or one established field rests on the department's traditional emphasis, which began with its first chairman, Albion Woodbury Small, and was later enforced by Thomas and Park, on a broadly defined sociological perspective that draws on various subfields of the social sciences. These men did not consider sociology in an antagonistic relationship with other disciplines but rather as a "methodology" for the social sciences and history. The striking similarity with Max Weber's view of sociology should be pointed out at this juncture. Clearly, Janowitz's metaphoric definition of sociology as "a sponge" and his conceptions of the profession are perfectly expressive of the Weberian/Chicago School heritage. He never has and would not consider himself a specialist in sociology, much less a military sociologist—an epithet he positively abhors—but rather as a social scientist. Given the versatility of his research, there is no doubt that Janowitz satisfies Small's ideal of the sociologist, "a consumate technician in his own specialty . . . and above that a reliable liaison officer between his specialty and all other divisions of knowledge . . . ," as described in a letter to Harry E. Barnes.

The impact of these traditions is also noticeable in Janowitz's conception of scientific inquiry and academic calling. His approach to the scientific enterprise is founded on the separation of ideological convictions from scholarship. Like Weber himself, Janowitz is not unaware of the relativity of the *Wertfreiheit* principle, but professes that the role of the social scientist is to respect it as much as possible, particularly in sensitive areas such as military affairs, which so easily lend themselves to value judgments. It is certain that the credibility of the IUS and the respect which the sociology of the military has acquired in military and academic quarters is linked to such an attitude. Morris Janowitz, and here again the Chicago School heritage of Thomas and Park is particularly obvious, refuses to assimilate the role of the social scientist to that of the social engineer, so fashionable in an era of academic technocracy and state interventionism, or to that of the social gospel's preacher.

This intellectual posture however must not be confused with an ivory-tower philosophy which postulates a separation between applied research and more abstract fundamental analysis. Janowitz believes that the pursuit of knowledge ultimately does have a social significance. If science cannot tell men how to live or society how to be organized, if it cannot set goals or offer solutions, it does independently of any self-conscious reformist efforts provide new basis for social relations. A partisan of what Edward Shils called the enlightenment approach, Morris Janowitz pursues the ideals set by men like Park and Znaniecki who believed that the mission of the social scientist is to clarify social trends and their attendant problems in order to help his audience, including the political elite, to understand the nature and the dynamics of the social world, to bring themselves to solutions for the issues at hand that they alone can solve.

Neither must academic detachment be confused with conservatism or callousness. His political preferences—"I am a social-democrat," he often claims—his attention to minority issues, and his occasional *Tagespolitik* writings in newspapers, are examples to the contrary. But like Weber, the main political virtues he emphasizes are realism, responsibility, and ideological restraint. Moreover, his high sense of personal obligations and his guiding attention by which so many of us have profited, his concern for moral values, sustains the humanistic aspect of his academic vocation.

## IX

Formerly a heterogeneous body of particular inquiries with little in common besides a curiosity for military affairs, the study of the *res militaris* has, over the last two decades acquired a scientific and academic legitimacy. Behind any such process of intellectual institutionalization, stands always a man, always an oeuvre. For the enterprise of the sociology of the military, which does not escape this rule, the organizational leadership and scholarship of Professor Janowitz has been decisive.

Under the form it has taken, this survey does not pretend to do complete justice to Janowitz's contribution, even limited as it is, to his "military writings." They are much richer and more diversified than could be conveyed in a selective treatment. The summary does, it is hoped, give an idea of the amplitude of Janowitz's work. First, his intellectual contribution exhibits most of the traits characterizing an *oeuvre fondatrice*. It defines for the benefit of a new field the basic themes, concepts, references and propositions, in other words a paradigmatic system, which makes possible a real accumulation of knowledge in the area of military sociological research.

As for his organizational contribution—the IUS and its subsidiaries—an institutional apparatus has been achieved such that the new discipline is now recognized as a distinctive and legitimate one on the thematic and epistemological horizon of the social sciences.

Nonetheless, the subject of armed forces and society is still a fresh field for research. As such, it remains fragile and exposed to various dangers. Structurally, its fragility results from the built-in ambiguity of the relationships between the researcher and the military; what the military and the academy see in one another and expect from one another rarely coincide. It is fragile also because there is clearly still not enough integration of independent teaching of military affairs in the university. As for the dangers which confront the new discipline, there are three. First, the continuing growth in the number of students attracted by military issues increases the likelihood of excessive specialization. This hazard is reinforced by the presence of military researchers and civilian experts who are under contract to the military establishment who willy-nilly tend to operate in narrow problem-solving perspectives. Second, because of the novelty of certain ideas, premature adulteration jeopardizes the conceptual continuity necessary to any young science; confusion here would ramify all the more given the politically sensitive nature of issues such as civil-military relations. It is within this context that Janowitz's criticism of Charles Moskos's view of the rise of the occupational outlook in the military finds its justification. The third danger facing the new discipline is the shift from an innovative toward a more reiterative style of research. This veering toward "normal science," to use Kuhn's terminology, was predicted by Janowitz. In a paper titled "On the Current State of the Sociology of Military Institutions," prepared for a round table held in Europe in 1978, he stated somewhat pessimistically, "I do not foresee any great theoretical breakthrough. . . . Nor do I even foresee any marked increase in the scope and the intensity of empirical work although . . . there is much work to be done. To the contrary, there is a real danger that the momentum of the last two decades will slow." In a more recent article, "Consequence of Social Science Research on the U.S. Military," which appeared in the summer of 1982, he repeated that he did not believe that social science research on military institutions met the highest intellectual standards. Considering that

many research centers in American and in Europe have become essentially preoccupied with bureaucratic expansion and public relations, academic Babbittry in sum; considering that they are often saturated with
redundant scholarship, "a sign," as Durkheim once wrote of German
social science, "of a certain lack of curiosity, a kind of self-withdrawal, of
intellectual plethora which opposes all new progress," Morris Janowitz's
diagnoses stand confirmed.

This is not to say, however, that scientific knowledge, in order to
progress, need necessarily pass through the patricidal phase, the sacrifice
of the founders, prescribed by Bachelard or Whitehead. For the time
being at least, the strengthening of the emerging discipline of the sociology of armed forces and society surely depends upon those ready to
emulate, rather than dispense with Morris Janowitz's example.

# Part I

## Theoretical Perspectives

# Continuity and Discontinuity in Civil-Military Relations

## JACQUES VAN DOORN

*The Institutional Approach of the Military*

Because the sociological study of the military covers a wide field, it is hazardous to make simple classifications. Nevertheless, a division into "internal" and "external" themes helps to clarify this study. Internal subjects are those connected with the relations between the soldier and his organization—varying from combat readiness to authority structure— whereas the external aspects can be placed under the heading "civil-military relations."

The way a soldier functions, both individually and in groups, is apt to catch the attention of scholars especially during and after wars: the *Kriegspsychologie* flourished in Germany after World War I, in the same way as *The American Soldier* was the fruit of World War II, and as reflections followed Korea and Vietnam.[1] Civil-military relations, on the other hand, are the subjects of research during times of peace: they are a political issue because they center on the maintenance of a balance between civil authority and military power.

Although the publications of Morris Janowitz cover a wide range of military problems, his main interest lies in the relationship between armed forces and society. His contributions are important for two reasons. First, he has freed the study of the external relations of the military . from the trammels of the civil-military relations concept; his approach covers every aspect of the relationship between the armed forces (including the subconventional forces) and the social and political order.

Second, he has placed the problem within classical sociology. This means that he does not confine himself to small-scale empirical research, but studies the general dynamics of the tensions between the military and social forces, normatively as well as empirically.

In his latest major work, *The Last Half-Century*, which may also be regarded as his intellectual autobiography, he has characterized his point of view quite clearly with the central notion of *social control*, that is, "the capacity of a social group, including a whole society, to regulate itself"; this self-regulation implies, according to Janowitz, "a set of 'higher moral principles' beyond those of self-interest".[2]

He does not stop at specifying the notion of social control, but gives it a definite shape in terms of social and political institutions. This emphasis on the institutional aspect pervades his entire work; he has focused, in fact, on a cluster of core concepts unmistakably interrelated both theoretically and normatively: professionalization, citizenship, institution-building, and legitimacy.[3] His contributions to the study of the military are no exception. The analysis is always centered around two concepts: professionalism and citizenship, embodied in the professional soldier and the citizen soldier.

Although both types appear in his work from the beginning, the study of the military profession evidently takes precedence. From the first publications, around 1960, onward, all attention is focused on the professional aspect of the career soldier,[4] and that at a time when the term "professional" was rarely considered applicable to military men.[5] He has never repudiated this approach, a consistency that gives him the right to plead for the preservation of "conceptual continuity"[6] in a discussion on recent changes in the social role of the military.

During the 1970s his interest in the relations between military service and citizenship continued to expand. Inspired by observations of nation-building functions of the military in new states, and apparently challenged by the establishment of the American all-volunteer force and the growing social and ethnic unrepresentativeness of military personnel which went with this,[7] he embarked on a study of the historical connection between nation-building, citizen rights, and military service.[8] He concluded that many classic authors unjustly created a contradistinction between the emergence of the nineteenth-century nation state and the development of the modern military. Instead, Janowitz argued:

> Political democracy is linked to the normative notion of "citizenship." To the extent that mass armies in the West defined their recruits in terms of political and normative ideas of citizenship, military service functioned as an essential contribution to political institutions.[9]

The analytical significance of both concepts—the professional and the citizen soldier—is essentially the same: a factual and moral connection between the armed forces and the society at large. In the case of military professionalism the connection develops from the military elite. After all, the idea of professionalism implies, apart from expertise and corporateness, a notion of service to the nation, responsibility, and sensitivity to the consequences of military activity.[10] More and more the professional soldier comes to serve an interest which surpasses his own; he is by definition not a mercenary. Nowadays the public interest is defined by the political community.

The concept of the citizen soldier links the armed forces and society in a different way. Whereas the military professional is an expert, serving the nation as a specialist, the citizen soldier is an active member of the political community, who puts his efforts at the service of this community because his political rights include the right to bear arms. In this case, the way in which armed forces are related to society is defined and controlled by the societal environment.

Both are ideal types in so far as they are hardly ever purely separate. Even where an all-volunteer force exists, it will primarily be the officer corps which is devoted to the professional ethos. On the other hand, within a citizen militia there will be at least a small elite of experts in command of the maintenance and training of military skills. Most systems are mixed: a predominantly professional elite and a mass of conscripts and short-term volunteers. Moreover, besides the professional military most countries have supplementary forces such as reserves and auxiliaries.[11]

The situation outlined above implies that the connection between armed forces and society can adopt at least two forms, which are not by definition mutually exclusive (indeed, at times they complement each other), but which can be expected to differ markedly as to effectiveness, legitimacy, social composition, functional specialization, and institutional outlook. In addition, the various conditions which are decisive for the rise and the maintenance of both models are historically determined.

These conditions are thus subject to change or even erosion, which, in turn, alters or weakens the relation between the armed forces and society.

This essay gives some general reflections on the present changes in these two relations between the military and society. In doing so, I will frequently refer to Morris Janowitz, because his writings often deal with the same subject, either in debates with himself, or with others. In a contribution to a *Festschrift* in honor of Morris Janowitz, it seems appropriate to tread onto the field which has fascinated him for so long.

## The Demilitarization of the Professional Soldier

In the Western world, the military profession has long been both effective and legitimate. On the one hand, professionalism is another term for expertise, based on a long, specialized training process, a high degree of corporate cohesion, and the ability to take initiative under difficult circumstances. On the other hand, the professional service to society is legitimate and widely recognized.

Nevertheless the military profession differs from other professions in that its central heroic role originates in older, often aristocratic and feudal, cultures. Surrounded with a system of peculiar symbols and norms, this role is alien to modern industrialized society. Even in the United States where these cultures were never indigenous, this ancient pattern has established itself.[12]

The pattern can be regarded as an evolutionary relic, but it is not without important institutional functions. Especially in societies where the values and virtues of the military profession are not immediately recognized, this "deviant" pattern helps to reinforce the necessary *esprit de corps*.

The heroic orientation of the professional military man needs to be protected and set apart all the more if the environment leaves little space for it: "in a nation where Spartan attributes are in short supply, any institution which feels a need for them must seek some protection by isolating itself from civilian society."[13] Besides the threat from without there is also a threat from within. Modern weapons, with their massive destructive power, render the traditional heroic attitudes obsolete. Even more important is the fact that because modernization of the European and American armed forces in the past century has been primarily technical, military effort now comes not from men but from machines.

Many military men had difficulty acknowledging this fact. Coming primarily from the landed gentry and the agricultural classes, they had an aversion to the destructive weapons offered by industrial civilization. The many years of unwillingness to accept the machine gun because of emphasis upon the frontal change and personal courage is an excellent example of this traditionalism.[14] It is furthermore not mere chance that the less tradition-bound Americans were the first to use the machine gun on a large scale (in the Civil War).[15]

This "industrialization" of war was part of a general process of rationalization and technicalization, which has for the moment found its terminal point in the present nuclear potential. Thus the differences between combatants and non-combatants have been largely removed, and many distinctions between the military and the members of civil society have become irrelevant.[16]

These and other developments have made a major part of the professional military into military technicians and managers. They are rightly called professional, but their ethos differs markedly from that of the traditional military. They resemble far more their civilian counterparts, who, incidentally, have started to fill the ranks of the armed forces to an increasing degree.

This convergence has led Moskos to the assumption that the American military, at least, is moving from an institutional—or professional—model to an occupational one.[17] The rapid penetration of unionism into the armed forces is a related phenomenon because it also implies contractual, instead of institutional, commitments.[18]

The supposition has grown that these changes influence the performance of military functions in circumstances of war. In any case, this type of professional cannot stand up very well against the challenge of sub-conventional warfare, as practiced in Vietnam. A sensational study by Savage and Gabriel is little less than a frontal attack on the scanty professional quality of the American officer corps in the Vietnamese war. The major cause of the debacle is sought in "its career obsession, and rapid rotation in and out of combat units for the sake of 'ticket punching.'"[19] Savage and Gabriel connect American problems in Vietnam directly with "the replacement of a traditional "gladiatorial" officer stereotype with the managerial combat nonparticipant, where efficiency instead of 'honor' becomes the performance standard."[20]

The demands of counter-guerrilla warfare are so high that the comparison by Savage and Gabriel of the American officer in Vietnam with the German officer in both World Wars is less correct than comparison with the French military in Vietnam. Nevertheless the facts remain, and they come as no surprise to those who are familiar with the doubts expressed by the French, some decades ago, concerning the Americans' managerial orientation.[21]

What is the significance of all this for the relation between armed forces and society? Our first impression is one of a certain degree of convergence, especially where the occupational model exists. However, this impression is only partly correct because the convergence merely suggests a similarity between military and civilian work attitudes.[22]

This work orientation cannot bridge the gap between armed forces and society. On the contrary, the contractual relation between the military and the state can certainly lead, in the case of officers, to a concern with collective self-interest, even at the expense of the public interest.

Moreover, the occupational orientation has been modeled on criteria valid in times of peace. War and the risks resulting from it can never be "paid off" with material compensations; war does not allow the unionist to weigh wages against work load, satisfaction against dissatisfaction.

But the major drawback of the demolition of the professional formula is the same as that of the disintegration of all institutions: the dissociation of self-interest and higher moral principles. After all, institutions are more than established patterns of behavior; they constitute value-oriented ways of handling essential societal needs, and as such they represent society's attempts to solve its problems in a responsible and orderly fashion. The military profession is a classic answer to the question of how violence can be kept within acceptable limits, and, more generally, how a civilization makes sense of the inevitable use of violence.

Military professionalism thus becomes an integral element in modern society. The professional ethos guards the moral boundaries of activities performed on behalf of the political community. If the number of such activities and their consequences increases—as the present forms of collective violence have—then institutionalization becomes all the more urgent. The professional responsibility becomes heavier. This is the reason why, in his discussion with Moskos on the development of the military profession according to occupation, Janowitz rightly states that the present peacetime situation demands "higher levels of professionalism," because "a clear recognition of purpose" is more necessary than ever.[23]

Sarkesian has tried to work out this idea further, using Janowitz's constabulary concept.[24] He believes that the military professional will have to acquire a wider orientation and more political insight. The military professional cannot accept the role of unconditional servant of the nation or become a paid employee of the state, but, within the rules of the game, he must defend the military point of view in political discussion. Sarkesian calls this a delicate affair but also the most obvious means to redefining the professional role.[25]

The institutional connection between the armed forces and society makes this formulation seem quite acceptable. But the question remains whether military professionalism is currently headed in a different direction, that is, whether the military elite is becoming deprofessionalized. If this is true, and the professional self-regulation weakens, then the societal control of the military will come to rest entirely with the political community. The citizen tradition is a historical formulation of a different kind and is therefore worth looking into.


## The Disappearance of the Citizen Soldier

As stated above, Janowitz has repeatedly pointed to the societal origin of the citizen soldier, connecting military service and political democracy, because control of the armed forces is in the hands of the people themselves. The normative definition of the citizen includes political rights as well as military duties, but the duty to bear arms was initially a revolutionary right, because it had previously been restricted to a small elite.

This theme is not merely historically interesting. The citizen tradition is not only still alive in various countries, but can be found in the more widespread derivative form of the military draft. In this sense, the draft can be contrasted with the volunteer force.

For a good understanding of this matter it is, however, necessary to understand that the purely citizen army was nearly always a revolutionary army. Thus, the citizen army is a transitional form of military organization, which either disappears or is transferred into a system of conscription in the post-revolutionary period.[26]

Moreover, the citizen army differs according to the structure of a given society. The American Revolution cannot be compared to European ones. In the American War of Independence, the militia drew large parts of the population into the revolutionary movement, but this took place within a society that showed strongly egalitarian characteristics: citizenship preceded military mobilization.[27]

In the European revolutions, however, recognition of the citizen was incomplete. This explains the fact that in nineteenth-century France and Germany the militia concept was a contra-concept, supported by radical and socialist movements. Where militias existed, they confronted the standing armies.[28]

Furthermore, the citizen is more than universal military service. The citizen concept not only implies universal civil rights but also points to peculiar national traditions in the relation between the state and its subjects.[29] To put it in another way: masses supporting national issues are not necessarily citizens in the modern democratic sense.

Thus, German militarism's success was based on a strong feeling of nationalism together with a semi-feudal social structure, but Germany was, nevertheless, the first nation to introduce universal military service at the same time that it abolished its militia. It would, however, be wrong to presume that this system of conscription strengthened the citizen rights of the German people. Instead, the system was part of a rigid authoritarian structure, supported by the armed forces. Rather than being dependent on the conscripts, the state had full power over them.

Therefore, the citizen soldier and the conscript soldier must be regarded separately, and much depends on the political and societal system within which their participation in the armed forces takes place.[30]

Citizen tradition has rarely been able to halt the continuing professionalization of the military elite. After all, this professionalization has been accompanied by an increasingly technical, complicated, and scientifically based method of warfare. This politically neutral development has helped the strong decline in popularity of the armed forces among the public.

> The armed forces were no longer seen, as they had been for a century and a half, as the embodiment of national pride, the cadre of the nation in arms . . . and although continental countries retained conscript service as a national institution, the core of the armed forces had to be found from highly-skilled professionals . . . .[31]

This dichotomy naturally leads to a hierarchical relationship between the professional and the citizen soldier. Whether they are complementary to each other or rivals[32] is less important than the fact that militias and other supplementary forces are often marginal in the military system, even in a country with such a strong citizen tradition as Israel.[33]

Finally, a few remarks on the progressive civilianization of the modern armed forces. At first, it seems possible to regard this penetration of civic values, norms, and lifestyles into the military community as a new form of community control over the military. This is partly right. Unions organizing military personnel are an extension of the civilian order; common educational facilities give opportunities for influencing military thought; convergence of military and civilian skills stimulate the contact between the two sectors of society.

This phenomenon does not, however, mean a return to the citizen tradition. On the contrary, the citizen soldier was the embodiment of civic militantism in the armed forces, whereas civilianization is often the expression of civilian anti-militarism or of non-military values. The citizen soldier competes with the professional as a military man, and the process of civilianization represents welfare state attitudes and norms in the military community. For this reason civilianization is not so much a way of bridging the gap between the military and its society as a unilateral process of the military's social adaptation.

Although the all-volunteer army shows a tendency to reinforce the internal rigidity of the military and demarcate more sharply the boundaries between the military and the civilian sector, civilianization is clearly not the solution. Rather, an answer may lie in what Janowitz and Moskos describe as the modern redefinition of the citizen soldier.[34] The starting point is an attempt to broaden citizen participation in the armed forces, by, for example, extensive personnel turnover. But the central values of the professional ethos ought not to be affected:

> It is not just another occupation. Whether we are dealing with a new recruit or a four star general, such men and women have undertaken a special obligation and assignment in the national interest. This is the definition of the situation that needs to be institutionalized.[35]

As they did in redefining the professional soldier, Janowitz and Moskos here speak in terms of ideals and images of the future. Whether the present political and social conditions are suitable remains uncertain. At base lies the need to preserve and reinforce existing formulas: the ethos of the professional soldier combined with the idea of the "citizen in uniform."

## The Demystification of the Military

The conclusion is not clear (indeed, disintegrating tendencies exist), but one can point to movements toward reconstruction which indicate that solutions are still possible.

Nevertheless this analysis will not suffice. Insufficient attention has been paid to the question whether the military can still be a viable formula for successfully institutionalizing collective violence. This is a question about the degree to which our great institutions still function. We should hesitate to deal with this question had it not already been discussed by Morris Janowitz. In his great work on America in the last half-century, which advocates an institutional approach, the "disarticulation of social institutions" is introduced at the very beginning; he returns to it in his last chapter, and his opinions show little optimism.[36]

In the case of the military such institutional disarticulation might have extremely dangerous consequences. The main function of military institutions is, after all, regulation of violence. As such violence, applied on a large scale during wartime, implies for the participant a direct confrontation with mutilation and death, all cultures develop institutional arrangements to control fear by giving meaning to these threats to life.

In more advanced societies, those participating in warfare are isolated, not only because this is technically efficient, but also, and particularly so, because their specific function entails an institutionalization of its own. This institutionalization is expressed in uniforms and symbolism, in indoctrination and socialization, and in separate communities, rooted in values and norms of their own.

This process of institutionalization was first applied to what Clifford Geertz has labeled primordial attachments: blood, religion, custom. Loyalties take the form of tribalism and communalism.[37] At a later stage of societal development these attachments become weaker, making way for the rise of specialized social institutions. The military is one of these; the institutionalizing of the use of violence takes on a pattern of its own, deviating from and even contrasting with the rest of society.

The military profession is an excellent example of such a process. The use of violence is entrusted to specialists who perform their task in the service of the political community. Their reward lies in the general recognition of their legitimacy and in the special status that is granted to them.

However, this mode of institutionalization is also a vulnerable one. Institutionalized violence, unlike violence between communities, which is seen as a primordial commitment, is now based on culturally determined arrangements which follow cultural change.

The first cultural transformation in Western history to have far-reaching consequences for the position of the military institution was the bourgeois-supported breakthrough of Enlightenment ideas in the nineteenth century. The military man came to be regarded as a representative of an obsolete, even barbaric, institution, that was doomed to disappear.

Late nineteenth-century nationalism changed this situation by providing a new basis for the military element in society and politics. Yet to a certain extent it was like rowing upstream. The glorification of collective violence often had a strong sense of artificiality, witness of a bad conscience. It was political adherents of the Counter-Enlightenment[38] such as Bakunin, Sorel, and Nietzsche who once more attached a mythical role to violence, both in the struggle between nations, and in revolutionary movements.

The militarization of modern totalitarianism shows how overstrained this mythification of violence has become. From a historical point of view, the totalitarian movements nevertheless constituted the last stronghold within which the military myth could flourish freely. After that it would be up to violent resistance movements where the myth experienced a revival, justified and even supported by Western philosophers like Sartre, Fanon, and others. But in the same period the military institution of the nation-state suffered from fundamental disenchantment and demythologizing.

Various causes of this process have been mentioned above. The media (especially television, which brought the war in Vietnam before our eyes) and the social sciences have also contributed to the debunking.[39]

However, we are not concerned here with what caused the process but with whether participation in collective violence and war is possible when it is not rooted in the irrational world of myths and symbols. Will not the disenchantment of civilization, heralded by Weber, and its rationalization, studied by Mannheim, produce a rationalization of the business of warfare, which will only lead to technically efficient killing on a large scale?

The question gains actuality with the observation that not only military institutions but the great professions too have been subject to the process of *Entmythologisierung*. The work of scholars like Freidson, Johnson, and Bledstein indicates that the crisis of the professional model extends far beyond the military sphere.[40]

Perhaps one can even go further and say that criticism of the major social institutions from family to church and state is now general. This is, evidently, what Morris Janowitz alludes to when he speaks of an "extensive disarticulation of social institutions"[41] in the Epilogue of his latest major work.

He nevertheless remains optimistic, and he bases this optimism on the assumption that the important contribution of the macro-sociology of advanced industrial societies must be sought in institution-building.[42] He speaks as a citizen of the United States, which, unlike European nations, is capable of surviving vast and often disruptive social change. American civilization, right from its beginning, has known, expected, and appreciated social change. In the recent past, radical discontinuity has had a destructive effect on Europe; America may well survive such discontinuity and profit by it.[43]

The future of the military depends upon American society to prove that disarticulation, or even disintegration, of the traditional military institutions need not mean the end of moral and political restrictions to violence.

## Notes

1. Paul Plaut, "Prinzipien und Methoden der Kriegspsychologie," *Handbuch der biologischen Arbeitsmethoden*, ed. Emil Abderhalden (Berlin and Vienna: Urban & Schwarzenberg, 1928), pp. 621–87; Samuel A. Stouffer, et al., *The American Soldier* (Princeton, N.J.: Princeton University Press, 1949, 2 vols.); Morris Janowitz, *Sociology and the Military Establishment* (New York: Russell Sage Foundation, 1959).

2. Morris Janowitz, *The Last Half-Century: Societal Change and Politics in America* (Chicago & London: University of Chicago Press, 1978), pp. 3, 546.

3. Janowitz, *The Last Half-Century*, pp. 397 ff.; also see his *Social Control of the Welfare State* (New York/Oxford/Amsterdam: Elsevier, 1976).

4. Morris Janowitz, *Sociology and the Military Establishment*, pp. 25 ff.; *The Professional Soldier* (New York: Free Press, 1960), chs. 1 and 20.

5. Samuel P. Huntington, *The Soldier and the State* (Cambridge, Mass.: Harvard University Press, Belknap Press, 1957), pp. 7 ff., 469.

6. Morris Janowitz, "From Institutional to Occupational: The Need for Conceptual Continuity," *Armed Forces and Society* 4 (Fall 1977), pp. 51–54.

7. Morris Janowitz, *The U.S. Forces and the Zero Draft* (London: IISS, Adelphi Papers nr. 94, 1973), pp. 21 ff.

8. Morris Janowitz, "Military Institutions and Citizenship in Western Societies," *Armed Forces and Society* 2 (Winter 1976), pp. 185–204.

9. Janowitz, *The Last Half-Century*, pp. 166 ff., 177 f.

10. Janowitz, *The Professional Soldier*, pp. 5 ff.

11. Louis A. Zurcher and Gwyn Harries-Jenkins, eds., *Supplementary Military Forces: Reserves, Militias, Auxiliaries* (Beverly Hills and London: Sage Publications, 1978).

12. See the penetrating observations by Philip Caputo in his book on Vietnam, *A Rumor of War* (London: Macmillan, 1977), pp. 8, 23, 31.

13. Laurence I. Radway, "Recent Trends at American Service Academies," in Charles C. Moskos, Jr., ed., *Public Opinion and the Military Establishment* (Beverly Hills: Sage Publications, 1971), p. 9.

14. John Ellis, *The Social History of the Machine Gun* (London: Croom Helm, 1975), pp. 16 ff.

15. Ibid., pp. 21 ff.

16. Albert D. Biderman, "What Is Military?" in Sol Tax, ed., *The Draft: A Handbook of Facts and Alternatives* (Chicago and London: University of Chicago Press, 1967), pp. 122 ff.

17. Charles C. Moskos, Jr., "From Institution to Occupation: Trends in Military Organization," *Armed Forces and Society* 4 (Fall 1977), pp. 41–50.

18. William J. Taylor, Jr., Roger J. Arango and Robert S. Lockwood, eds., *Military Unions* (Beverly Hills and London: Sage Publications, 1977).

19. Paul L. Savage and Richard A. Gabriel, "Cohesion and Disintegration in the American Army," *Armed Forces and Society* 2 (Spring 1976), p. 371.

20. Savage and Gabriel, p. 340.

21. Raoul Girardet, *La crise militaire française 1945–1962* (Paris: Armand Colin, 1964), pp. 222 f.

22. Roger W. Little, "Convergence of the Civilian and Military Occupational Structures," in N. A. B. Wilson, ed., *Manpower Research* (London: The English Universities Press, 1969), pp. 442–448; David R. Segal, Barbara Ann Lynch and John D. Blair, "The Changing American Soldier: Work-Related Attitudes of U.S. Army Personnel in World War II and in the 1970s," *American Journal of Sociology* 85 (July 1979), pp. 95–108.

23. Janowitz, "From Institutional to Occupational," p. 53.

24. Janowitz, *The Professional Soldier*, pp. 418 ff.

25. Sam C. Sarkesian, "Professional Problems and Adaptations" in Ellen P. Stern, ed., *The Limits of Military Intervention* (Beverly Hills and London: Sage Publications, 1977), pp. 306 ff., 313 ff., 318 ff.

26. John Ellis, *Armies in Revolution* (London: Croom Helm, 1973), pp. 238 ff.

27. John Shy, *A People Numerous and Armed: Reflections on the Military Struggle for American Independence* (London/Oxford/New York: Oxford University Press, 1976).

28. Felix Gilbert, ed., *The Historical Essays of Otto Hintze* (New York: Oxford University Press, 1975), pp. 206–15; Michael Howard, *War in European History* (London/Oxford/New York: Oxford University Press, 1976), pp. 94 ff.

29. Carl Brinkmann, "Citizenship," in *International Encyclopedia of the Social Sciences* (New York: Macmillan, 1930), vol. III, p. 471.

30. Jacques van Doorn, *The Soldier and Social Change* (Beverly Hills and London: Sage Publications, 1975), pp. 95 f.

31. Howard, *War in European History*, pp. 141 f.

32. Zurcher and Harries-Jenkins, eds., *Supplementary Military Forces*, pp. 12–16.

33. Baruch Kimmerling, "The Israeli Civil Guard," in Zurcher and Harries-Jenkins, eds., *Supplementary Military Forces*, pp. 107 ff.

34. Morris Janowitz and Charles C. Moskos, Jr., "Five Years of the All-Volun-

teer Force: 1973–1978," *Armed Forces and Society* 5 (Winter 1979), pp. 209 ff.

35. Janowitz and Moskos, p. 211.

36. Janowitz, *The Last Half-Century*, pp. 16 f., 548.

37. Clifford Geertz, "The Integrative Revolution: Primordial Sentiments and Civil Politics in the New States," in Clifford Geertz, ed., *Old Societies and New States* (New York: Free Press, 1963), pp. 109, 111.

38. Isaiah Berlin, "The Counter-Enlightenment," in *Against the Current: Essays in the History of Ideas* (London: The Hogarth Press, 1979), pp. 1–24.

39. Recent examples: Norman Dixon, *On the Psychology of Military Incompetence* (London: Jonathan Cape, 1976); John Keegan, *The Face of Battle* (New York: Vintage Books, 1977).

40. Eliot Freidson, *Profession of Medicine* (New York: Dodd, Mead, 1970); Terence J. Johnson, *Professions and Power* (London: Macmillan, 1972); Burton J. Bledstein, *The Culture of Professionalism* (New York: W. W. Norton, 1976).

41. Janowitz, *The Last Half-Century*, p. 548.

42. Janowitz, *The Last Half-Century*, p. 551.

43. Stanley Hoffmann, "Fragments Floating in the Here and Now," in "Looking for Europe," *Daedalus* 108 (Winter 1979), pp. 8–10.

# 2

# Convergence and Structural Linkages Between Armed Forces and Society

MOSHE LISSAK

The issue of institutional linkages between the military and civilians is rather old and well known. Lately it has become a focus of attention in the literature dealing with military–civilian relations of both developing and developed, post-industrial countries. In the latter case, the concept of convergence has often been brought up. The two sectors, which in the recent past were very different from each other in terms of structure, mode of operation, and social norms, have begun to converge.[1] Convergence may be achieved either simultaneously, although at different rates, or by the adoption by one sector of the attributes and functions of the other. It is currently generally accepted that it is the military system that has changed and is becoming more and more like a large-scale civilian bureaucratic system.[2]

One may raise some basic questions concerning this definition of convergence, such as:

1. What are the conditions conducive to the development of convergence, or, alternatively, of divergence of the two sectors?

2. Is the convergence trend operating simultaneously and at the same intensity at all levels of the two sectors, and does it have the same impact on all their attributes and functions? For example, one may ask whether convergence or divergence has the same impact on structure (e.g., division of labor between the various military services), on mode of operation (e.g., decision-making processes), and on the normative dimension (e.g., military discipline, or source of authority within the military system).

3. What is the possible impact of these processes on the various institutional linkages between the military establishment and the civilian sector?

The first question has been extensively covered. There is a basic consensus as to what conditions are conducive to the development of trends of convergence or divergence. Therefore, we will refer to this question only very briefly.

Among the most important factors promoting the process of convergence is the role expansion of the military. With the technological revolution, the process of professionalization, internal differentiation between the services and their branches, and the need for more concern with civilian issues, both in peacetime and in emergency, diversified organs intended to cope with these problems have grown rapidly. Within these organs one can find many roles and functions which parallel civilian occupations.[3] Thus military occupations have become increasingly interchangeable with civilian occupations.[4] This is certainly true in developed societies within Western and communist regimes. However, one may notice similar trends in the more developed countries of the third world. The trend toward convergence between the military establishment and the civilian sector is, then, a result, on the one hand, of the role expansion (characterizing especially developing countries), specialization, and professionalization of the armed forces, and, on the other, of the democratization and liberalization of the civilian sector, which does not stop at the gates of military bases. The last trend is obviously more salient in Western democratic societies.

Still, outside of the trend of convergence, one can discern built-in constraints preventing major overlaps between the two sectors. These sectors and even more so certain sub-systems within them (for example, the rural sector in many of the third world states) are not exposed to the same pressures for structural changes, and thus their motivations to adopt new modes of operation and normative principles are different. In addition, over a period of time, it has become evident that overall convergence is more limited than it first looked.[5] This mistake can be explained by the illusion caused by the external similarities between civilian and military occupations in industrialized countries. Role expansion is rather limited as far as Western democratic societies are concerned, although it was rather widespread in many developing societies in the 1950s and 1960s.[6] However, as we must avoid the illusion that the military and civilian sectors are converging, so must we also avoid the idea that they are sharply diverging.[7] It is more reasonable to assume the simultaneous co-existence in most of the armed forces of convergence and divergence trends between the two sectors and within the military establishment itself. It was Moskos who suggested naming this sort of army the "Segmented or Plural Army."[8] The "plural" aspect is evident in the variety of trends within the military establishment; the "segmented," in the fact that the various trends have differing validity within the different components and branches of the military. Possible lines dividing these components may be, for example, those between officers and NCOs, or between combat units and administrative units.[9] The pluralistic and segmented character of convergence and divergence trends in many armed forces, especially within Western democratic societies, are realities which will not disappear in the near future, although one can expect variations on these trends. Thus we must ask how these multiple and contrasting phenomena will influence the institutional linkages between the military and civilian sectors.

One-sided and generalized conceptions about convergence patterns have led in the past to misleading conclusions about the future of the institutional linkages between the two sectors. Institutional linkages are all formal and informal frameworks that serve as meeting points for military men and civilians. Governmental committees for research and development or for political-strategic planning serve as links in some countries; educational institutions operated both by military and civilian authorities or agrarian reform activities supported by military commanders, in others.

Some scholars have assumed that divergence patterns will weaken the linkages between the military and civilian sectors,[10] whereas others have argued that divergence will intensify the dependence of the military establishment on the civilian sector and thus will strengthen institutional linkages.[11] These two contentions need to be reconciled. It would be wrong to assume the existence of an exclusive and clear-cut relationship between convergence or divergence, on the one hand, and the strengthening or weakening of linkages between the armed forces and the civilian population, on the other. The hypothesis that in certain cases divergence processes are indeed weakening the institutional linkages, while in other cases the reverse is true, must be tested. Is there any relationship, direct or indirect, between all the factors that cause a weakening or a strengthening of institutional linkages? Do changes in the structure, mode of operation, and norms of the armed forces have a differential impact on the institutionalization of the linkages between the two sectors?

The hypothesis that no consistent correlation between convergence and divergence processes and the strength of the linkages between the two sectors exists is based on the assumption that there are a number of possible interactions between these two variables. The following chart presents four prototypes:[12]

|  |  | *Institutional Linkages* | |
| --- | --- | --- | --- |
|  |  | strengthened | weakened |
| *Trend* | convergence | A | B |
|  | divergence | C | D |

1. Prototype A illustrates the possibility that convergence may bring about the strengthening and institutionalization of linkages between the civilian and military sectors.
2. Prototype B, that convergence may be followed by the weakening of these linkages.
3. Prototype C, that the process of divergence strengthens the institutional linkages.
4. Prototype D, that divergence weakens the linkages.

Various investigations concerning military-civilian relationships, both in democratic and non-democratic societies, and in developed and developing countries, contain many examples of A.[13] One of the most obvious is the interaction between military and political elites. The necessity of combining strategic and political considerations in many cases of national security analysis requires a great deal of specialization in these two fields, not only by the civilian experts and political leaders but also by military officers. It also requires meetings between the two elites who create "national security policy."[14] As the specialization increases in strategic policies and related fields, this sort of meeting will, out of necessity, become formalized. In both Western and Eastern-European societies political-strategic considerations are generally linked to global and regional balances of power. In many of the developing countries decisionmaking in this area is usually part of a counter-guerrilla warfare.[15]

Another prominent example, typical only of Western European societies, is the phenomenon of unionization within the armed forces. In contrast to the preceding example, meeting formats here are between the middle and the lower ranks of the civilian and military hierarchies. In recent years the rapid expansion of unions, especially among enlisted men and NCOs, has been aimed at protecting personal interests (the freedom of the individual), and professional interests (conditions of service). In some cases the military trade unions have connections with civilian trade unions and even political organizations.[16] This phenomenon did not result from the switch to a volunteer-based army, although it is very possible that unionization will crystallize and institutionalize even more in an all-volunteer army. It will certainly be unavoidable if the military establishment, or parts of it, adopts the rules of the civilian labor market in order to compete there. A rather substantial segment of the available manpower is already composed of civilians who are working for the military in non-combat positions and who already belong to civilian trade unions.[17]

One of the best documented examples of prototype A is the growth of the number of military occupations that are similar, or even identical, to civilian occupations.[18] This phenomenon diverts our discussion from the politico-economic aspect to the socio-economic one. In the more sophisticated military systems where the trend of convergence is dominant, and especially in the structural sphere, many are employed as technicians, physicians, lawyers, social workers, etc., and maintain, or are willing to maintain, some sort of allegiance to civilian professional organizations. The more these allegiances strengthen, the more important civilian professional organizations become in molding the linkages between the civilian and military sectors. This development may bring about a conflict of interests between the bureaucratic and the professional aspects of the above-mentioned positions, or, more specifically, antagonism between loyalties to the military and commitment to the profession.[19]

Another illustration of the correlation between the process of convergence and the strengthening of the linkages between the military and civilian sectors may be found in the area of social stratification. Many scholars argue that a mass army based on conscription is the best guarantee for optimal representation of the various economic, ethnic, religious, and other groups within the society concerned. This is particularly true for the lower echelons of the armed forces. Moreover, the existence of a comprehensive conscription system drawing draftees from all parts of society creates, at least theoretically, optimal conditions for qualified personnel to move upward. Under these conditions the armed forces are the most balanced representation of a given country's different social groups.[20] This balanced representation ensures, to a large extent, the continuing existence of linkages, albeit not necessarily formal ones, between various segments of the military with socially corresponding segments of the civilian sector.

Another important illustration of the interrelationship between trends of convergence and the strengthening of the linkages between the civilian and the military sectors is the existence of a large-scale reserve force, drawn from the entire eligible population. The continuation of professional and institutional civilian allegiances to the armed forces by long periods of reserve service strengthens perhaps more than any other mechanism the linkages between the two sectors. This assumption is certainly true when reserve duty entails not only personal sacrifice but also social reward—such service symbolizes membership in the national collective and identification with its most important goals.[21] From the military standpoint, the existence of a reserve force encourages the continuation and institutionalization of social contact between career personnel and the reservists in all ranks and all occupations within the armed forces. Thus one may look at the reserve forces as a military-social complex or a military-community complex, which is larger and even more comprehensive than the military-industrial complex. Moreover, in contrast to the military-industrial complex, with which many associate negative functions,[22] the reserve establishment may substantially reduce the danger of a professional military caste's emergence, and thus contribute to a better integration of the military professionals into the overall social hierarchy.

A final example of prototype A is the involvement of the armed forces in civic action. Military participation in civilian projects is a common and widespread phenomenon in many developing countries.[23] Some European military organizations also have experience in this sort of activity, especially in emergencies (for example, natural disasters). This extension of activities certainly strengthens the linkages between the two sectors.

The second prototype (B) represents a reverse trend. In this case the process of convergence between the two sectors may have a negative effect on how the linkages fulfill their roles. These two contrasting prototypes are not mutually exclusive. They may operate simultaneously within the same military organization, although their significance and weight may differ. A typical example is the extensive convergence be-tween the higher echelons of the military and the civilian political sys-tem. One possible result of this process is the personal and conceptual dominance of the civilian defense ministry by the military elite. In these circumstances, the ministry of defense loses its ability to serve as a buffer and mediator between the general staff and the political elites and be-comes, in fact, the representative of the military on defense and foreign policy. It goes without saying that the effectiveness of the civilian sector in influencing defense policy generally diminishes under these circum-stances, if it is not lost entirely, as in a case of a coup d'état.

Another illuminating example which has already drawn a great deal of academic and general attention is the phenomenon of the military-industrial complex (the MIC). However, the fact that the process of convergence means the reduction of the scope of the MIC has been neglected. Convergence in this context means that the research and development of weapons is nationalized in the form of a "military indus-try." On the other hand, when the armed forces abandon, for whatever reason, the policy of having the defense ministry itself responsible for research and development, the conditions are much more conducive to the strengthening of the linkages between the two sectors. It is, however, clear that, due to the technological sophistication of warfare, the inter-dependence of civilian and military industries is unavoidable, necessitat-ing at least an elementary form of MIC. This necessity is not in force, of course, in the many developing countries which lack industrial infrastructures.

The interpersonal relationships between military personnel and the civilian population are another prominent example of a possible negative relationship between convergence and the weakening of the ties between the two sectors. The increasing trend toward housing military personnel with their families on military bases and providing them with all the services available in the civilian sector may change the military base into a pseudo-total institution, not only for the soldier but for his family as well. In these circumstances, the network of primary and secondary prelationships with the civilian population may be weakened.[24]

The military monopoly on the professional training of soldiers and officers is a similar phenomenon. Convergence here is expressed in the inclination of military academies to choose all their professional and academic teaching staff from among military personnel and to limit its contact with the civilian academic community to sporadic discussions of esoteric subjects.[25] This monopoly on both the transfer of professional knowhow and general education has reduced the possibilities for relationships with various segments of the civilian sector which could help the military in precisely these matters of education and professional training. The rather wide judicial autonomy employed by the military in democratic societies, and especially in many of the developing societies, denying civilian courts jurisdiction over military personnel even in cases of civilian offenses, is also significant evidence of the possible negative relationship between trends of convergence and a weakening in the institutionalization of the meeting points between the two sectors. [26]

The third prototype (C) describes the relationship between the trend of divergence and the institutionalization of meeting points. A typical example of this sort of relationship exists in societies where the armed forces are actually giving up their absolute autonomy in research and development. Intensive cooperation between civilian and military industries produces a large-scale MIC. Such a complex may have negative implications, especially in the political field—the civilian political elite might effectively control the military establishment. These apprehensions, however, do not negate the potential contributions of the MIC to the strengthening and institutionalization of the meeting points between the two sectors. Lacking research and development frameworks, many developing countries are actually denied such a potential meeting point. Cooperation between the representatives of the armed forces and civilian officials in purchasing arms from abroad may serve as a substitute.

Another typical example of the third prototype is the situation where the armed forces are giving up, if feasible (as it is in most of the Western and communist societies), the absolute monopoly of military academies on education and training of officer candidates. The result in the case of Western democratic societies, for example, is increasing cooperation between military academies and universities. A university education becomes an integral part of an officer's curriculum. [27] In this case we find divergence at the structural level and in the military mode of operation, but the promotion of convergence at the normative level. The inclination to reduce the judicial autonomy of the armed forces may also bring about stronger meeting points between the two sectors.

In the fourth and last prototype (D) the process of divergence may have a destructive impact on the institutional linkages between the two sectors. One example is from the political-strategic sphere. A possible result of divergence in this case would be a low level of coordination between strategic planning executed by general staffs and political planning made within the civilian administration. In periods of consecutive emergencies, a low level of this kind of coordination may give military intelligence (MI) an almost complete monopoly on intelligence both at the tactical and the strategic levels. In other words, communications would be one way, especially if political elites do not have the personnel and instruments to evaluate the validity and reliability of the raw intelligence provided by MI, as is the case in most third world states. The danger in this case is that tactical and strategic considerations which lack a social or political dimension may lead to misleading estimates of the enemy's strength and intentions.

The second careers of military personnel present a related problem. One can envision a situation where, despite fewer quasi-civilian jobs in the military establishment, the military authorities do not provide a system of training for second careers in the civilian labor market. The absence of a clear policy regarding the change-over from a military to a civilian career may harm the relationship between the two sectors. In this case, it would be hard to control and channel the social, political, and economic by-products of the influx of unprepared soldiers and officers into the civilian labor market.[28] A lack of policy here is especially destructive in societies where military service is based on generally long periods of voluntary service which make adaptation to civilian life more complicated.

Another potential by-product of the establishment of an all-voluntary army is an example of prototype D. Volunteer recruitment is correctly linked by some scholars to a selective and uneven representation of the various social groups.[29] An even greater distortion may emerge when the distinction between "aristocratic" and "non-aristocratic" units is based on social origin and on traditional allegiance of certain status, ethnic, or tribal groups in the civilian population to certain military units. A large-scale reserve system may mitigate the negative effect of the armed forces uneven social composition, but the general trend of not relying on large reserve forces intensifies the negative effect of divergence upon the structural linkages between the civilian and military sectors.

The above examples are intended to show that the direct and indirect effects of convergence and divergence trends within the military establishment generate many unforeseen by-products. These examples also emphasize that many of these by-products exist simultaneously and may even work against each other. This is the case when one looks at these processes over time. For example, it is contended that since World War II a process of alienation and segregation between the two sectors has become evident, in many cases and especially in democratic societies. This phenomenon can be seen as a shift from the first to the fourth of our prototypes.

One can criticize this contention as ignoring some of the undercurrents that operate simultaneously with the general trend. But a belief in the validity and authenticity of this general trend is supported at the normative-symbolic level by the shrinking of the armed forces' prestige and symbolism. It has not been our intention to disprove the reliability of this particular diagnosis but rather to emphasize that parallel to this development other trends are noticeable. One can especially see the institutionalization of new meeting points between the military and civilian sectors or the re-institutionalization of traditional ones. Our contention is that, although at a certain stage one may notice an accelerated movement from the first to the last prototype, eventually this process will halt. In the armed forces of most democratic societies one can observe the symptoms of prototypes A and D, as well as those of B and C. In the long run, the problem of the co-existence of various prototypes operating simultaneously is less important than the different emphases put on one prototype or the other by various military establishments. Theoretically, one can classify various societies even if they belong to a more or less homogeneous political culture (for example, democratic societies) according to their similarity to one prototype or another. Despite this, one should not forget that the similarities between various societies regarding relationships between civilian and military sectors may be attributed to different causes. In addition, the legitimacy of a certain status quo might not be the same in the civilian sector as it would be in the military sector.

In summary, processes of convergence and divergence operate simultaneously in most of the armed forces. One should not *a priori* assume positive or negative correlations between these processes and the character of the structural linkages between the two sectors. The fact that two-way processes exist calls for revised descriptions of the "social crisis" attributed to the various armed forces and of the chances for this crisis' resolution.[31] A more balanced evaluation of this issue is needed.

I have tried to contribute to such a balanced perspective. More empirical evidence needs to be accumulated, and the theoretical sociological issues relevant to these issues must be clarified. For example, the phenomenon of boundary permeability between various institutional spheres within the society at large, and specifically between various civilian subsystems and the armed forces needs further elaboration.[31] The respective concepts of convergence and divergence need to be better defined. It is crucial to understand much more about these two processes at the structural level. The development of this sphere of research also requires a better definition of the types of social, economic, and symbolic exchange that occur between the military establishment and various civilian subsystems.[32] The understanding of these diversified processes of input and output will certainly shed more light on the structural linkages between the two sectors and the character of the key men that operate in these frameworks. Finally, theoretical development in this direction may enable us to understand more clearly the contribution of each of our suggested prototypes to the social and political stability of societies that depend so heavily on the quality of relations between civilian and military elites.

## Notes

1. Morris Janowitz, *The Professional Soldier* (New York: Free Press, 1960), pp. 15–72; Charles C. Moskos, Jr., "Armed Forces and American Society: Convergence or Divergence?" in Charles C. Moskos, Jr., ed., *Public Opinion and the Military Establishment* (Beverly Hills, Calif.: Sage Publications, 1971), pp. 271–94; Charles C. Moskos, Jr., "The Emergent Military: Civilian, Traditional, or Plural?" *Pacific Sociological Review* 16 (April 1971): 255–80; Albert D. Biderman and Laure M. Sharp, "The Convergence of the Military and Civilian Occupational Structures: Evidence from Studies of Military and Retired Employment," *American Journal of Sociology* 73 (January 1968): 381–99; David R. Segal, John Blair, Frank Newport, and Susan Stephens, "Convergence, Isomorphisms, and Interdependence on the Military Interface," *Journal of Political and Military Sociology* 2 (Fall 1974): 159.

2. Morris Janowitz, "Armed Forces in Western Europe: Uniformity and Diversity," *Archives Europeenes de Sociologie* 6 (1965): 225–37; Moskos, "Emergent Military," p. 207; Albert D. Biderman, "What is the Military?" in Sol Tax, ed., *The Draft* (Chicago: University of Chicago Press, 1967), pp. 122–25.

3. Biderman and Sharpe, "Convergence of Military," pp. 381–99; Kurt Lang, *Military Institutions and the Sociology of War* (Beverly Hills, Calif.: Sage Publications, 1972), pp. 179–204.

4. Lang, *Military Institutions*, pp. 92–93, 97.

5. Roger W. Little, "Convergence of the Civilian and Military Occupational Structures," in N. A. B. Wilson, ed., *Manpower Research* (London: English University Press, 1969), pp. 442–48; Segal et al., "Convergence," pp. 157–72.

6. Moshe Lissak, *Military Roles in Modernization: Civil-Military Relations in Thailand and Burma* (Beverly Hills, Calif.: Sage Publications, 1976), pp. 13–46.

7. Biderman and Sharpe, "Convergence of Military," p. 282.

8. Moskos, "Emergent Military," p. 275.

9. Biderman and Sharpe, "Convergence of Military," p. 282; Moskos, "Emergent Military," pp. 275–77; Segal et al., "Convergence," p. 170.

10. Morris Janowitz, *Military Conflict* (Beverly Hills, Calif.: Sage Publications, 1975), p. 85.

11. Segal et al., "Convergence," pp. 159, 162–65.

12. As these prototypes are an illustration of hypothetical interrelationships between two variables, they are certainly capable of suffering from over-generalization and oversimplification. For example, the frame of reference for this diagram is the armed forces in general. In fact, it is possible, and even necessary, to break this framework down into several sub-systems. For example, it is reasonable to compare the officer corps to the NCO and enlisted ranks, combat units to support units, or highly technological units to units with simple functions. The same is true of the other variable. One may break down the institutional linkages into various subtypes, as, for example, the distinction between formal and informal linkages or between highly institutionalized and less developed linkages. Another possibility is the comparison of the different institutional spheres, such as political, economic, educational, etc. The oversimplification of the diagram is also reflected in the fact that we have not attempted here to distinguish between convergence-divergence processes at individual, structural, operational, or normative levels. This diagram, which is essentially a result of analytical deduction, is intended, rather, to suggest only general correlations between the two variables concerned with here. Undoubtedly, any systematic, empirical research will have to resort to more sophisticated models. Thus the following illustrations are not supposed to replace more comprehensive and empirical research. They are intended only to suggest possible hypotheses for testing and to show the value of these prototypes.

13. There is some similarity between this prototype and what van Doorn calls "Reactive Civilization." Jacques van Doorn, "Models of the Emergent Military: Civilisation or Remilitarization," *Royal United Service Institute for Defense Studies Journal* (March 1975): 35–37.

14. Jacques van Doorn, "The Military Profession in Transition," in Wilson, *Manpower Research*, p. 456; Lang, *Military Institutions*, p. 48; Stanley Hoffman, "The Acceptability of Military Force," in *Force in Modern Society*, Adelphi Paper No. 102 (London: International Institute for Strategic Studies, 1973).

15. Eliezer Ben Rafael and Moshe Lissak, *Social Aspects of Guerilla Warfare and Anti-Guerilla Warfare* (Jerusalem: Magnes Press, Hebrew University, 1979).

16. Moskos, "Emergent Military," p. 268; *Armed Forces and Society*, "Special Symposium on Trade Unionism in the Military" (Summer 1976): 475–612.

17. For the issue of the impact of civilian employees on the autonomy of the military framework, see Biderman. "What is Military," in Tax, ed., *The Draft*, pp. 133–34.

18. Biderman and Sharpe, "Convergence of Military," p. 383; Moskos, "Emergent Military," p. 273.

19. Jacques van Doorn, *Soldier and Social Change* (Beverly Hills: Calif.: Sage Publications, 1975), pp. 29–50.

20. Janowitz, "Armed Forces in Western Europe," p. 232; Moskos, "Emergent Military," pp. 271–75; Lang, *Military Institutions*, p. 87.

21. Dan Horowitz and Baruch Kimmerling, "Some Social Implications of Military Service and the Reserves System in Israel," *Archives Européennes de Sociologie* (15): 265, 278.

22. Stanley Lieberson, "An Empirical Study of Military-Industrial Linkages," in Sam C. Sarkesian, ed., *The Military-Industrial Complex: A Reassessment* (Beverly Hills, Calif.: Sage Publications, 1972), pp. 53–94; C. Wright Mills, *The Power Elite* (New York: Oxford University Press, 1956), pp. 198–204; Charles C. Moskos, Jr., "The Military-Industrial Complex: Theoretical Antecedents and Conceptual Contradictions," in Sarkesian, ed., *The Military-Industrial Complex*, pp. 6–17; Marc Pilisuk and Thomas Hayden, "Is There a Military Industrial Complex Which Prevents Peace?" *Journal of Social Issues* 21 (July 1965): 65; Charles Wolf, Jr., "Military-Industrial Simplicities, Complexities, Realities," in Sarkesian, ed., *The Military-Industrial Complex*, pp. 25–52.

23. Lissak, *Military Roles*, pp. 13–46.

24. Segal et al., "Convergence," pp. 160–62.

25. Maurice Garnier, "Some Implications for the British Experience with the All Volunteer Army," *Pacific Sociological Review* 16 (April 1973): 190; C. M. A. Hartman, "The Service Academies as a Social System," in M. R. van Gils, ed., *The Perceived Role of the Military* (Rotterdam: Erasmus University Press, 1971), pp. 42–44.

26. Bengt Abrahamson, *Military Professionalization and Political Power* (Beverly Hills, Calif.: Sage Publications, 1972), p. 147; Morris Janowitz, "Strategic Dimensions of an All Volunteer Armed Forces," in Sarkesian, ed., *The Military-Industrial Complex*, p. 53.

27. Garnier, "Some Implications," p. 190; Hartman, "The Service Academies," pp. 42–44; Janowitz, "Strategic Dimensions," pp. 153–55.

28. Albert Biderman, "Retired Soldiers within and without the Military-Industrial Complex," in Sarkesian, ed., *The Military-Industrial Complex*, p. 122.

29. Garnier, "Some Implications," pp. 187–96; Moskos, "Armed Forces," p. 277.

30. We are not concerned here with the quality of combat units. Nevertheless, there is certainly a substantial correlation between the social and the professional aspects.

31. Moshe Lissak, "The Defense Establishment and the Society in Israel: Boundaries and Institutional Linkages," Prepared for the IUS Conference, Chicago, October 1980; Segal, et al., "Convergence."

32. Lissak, "Military Roles," pp. 13–46.

# 3

# Military Service, Nationalism, and the Global Community

JOHN LOVELL

## Nationalism and Modern War

The twentieth century has witnessed the hypertrophy of war, in Walter Millis's apt phrase.[1] Weapons of war have been perfected to a point that warring states are able to inflict death and destruction on one another to unprecedented levels with unprecedented speed. Moreover, the tiny sector of the population that was called upon to do battle in the past has been superseded by entire societies mobilized in the name of patriotic duty. The nation-in-arms concept that took root in revolutionary slogans in America in 1776 and in France in 1789 reached its full expression in two world wars in the twentieth century. In the nuclear era, war planning proceeds on the assumption that if entire societies are not devas-

I have benefited from comments and criticisms on an early draft of this chapter offered by my colleagues, Edward H. Buehrig, Byrum E. Carter, James B. Christoph, Norman Furniss, and Harvey Starr.

tatingly affected by an initial violent exchange at the outset of war, rapid mobilization will be required to sustain the conflict.

It is no wonder that thoughtful men and women have cried out not only in protest at the ever-more-awesome arms race among the nuclear powers, but also at parochial expressions of loyalty that may convince governments that war remains a viable, perhaps a required, option. On the eve of the twentieth century, a Cambridge professor of law, John Westlake, observed that it had become "almost a truism to say that the mitigation of war must depend on the parties to it feeling that they belong to a larger whole than their respective tribes or states, a whole in which the enemy too is comprised, so that duties arising out of that larger citizenship are owed even to him."[2] Half a century and two world wars later, Arnold Toynbee also wrote of the need to transcend the identification with "the particular tribe of which we happen to be tribesmen. . . . If the human race is to survive," he warned, "we shall have to make a revolutionary break with the traditional order of priorities in our loyalties. We shall have to transfer our paramount loyalty from our respective national fragments of the human race to the human race itself."[3]

However, the painful experience of the twentieth century suggests that the wishful quality of proposals such as those of Westlake and Toynbee has rendered them politically impotent. Moreover, to focus exclusively on the pernicious uses to which armed forces have been put in the name of modern nationalism is to fail to acknowledge fully the paradoxical relationships among military service, nationalism, and global community. Military service, nationalism, and a sense of global community assume distinctive forms and meanings within particular contexts, of course, and most notably differ considerably from the less developed countries to complex industrial societies. Given space limitations, we focus here especially on the pattern of interrelationships that is discernible in the latter.

## Military Service and the Roots of Commitment

The proposition that military service in defense of the state was an obligation inherent in citizenship is evident in the writings of Plato and Aristotle. In the revival of classical thought in the late Middle Ages, military service emerged again as an essential attribute of active citizenship (*vivere civile*) in a republic.[4] Although military service his continued to be linked at least symbolically to citizenship in modern nation-states, the size of several of the most populous modern states, the professionalization of armed forces in them, and changing perceptions of the demands of loyalty in the light of the nature of modern warfare are among the factors that have altered the manner in which the linkage has been maintained.[5]

No state should expect to elicit unconditional loyalty. Nor can the demand to bear arms on behalf of the state fail to arouse questions regarding the legitimacy of the cause for which death may be risked or inflicted on other human beings. Whatever moralistic justifications may be invoked on behalf of the demands for ultimate loyalty, the state itself remains essentially amoral, and the individual must thus weigh the demands according to his own conscience.[6]

Especially in the light of twentieth-century experience, the bloodshed in the name of loyalty to the nation-state devalues future claims to such loyalty. The spectacle of World War I, which exacted a toll of ten million lives—virtually an entire generation of young men from the major European participants—triggered disaffection and disillusionment throughout Europe and America. In Great Britain in the early 1930s, for example, student unions at Oxford and a number of other colleges passed resolutions affirming that they would "in no circumstances fight for [their] King and country." Of course it is testimony to the continuing appeal of national loyalty that with the outbreak of World War II large numbers of those who had supported the "Oxford oath" volunteered for military service. A similar change of heart was experienced by thousands of young men in other countries.

But again the price of loyalty was enormous. Moreover, the smoke had scarcely cleared from World War II before the two most powerful victors in that contest were cementing alliance systems in apparent anticipation of still more bloodletting. As Camus noted at the time, "We are asked to love or to hate such and such a country and such and such a people. But some of us feel too strongly our common humanity to make such a choice."[7]

Paradoxically, however, the bonds of common humanity may be forged more effectively by those who acknowledge the continuing reality of national citizenship and the set of obligations that go with it than by those who reject such ideas completely. Mazzini, Woodrow Wilson, Masaryk, and Sun Yat-sen are among the leading champions of nationalistic causes who envisioned that world community and peace would emerge from the roots of nationalism.[8] One may grant the element of naiveté that characterized some of these more idealistic arguments. However, contending that nationalism may be an essential building block need not mean making the preposterous argument that internationalism is best served by the promotion of zealous nationalism. Rather, one may merely suggest, as Reinhold Niebuhr has done, that "A valid moral outlook must be based upon an honest regard for the facts in the human situation, and must not construct norms which are impossible to achieve in view of the persistence and power of man's self-concern, and more particularly of his collective self-concern."[9]

The "facts of the human situation" that are observable in the attitudes of soldiers in combat provide some fascinating clues regarding the links between individual and collective self-concern, on the one hand, and responsibility to the global community, on the other. Illustrative are the findings of the pioneering studies of the Wehrmacht by Shils and Janowitz, and of the American Army in World War II by Stouffer and associates. These studies reveal that even in armies at war, the proliferation of patriotic appeals has less salience for the soldier than the casual observer might suppose. Instead, the soldier in combat is sustained primarily by bonds of camaraderie—mutual trust and mutual dependence among members of a common military unit.[10] Patriotism is not irrelevant, but commitment to the nation is more remote and abstract than the immediate commitment to one's comrades-in-arms.

As Moskos has noted, field research among American soldiers in Vietnam has shown that commitment to comrades-in-arms is to be understood more in terms of a pragmatic appreciation of the requisites of survival than in terms of a mystical capacity for transcending self-interest.[11] Consequently, when trust is absent, especially followers' trust of those in positions of authority, the soldier's willingness to risk death on behalf of his comrades—and thus on behalf of his nation—is likely to be absent. Instead, the soldier may yield to his felt need to "take care of number one" by going AWOL or deserting his unit.

Often, however, primary group loyalties remain even among disaffected soldiers. Allegiance is transferred from the formal organization represented by authority to a dissident informal organization. Doubtless mutiny is a more common occurrence than one might suppose from the number of mutinies officially reported. As Elihu Rose has noted, governments and military organizations abhor mutiny, and prefer to employ euphemisms such as "strikes," "unrest," "breakdowns in discipline," "combat refusals," or "disaffection" to refer to collective insubordination. Analysis of such acts, however labeled, reveals that a sense of solidarity among dissident members of a group is as essential to rebellion as bonds of mutual dependence and camaraderie are essential to maintaining commitment to officially sanctioned organizational goals.[12]

Especially instructive is the research finding that loyalty at the level of primary-group interaction may be an essential ingredient of loyalty to a more remote collective association. To the extent that mutual trust and obligation exist at the primary group level, the individual is provided with a sense of security which, in turn, helps to establish a readiness to accept responsibilities to the larger community of which the group is a part. Pye's analysis of the function which armies in developing nations have played in providing a structured, disciplined environment in societies experiencing abrupt and sweeping social changes illustrates the point.[13] Moskos's study of the attitudes and behavior of military participants in a United Nations peacekeeping operation suggests the further important conclusion that the development of cohesion at the level of the operating unit may sustain a commitment to an international cause as well as to a national one.[14]

To discover that the training and discipline of military organizations may be put to the service of goals that promote peace rather than hinder it is not to indulge in a flight of fancy in which the training of national armies is transformed into a celebration of the virtues of global community and peace. It is to suggest, however, that the relationship between the cultivation of nationalism and the promotion of internationalism is complex, and that the former is less intrinsically antithetical to the latter than is commonly assumed. Numerous scholars in recent decades have begun to explore the complexities of that relationship.[15] This is not the place to rehearse the voluminous analyses and conclusions that are products of such scholarship. However, it will be useful to sketch some of the nationalist-internationalist fluctuations in public mood that have occurred in complex industrial societies, with particular reference to changing attitudes toward military service. Doing so highlights the pertinence of the above findings about the sources of organizational and societal loyalty and cohesion and calls attention to problems which complex industrial societies have yet to resolve.

*From the 1940s to the 1970s:*
*Growing Controversy over Military Service*

One can distinguish between the degree of social cohesion that is evident in a polity and the consensus or dissension that is elicited by governmental policies. This basic distinction is essential to an understanding of the fluctuations in expressions of nationalism and attitudes toward military service that have been evident in complex industrial societies over the past quarter century. A brief overview reveals periodic surges of nationalism, up to and including the present, which provide at least a partial basis for policy consensus. However, social fragmentation, which appears to have increased in recent years, has undermined civic commitment and durable national unity.

From the end of World War II to the late 1950s, popular as well as governmental attitudes in countries that had fought the war were profoundly shaped by the wartime experience, the exigencies of postwar recovery, and by the extraordinary dependence of Western war-torn countries on the United States and of the Eastern ones on the Soviet Union. These were circumstances that fostered what Hoffmann has aptly termed the "Atlantic mythology" among peoples of North America and Western Europe—Jean Monnet's vision of a community of shared values and institutions that would transcend parochial national interests.[16] Military service was a widely accepted expression of citizen obligation within the NATO states, fortified by a pervasive recognition of the threat posed by communist adversaries.

Paradoxically, however, the continued salience of Cold War concerns and the resource demands associated with these concerns brought to a head policy issues that tended to revive nationalistic fears and jealousies. The French accepted only with great anguish and reluctance the decision, pushed by the Americans, to rearm West Germany.[17] The concurrent American decision to place increasing emphasis on nuclear deterrence (including tactical nuclear weapons), while pressuring NATO allies to increase their force commitments, succeeded primarily in heightening intra-alliance frictions and encouraging allies to reduce rather than increase force commitments.[18] Bitter differences among the Western allies over American policies during the Korean War, the French decision to withdraw its support for a European Defense Force, the Geneva accords that brought the first Indochina War to a conclusion in 1954, and the Suez Crisis of 1956 revealed vividly the frailty of the contemporary community structure.

Not surprisingly, the legitimacy of military service came to be questioned by many citizens. In the Federal Republic of Germany and Japan, the citizenry, having been subjected to the ideological exorcism of the early occupation years, underwent in the 1950s a curious reversal of policy by the principal occupying power. With the encouragement provided by the American commitment to a security treaty with Japan in 1952, the Japanese transformed their National Police Reserve into a National Self-Defense Force. A majority of Japanese polled at the time favored such rearmament, but less than half of this number expressed support for any member of their family's joining the military service.[19]

When the Federal Republic of Germany launched the new Bundeswehr in 1956, it was able to man the force entirely with volunteers. Military conscription was introduced the following year, although it still was possible to recruit approximately 90 percent of the force from volunteers. The number of volunteers declined steadily, however, to the point where by the late 1960s more than half of the Bundeswehr was composed of conscripts.[20]

In the Netherlands, France, and Great Britain, popular acceptance of military service tended to be undermined, not only by growing policy differences among NATO allies, but also by the assignment of military forces to controversial colonial roles. Indonesia for the Dutch (assisted initially by the British), Indochina and Algeria for the French, Malaya and Kenya for the British, and finally Suez for both the British and French came to symbolize in the minds of many citizens the distasteful purposes for which military service could be utilized.

Although the Dutch and the French continued to maintain conscript forces, the British abolished conscription beginning with a Defence White Paper of 1957. The act has been described by one critic as "surely one of the most catastrophically cocksure and mistaken documents in British defence history."[21] More charitably, it can be described as a means of adapting to the nuclear emphasis in strategy favored at the time by the United States, enabling the British to get by with reduced numbers of personnel (volunteers) and thereby placating popular opinion.

For the United States, the great challenge to the legitimacy of military service came with the Vietnam involvement of the late 1960s and early 1970s. Like the British, the American government responded by abolishing conscription. In fact, the tactic largely succeeded in defusing antiwar protest, but not before schisms of hitherto unimagined dimensions in American society had been revealed.

Violent protests also racked Japan, Great Britain, France, West Germany, and other European states in the 1960s and 1970s. As in America, students and others of draft age constituted the core of the protest movements. In Japan, the government continued to rely on voluntary recruitment into the Self-Defense Force (SDF), although a pledge that conscription would not be introduced was included in a draft of a Defense White Paper in 1970, only to be deleted from the published version. Defense policy in general continued to be a delicate issue in Japanese politics. Larger numbers of Japanese favored weakening the SDF rather than strengthening it, with young men under 30 considerably more hostile to the SDF than were men over 30.[22]

Despite intense public criticism of the military in the various continental European NATO states in the late 1960s and the 1970s, coupled with various protests from within the ranks of the armed forces themselves, personnel procurement systems were scarcely modified. Response to protests did come in several cases in the form of reducing the length of compulsory service, in altering barracks life in the direction of civilian occupations, and in accommodating greater participation by soldiers in decisions affecting their welfare (through unionization, for example, as in the Netherlands, Belgium, and the FGR). However, military conscription continued to be used to augment voluntary recruitment. The former approach accounted for roughly half of the new entrants into the French, German (FGR) and Dutch forces in the mid-1970s, and for approximately 70 percent of new entrants into the Italian forces. Support for the continuation of conscription came from the curious combination of conviction on the political right that military training was a useful element of political socialization, instilling discipline and respect for authority, and belief shared by many on the political left that conscript soldiers provided a check on military intervention in domestic politics.[23]

## The 1980s: Social Fragmentation and the Loss of Civic Obligation

Pragmatic economic and political arguments continue to be advanced in the 1980s for continuing military conscription in continental European countries, or for reviving military conscription in Great Britain and the United States. Such arguments should not be interpreted as evidence of widespread feelings of citizen obligation, defining military service as a primary means of fulfilling that obligation. On the contrary, whatever national consensus existed in complex industrial societies of the West in the early postwar decades regarding civic obligation has been substantially dissipated.[24] More broadly, one can speak of a decline in the sense of community that characterizes these societies. Surveys comparing the attitudes of American college students in the late 1970s with those of the late 1960s are illustrative. The characteristic pattern was one of diminished feelings of community, of greater isolation, of disillusionment, and of narcissism.[25] One need not accept McWilliams's bleak conclusion that "political fraternity . . . is impossible in the great industrial states" to recognize that sentiments documented among American youth to some extent have become characteristic of the society as a whole, and are evident in varying degrees throughout complex industrial societies.[26]

A conservative mood, often punctuated by outbursts of nationalism, had become evident throughout much of the industrialized West by the early 1980s. However, a pervasive longing for a restoration of national pride should not be confused with abundance of civic consciousness and commitment at the wellspring. When policy consensus has been achieved in the 1980s in the states under review, it has typically been on terms that can only provide distraction from, not cures for, underlying social and political differences.

Examples of such differences are too obvious to merit detailed recitation: the rift between French and English-speaking Canadians, and more recently between the western and eastern provinces; religious feuding in Northern Ireland, the resurgence of Scottish and Welsh nationalism and of racial strife attendant on the assimilation of new waves of immigrants into British society; fragmentation along linguistic and cultural lines in Belgium; class and generational differences in France and the Federal Republic of Germany; rural and urban differences in Japan; divisions in the United States along racial, ethnic, and regional lines.[27]

America in the 1980s provides a striking illustration of the limited ability of modern nationalism to unify disparate sectors of a politically as well as socially heterogeneous society. Jingoistic slogans have evoked memories of the Cold War mood of the 1950s but not the broad policy consensus that characterized that period. Despite the high levels of popular support that have been mobilized for increases in defense spending, a renewed debate over military conscription will surely reveal deep divisions within the society.[28] Moreover, the Reagan administration's inability to elicit a policy consensus on such pressing issues as energy, health, environment, and the appropriate foreign policy response to revolutionary change is already evident.[29]

In part, the failure of nationalistic appeals to provide a solid basis for sustained unity is attributable to the tendency of policymakers to define national needs narrowly in terms of defense against external threats. As Robert S. McNamara observed recently, there has been "an almost universal tendency to think of the security problem as being exclusively a military problem, and to think of the military problem as being primarily a weapons-system or hardware problem."[30] That being the case, security has proven to be ephemeral. The weapons of war which nation A has acquired in the name of "security" so threaten nation B as to require a comparable or greater investment by B. And so it goes.[31] Moreover, to the extent that the underlying sources of societal insecurity lie in the realms of economic conditions, internal political unrest, and social malaise, the investments made in the name of security cannot provide real solutions and may in fact aggravate the problems.[32]

It may be useful to define the analytical requirement confronting complex industrial societies as that of devising a "moral equivalent of national security," much as William James proposed that a "moral equivalent of war" be devised in an earlier era.[33] That is, lest "national security" be nothing more than a rallying cry around which modern garrison states are organized (as some critics contend),[34] the concept needs to be broadened in ways that accommodate both a societal understanding of needs that transcend (but include) protection from military attack and a responsibility to the global community.

The originality of James's analysis lay not in his elucidation of the folly and horror of modern war, but rather in his recognition of features of military organization and training which, if redirected, might contribute to the cause of peace. The findings from research on military organizations completed since James wrote give renewed relevance to his analysis. As noted above, the findings highlight the sources of group cohesion and suggest how loyalty at the small group level may serve to sustain the individual's sense of responsibility to the national or even to the global community.

Yet even when augmented by more recent research, the James analysis offers no panacea for current problems. No rush to revive or expand military conscription is likely to produce increases in levels of civic commitment in complex industrial societies (the reverse effect is more likely). Moreover, expansion of surrogate forms of endeavor such as the Peace Corps (which James implicitly anticipated) can come only in response to, not in anticipation of, broadened desires for citizen involvement in public service. However, if complex industrial societies are to come to grips with the need to re-examine and perhaps to redefine the concept of civic obligation, they would do well to remain attentive to the close but evolving relationship of military service to citizenship.

## Notes

1. Walter Millis, *Arms and Men* (New York: G. P. Putnam's Sons, 1956), Chap. 6.

2. John Westlake, *Chapters on the Principles of International Law* (Cambridge: At the University Press, 1894), p. 267.

3. Arnold J. Toynbee, "Again Nationalism Threatens," *New York Times Magazine* (Nov. 3, 1963), p. 110.

4. The writings of Leonardo Bruni d'Arezzo in the early fifteenth century have special importance in developing this view. See John G. A. Pocock, *The Machiavellian Moment: Florentine Political Thought and the Atlantic Republican Tradition* (Princeton, N.J.: Princeton University Press, 1975).

5. Space limitations preclude a thorough discussion of the changes that occurred with the evolution of the nation-state system and the emergence of modern military professionalism. See Gerke Teitler, *The Genesis of the Professional Officers' Corps*, trans. Mrs. C. N. Ter Heide-Lopy (Beverly Hills, Calif.: Sage Publications, 1977); Maury D. Feld, *The Structure of Violence: Armed Forces as Social Systems* (Beverly Hills, Calif.: Sage Publications, 1977); Samuel P. Huntington, *The Soldier and the State* (Cambridge, Mass.: Harvard University Press, Belknap Press, 1959); Morris Janowitz, *The Professional Soldier* (New York: Free Press, 1960).

6. The state of course may "compel a man to be free," as Rousseau put it. It is interesting to note, however, that Rousseau reached that conclusion on the basis of his recognition that the state was merely a "rational abstraction," obligations to which the individual might well ignore in the absence of compulsion. Jean-Jacques Rousseau, *Treatise du Contrat Social*, included in *Social Contract: Locke, Hume, Rousseau*, ed. Sir Ernest Barker (New York and London: Oxford Univeristy Press, 1960), p. 184.

7. Albert Camus, *Neither Victims Nor Executioners*, trans. Dwight MacDonald for *Politics* (July–August 1947), reprinted in pamphlet form (Chicago: World Without War Publications, 1972), p. 53.

8. A useful discussion of the views of these and other leaders within the context of an analysis of "The Virtues of Nationalism" is provided by Rupert Emerson, *From Empire to Nation* (Cambridge, Mass.: Harvard University Press, 1962), Chap. 19.

9. Reinhold Niebuhr, *The Structure of Nations and Empires* (New York: Charles Scribner's Sons, 1959), p. 30.

10. Edward A. Shils and Morris Janowitz, "Cohesion and Disintegration in the Wehrmacht in World War II," *Public Opinion Quarterly* 12 (Summer 1948): 280–315; Samuel A. Stouffer et al., *The American Soldier*, 4 vols. (Princeton, N.J.: Princeton University Press, 1949).

11. The cynicism that American GIs expressed regarding the cause for which they were fighting in Vietnam has been described vividly by Charles C. Moskos, *The American Enlisted Man* (New York: Russell Sage Foundation, 1970), chaps. 6 and 7. See also Moskos, "The American Combat Soldier in Vietnam," *Journal of Social Issues* 31, no. 4 (1975): 25–37. On the point at hand, also see Frederick J. Kviz, "Survival in Combat as a Collective Exchange Process," *Journal of Political and Military Sociology* 6 (Fall 1978): 219–32.

12. Data on acts of disobedience in American Army units in Vietnam, ranging from blatant drug use, desertion, and combat refusal to "fragging" are analyzed and compared to the experience of armies in other wars by Paul L. Savage and Richard A. Gabriel, *Crisis in Command: Mismanagement in the Army* (New York: Hill and Wang, 1978). A perceptive historical overview and analysis of the dynamics of collective disobedience in military organizations has been provided by Elihu Rose, "The Anatomy of Mutiny" (Paper

presented at a conference on civil-military relations, U.S. Naval Academy, Annapolis, Maryland, March 27, 1981). Walzer notes that "Disobedience, when it is not criminally but morally, religiously, or politically motivated, is almost always a collective act, and it is justified by the values of the collectivity and the mutual engagements of its members." Michael Walzer, *Obligations: Essays on Disobedience, War, and Citizenship* (New York: Simon and Schuster, 1971), p. 4.

13. Lucian W. Pye, "Armies in the Process of Political Modernization," in *The Role of the Military in Underdeveloped Countries*, ed., John J. Johnson (Princeton, N.J.: Princeton University Press, 1962), pp. 69–89.

14. This is not to suggest that performance of an international peace-keeping role "comes natural" to the soldier. The tensions inherent in such a role are described in Charles C. Moskos, Jr., *Peace Soldiers: The Sociology of a United Nations Military Force* (University of Chicago Press, 1976). See also the analysis of potential conflicts of loyalty by Henry V. Dicks, "The International Soldier—A Psychiatrist's View," in *International Military Forces*, ed. Lincoln P. Bloomfield (Boston: Little, Brown & Co., 1964), pp. 236–56.

15. A relatively comprehensive review of current findings is provided in Richard L. Merritt and Bruce M. Russett, eds., *From National Development to Global Community: Essays in Honor of Karl W. Deutsch* (Winchester, Mass.: Allen & Unwin, 1981).

16. Stanley Hoffmann, *Gulliver's Troubles, Or the Setting of American Foreign Policy* (New York: McGraw-Hill, for the Council on Foreign Relations, 1968), Chap. 11. See also Ernst B. Haas, *The Uniting of Europe* (Stanford, Calif.: Stanford University Press, 1959).

17. See Laurence W. Martin, "The American Decision to Rearm Germany," in *American Civil-Military Decisions*, ed., Harold Stein (Birmingham, Ala.: University of Alabama Press, for the Twentieth Century Fund in cooperation with the Inter-University Case Program, 1963), pp. 643–63.

18. Deterrence in NATO is largely a "collective good." If the United States was going to ensure deterrence through the threat of massive nuclear retaliation, there was little real incentive for the smaller allies to invest heavily in supporting large numbers of armed forces. See Bruce Russett, *What Price Vigilance? The Burdens of National Defense* (New Haven, Conn.: Yale University Press, 1970), Chap. 4.

19. Douglas H. Mendel, Jr., *The Japanese People and Foreign Policy* (Berkeley & Los Angeles, Calif.: University of California Press, 1961), p. 69. See also James H. Buck, ed., *The Modern Japanese Military System* (Beverly Hills, Calif.: Sage Publications, 1975).

20. Federal Ministry of Defense, *White Paper 1970: On the Security of the Federal Republic of Germany and on the State of the German Federal Armed Forces* (Bonn: Press and Information Office of the German Federal Republic, 1970), p. 88, cited with commentary by James A. Linger, "The Emergence

of the Bundeswehr as a Pressure Group," *Armed Forces and Society* 5 (Summer 1979): 560–89. The entire issue of the journal is devoted to an examination of civil-military relations in the Federal Republic of Germany.

21. W. Correlli Barnett, "The Military Profession in the 1970s," in *The Armed Forces and Society*, ed., J. N. Wolfe and John Erickson (Edinburgh, Scotland: Edinburgh University Press, n.d.), p. 8. But see the discussion by John Erickson, pp. 17–21.

22. Data on governmental and popular reactions to the SDF are reported in Thomas M. Brendle, "Recruitment and Training in the SDF," and in Douglas H. Mendel, Jr., "Public Views of the Japanese Defense System," in *The Modern Japanese Military System*, (See n. 19, line 3) (1975), pp. 67–96, and 149–80.

23. Catherine McArdle Kelleher, "Mass Armies in the 1970s: The Debate in Western Europe," *Armed Forces and Society* 5 (Fall 1978): 3–29. Also Gwyn Harries-Jenkins and Jacques Van Doorn, eds., *The Military and the Problem of Legitimacy* (London: Sage Publications, 1976).

24. Cf. Gabriel A. Almond and Sidney Verba, *The Civic Culture: Political Attitudes and Democracy in Five Nations* (Princeton, N.J.: Princeton University Press, 1963), and Almond and Verba, eds., *The Civic Culture Revisited* (Boston: Little, Brown & Co., 1980).

25. Arthur Levine, *When Dreams and Heroes Died: A Portrait of Today's College Student* (San Francisco: Jossey-Bass for the Carnegie Foundation for the Advancement of Teaching, 1980). See also Christopher Lasch, *The Culture of Narcissism* (New York: W. W. Norton & Co., 1979).

26. Wilson Carey McWilliams, *The Idea of Fraternity in America* (Berkeley & Los Angeles, Calif.: University of California Press, 1973), p. 65.

27. Social fragmentation in America has been described by Kevin Phillips, with perhaps a bit of hyperbole, as "The Balkanization of America," *Harper's* 256 (May 1978): 37–47.

28. E.g. see the discussion in a speech symposium on "The Rise and Fall of the Volunteer Army," *Society* 18 (March–April 1981).

29. Cf. Milton J. Rosenberg, "The Decline and Rise of the Cold War Consensus," *Bulletin of the Atomic Scientists* 37 (March 1981): 7–9; eleven articles examining "The End of Consensus?" in *Daedalus* 109 (Summer 1980); George Quester, "Consensus Lost," and Thomas L. Hughes, "The Crack-Up," in *Foreign Policy* (Fall 1980): 18–32, 33–60.

30. Robert S. McNamara, remarks made upon receipt of the Albert Pick, Jr. Award, University of Chicago, May 22, 1979.

31. The continuing arms race between the superpowers is the obvious case in point, although the cycle is not peculiar to that relationship. The Arab-Israeli conflict provides another example. See especially the analysis of empirical data on military expenditures by Israel and her Arab neighbors

during the period 1948–1967, by Nadav Safran, *From War to War* (New York: Pegasus, 1969), Chap. 4.

32. It is not my intent either to deny the social welfare expenditures of complex industrial societies in recent decades, nor to suggest that tradeoffs between defense expenditures and domestic expenditures invariably occur (often they do not). James L. Clayton, *Does Defense Beggar Welfare? Myths Versus Realities*, Agenda Paper no. 9 (New York: National Strategy Information Center, 1979). The point is simply to elaborate on McNamara's observation by suggesting that a narrow view of national security reduces the probability that adequate solutions to the multiple problems of national insecurity will be devised.

33. William James, "The Moral Equivalent of War," in *Memories and Studies* (New York: Longmans, Green and Co., 1911). The essay was written for and first published by the Association for International Conciliation (leaflet no. 27) and also published in *McClure's Magazine* (Aug. 1910) and in *The Popular Science Monthly* (Oct. 1910).

34. See for example Daniel Yergin, *Shattered Peace: The Origins of the Cold War and the National Security State* (Boston: Houghton Mifflin Co., 1977). Also Marcus G. Raskin, *The Politics of National Security* (New Brunswick, N.J.: Transaction Books, 1979).

# Part II

## Historical Perspectives

# 4

# Machiavelli's Militia
# and
# Machiavelli's Mercenaries

MAURY D. FELD

*I*

As in so many other things, it is Machiavelli most of all who must bear
the responsibility for having given mercenaries a bad name. For him, the
issue is clearly one of public morality. In an author who took pride in a
power of judgment, pragmatically motivated and unhindered by conventional or sentimental considerations, this is worthy of note. Nothing in
the annals of his contemporary Italy or its neighbors justifies the belief
that local troops who fought out of a sense of civic obligation were
superior to imported combatants who fought because they had been hired
to do so. There were, of course, the Swiss. But they were equally effective in defending their home cantons as in carrying out some contracted
aggression. Their Spanish rivals were, it is true, imbued with national
sentiment, but as an army of professional long-term soldiers who spent
most of their active life abroad, and who had the nasty tradition of
putting patriotism aside and mutinying when regular pay was not forth-

coming, they could hardly be regarded as a civic militia. Against both the Swiss and the Spaniards, Italian local forces had not been able to put up much more than a token resistance.

Nor, taking mercenaries as individuals, can we say that Machiavelli's condemnation is based on his belief in the necessity of some conventional ethic. The practices he condemns in hired soldiers as a class strongly resemble those he commends in his individual ideal prince: keeping faith only when it serves your interest, pursuing and prolonging wars in order to promote your own security, being most dangerous to those upon whom or to whom you think yourself dependent or indebted, etc. It clearly could not have been the style itself he disliked; it was the social level of its execution.

This leaves us with a third explanation: that Machiavelli's political prescriptions were based on a patriotism so intense as to justify every measure only by its results. Native mercenaries, however they behaved, had been the instrument of Italy's downfall. Native princes, on the other hand, devoid of scruples and utilizing the forces of nascent nationalism, had just unified France and Spain and driven out their alien oppressors. One of similar stamp might, in turn, do the same for Italy.

This explanation, the most plausible and also the most generally sympathetic, has a good deal to recommend it. It can be reconciled with much of Machiavelli's own behavior and many of Machiavelli's own words. But this is the behavior and these are the words of a crippled Machiavelli, of a life shattered by the downfall of the Florentine Republic in 1512, the Machiavelli of the Preface and Conclusion to The Prince (1513). Before this time, during a period when Machiavelli had reason to believe himself in command of his own destiny, he was a pronounced republican and an outspoken opponent of princes in general, of the Medici in particular, and of despotic rule. His favored instrument, a civic militia, was designed to be a bulwark of popular government. Moreover, his three other major political treatises, the Discourses (1513–1517), The Art of War (1521), and The History of Florence (1525) are all imbued in guarded but unmistakable fashion with the spirit of classical civic morality.

It must be borne in mind that Machiavelli's literary career begins exactly when his political career ends. As a public servant he had been free, trusted, and honored by the powers that be. As a literary man he had been tortured, despised, exiled, and rejected by those upon whom his life and prosperity had become dependent. The contrast between these two states is the corrective lens through which his expressed opinions and his various doctrines must be scrutinized.

There is, nonetheless, a central theme which runs through his active public life as well as all four of his major political works: only those institutions which make a state or community strong and secure are desirable. The strength and security of the state are, as a matter of fact, the sole criteria according to which political and social behavior is to be judged. A prince, provided that his amorality is directed in a rational and pragmatic fashion, may advance the interests of the state. Mercenaries, no matter what the motivation of their behavior, are inherently incapable of doing so. With this his argument rests.

## II

This is something of a paradox. On the one hand we have a Machiavelli whose name has become a byword for the advocacy of amorality as a principle and of self-interest as a standard in the conduct of politics. On the other hand, we have him condemning a conventional instrument (mercenaries) of a regular feature of politics (war) as incurably tied to such practices. The conduct of war, one has to conclude, is for Machiavelli something too noble and too important to be subjected to those principles which govern the rest of political life.

That a proposition of this kind will invariably be read as ironic or facetious is a measure of the modern temper. The nobility of a military career was certainly plausible, if not indeed self-evident, for Machiavelli and his contemporaries. Up to 1914 it was, in fact, subscribed to, with varying degrees of sincerity, by a large part of the population of Western Europe. But that is not a matter which concerns us here. What I would like to investigate are the grounds on which Machiavelli, a paradigm of political realism and a model of civic devotion, was able to adopt and maintain such an attitude.

As even a casual reading of Machiavelli makes abundantly clear, the art of political rationality was for him the process of detecting and anatomizing the apt historical example, thus extracting the expedient present solution from the lessons of the past. He is equally explicit as to the particular sources from which examples are to be drawn: Italy of the last century or so, for examples of the disasters which follow from the inability to see events in their true light, and the Italy of the classical Roman republic, for examples of the public benefits which ensure from the judicious application of the art of political memory.

The ideal political commentator was thus to be found in the society of resident Italian humanists who since the late fourteenth century had provided the core of professional public servants to the various Italian states, and who, thus, by personal and by directly transmitted experience, had been witness to and participants in the latters' train of disasters. These very humanists were also the official guardians of the records of the distant past when public affairs had been better managed.[1]

The major source for his stream of exemplary events and his model for both the structure of history and the constitution of an ideal commonwealth is antique Rome, and in particular the Roman republic in its pristine form, prior to the decay that set in with victory in the Punic Wars. For the history of Rome, his most frequently cited source, and the scriptural framework for the most lengthy of his political treatises, is the *Ab urbe condita* of Livy whose first ten books (Decade) provide the texts for the string of republican sermons which make up Machiavelli's *Discourses*.[2]

The incidents of Livy's first decade furnish strange materials for an exemplary text. The sections dealing with the earliest, the purest, and the most heroic days of Rome present a series of acts of unbridled violence; arbitrary murders of sisters, brothers, sons, kinsmen, and neighbors. All of these, however, are rendered virtuous and heroic by the fact that they were carried out under the discipline of arms, and motivated by a concern for the glory and growth of the city of Rome, that is to say, of its cults, its altars, and the images of its gods. According to Livy, Rome prospered most when its spoils of war were dedicated, not to private ends, but to the adornment of its common temples. In a real sense, the multiplication of public shrines was, for the early Romans, the ultimate reason for waging war. A successful war was one which ended with the gods of the conquered community being triumphantly transplanted to a Roman site. The progressive universalization of Roman holiness was the unfolding record of its divine mission.[3] Carried one step further and observed through Machiavelli's Livian lens, war was the supreme religious sacrament, the moral equivalent of that radical evil, materialist self-interest, or, as Professor C. B. Macpherson would have it, possessive individualism. It was only through war that man entered into communion with the ideal, divinely inspired, and therefore inherently self-justifying social condition.

Among his contemporaries, Machiavelli singles out for praise Francesco Valori, "because no country ever had a citizen who more desired her good than he did or who was so much and *with fewer scruples* (my italics) her defender. His courage and good character [were] proven by his always holding high office and dying poor, to such an extent that his grandchildren refused their inheritance from him."[4] From the Roman perspective Francesco Valori was a modest hero. Under Florentine conditions, he indicated the direction wherein salvation lay.

The poverty of Francesco Valori was, as Machiavelli insinuates, not an instrument of ascetic purification. It did not rid him of the desire or the motives for worldly success. Nor did it make him indifferent to the behavior of his fellow citizens and the conventions of his society. He was ambitious, courageous, even rash, and "had fear only of measures that were unlawful."[5] Valori devoted to the commune of Florence those sentiments and ambitions which less patriotic men employed for the benefits of their own persons and their own families.

"I shall never depart," Machiavelli remarks at the onset of his *The Art of War*, "in giving examples of anything, from my Romans."[6] Valori was a quintessential exemplar of the primitive Roman morality—without scruples, and with a lust for power, yet untainted by any desire for personal material gain. His spirit had animated the Rome of Livy's First Decade, where quarrels which repeatedly arose between the rich and the poor, and which repeatedly threatened to erupt into civil war, were repeatedly resolved by wars of external conquest. Within Florence itself, however, Francesco Valori was an eccentric and an anomaly.

Why he was such, and why traits and motives so common and so fruitful in the history of early Rome were so rare and so barren in Renaissance Florence is the crucial Machiavellian question. *"Quid enim est omnis historia, nisi Romana laus?"* ("What then is all history but the praise of Rome?") wrote Petrarch (1304–1374), the herald of the Italian Renaissance and the proto-patriot of Italian national consciousness. This sentence with its downhill assumption can be taken as the unifying motto of Renaissance humanism. Rome is the critical model for the study of humanity, and decay is the destined human state.

The anatomy of this model is yet another matter. It does not lie in the peculiar nature of those who were Roman citizens. As Machiavelli himself repeatedly states, and as he finds abundant evidence in Livy, mankind is everywhere and at all times the same, corrupt and contemptible. Its occasional elevations are due to the presence and the force of wise leaders and intelligent institutions. This is nowhere more true than among the Italians, the decadent but not decayed remnants of the ancient Roman stock.

Every institution, as he repeatedly notes, is subject to its generic form of decay. The human element which can never be removed from politics represents a natural source of corruption. The weakness of the state places it at the mercy of its more successful neighbors. The strength of the state presents, on the other hand, the temptation and provides the means for the private ambitions of its leading citizens. In either case, the original constitution, whatever its merits, is prey to the forces of violent change.

The remedy, it is clear, must rest in recourse to supernatural forces. But Machiavelli does not, as he makes abundantly clear, believe that there is really such a thing as a numinous being, or powers from on high. Whatever evidence exists in that direction is a product of either the ignorance of the many, or the wiles of the few—or, to be strictly accurate, of a combination of both. Religion is an institution devised by the founders of states in order to incorporate their governing principle into a form capable of outliving particular mortal careers. Whatever his particular prescriptions and analyses, Machiavelli never deviates from his belief that, the message of Holy Scripture notwithstanding, human history is the sole and exclusive creation of human beings, Cyrus, Moses, Romulus, and Theseus, for example. The greatness of republican Rome, as his *Discourses* so abundantly and vividly illustrate, is that never, especially in the two centuries immediately following its foundations, was a human community and its members so actively and firmly in control of its destiny.

Nonetheless, Machiavelli not only concedes the existence of a Roman religion but even gives it a major role in his constitution. The manner in which this is accomplished is, however, highly unusual, and is peculiar to Rome and to Machiavelli's private vision of politics. What is striking about the religion of the *Discourses* is the central role played by the Roman people. It is their collective behavior, not the presence of the gods, nor the rituals of the priesthood, that is the focus of the civic cult.

It would not be altogether just to describe this vision of Roman society and religion as a factitious creation, springing entirely from Machiavelli's private imagination and designed to serve and fortify his own particular purposes and beliefs. Recent scholarship on the nature of the Rome religion has tended to support him in this approach. "The Romans," as Stefan Weinstock has remarked, "had no sacred books on which one [that is to say, they or anyone else] could base a discussion of their religion." The evidence of worship were to be found in the behavior of individual citizens, in their devotions to their household gods, their local gods, and to the public cults of the state.[7]

The source material of Machiavelli's Roman model is, therefore, to be found in the Roman histories he had at his disposal, especially those relating to the earliest period, his designated era of civic excellence. Most specifically and directly, it is to be found in Livy whose narrative history furnishes the text for Machiavelli's republican sermons, and whose old-fashioned piety provides the raw data for Machiavelli's critique of what he takes to be the civic blasphemy of his own era.

There is at least one major difficulty in all this. Livy's rather simple-minded and uncritical narrative does not support the full weight of Machiavelli's Roman constitution. Livy gives us the events of Roman history, but not the theory of the Roman state. Machiavelli the supreme realist was writing for a circle of like-minded friends.[8] If his justification of the Roman state was not much more than a fanciful reconstruction and he one of the "many" who "have imagined republic and principalities never seen or known in fact,"[9] he stands condemned out of his own mouth.

It is at this point that the second great historian of early Rome, Polybius, comes to the aid of Machiavelli and supports his hypothesis of Roman civic religion. In his *Histories*, Book VI, 14, 3–5, Polybius declares: "there is a part and a very important part left for the people. For it is the people which alone has the right to confer honours and inflict punishment, *the only bonds by which kingdoms and states and in a word human society in general are held together*. For where the distinction between these is overlooked or is observed but ill applied, no affairs can be properly administered" (italics mine). This remark summarizes in the most succinct manner possible Machiavelli's equation of popular religion and popular government. It is the hard fact of the people acting as the embodiment of divinity and the ultimate judge that creates and maintains the social bond.

The relationship between Machiavelli and Polybius is a subject on which much ingenuity and much ink have been expended.[10] The crux of the matter lies in the probability that *Discourses* I,ii, almost literally, and *Discourses* I,i–xviii by implication, betray an acquaintance with the text of Book VI of the *Histories* of Polybius. Yet at the time Machiavelli was writing only Books I–V had been published in Latin translation. It is almost certain that Machiavelli knew no Greek, and that the earliest publication of a translation of the entirety of the surviving fragments, and especially those expounding Polybius' theory of mixed constitutions, the substance of Discourses I,ii was in 1546, long after Machiavelli's death.

Less attention, however, has been paid to the more persistent parallels between Polybius' discussion in Book VI of Roman military institutions and Machiavelli's ultimate act of Roman worship, his *Art of War*, at the onset of which he declares his undeviating devotion to the Romans as exemplars. There is indeed one passage where Machiavelli seems to have literally transcribed Polybius, and where the resemblance is so close that it is difficult not to believe that he had the latter's text before him. This is the section in Book VI of *The Art of War* dealing with breaches of discipline, and which is a rough literal translation of Polybius, Book VI, 37, 2–5.[11]

That Machiavelli should stress the military aspects of Polybius is highly significant. In the Florentine humanist circle he frequented Polybius was singled out—in contrast to Livy—as having extracted a philosophical theory of government from the raw annals of republican Rome.[12] The fact that Machiavelli, a zealot for Roman institutions, should have found the most pertinent exposition of this theory in a discussion of Roman military institutions illuminates the sense of his inquiry. This interest in the military rather than the constitutional aspects of Polybius is, moreover, not unique. Between 1525 and 1550, there were at least four translations of the military chapters of Book VI, one of which, the *De Militia Romanorum* (1529) of Janus Lascaris was circulating in manuscript in Florence during the lifetime of Machiavelli and was, in all likelihood, known to him.

It is nevertheless striking that Machiavelli should use not the discussion of constitutions but the section devoted to military punishments and rewards as his point of entry into the Polybian text. For Polybius himself in a passage that was surely familiar to Machiavelli (Book VI, 3, 39) places such rewards and punishments in a religious context. The transgressors are either sacrificed or exiled, that is, banished from their homes and shrines, whereas the recipients of military glory "quite apart from becoming famous in the army and famous too for the time at their homes, are *especially distinguished in religious processions after their return, as no one is allowed to wear decorations except those on whom these honours for bravery have been conferred by the consul*" (39, 7–12).

The "punishments and rewards" which it is the constitutional function of "the people" to confer and which are the "only bonds" by which "human society in general is held together" operate most naturally, effectively, and indeed exclusively, in a military context. The message then is quite clear. Military service is the public cult of the state. The people assembled under arms represent the active presence of divinity in a civic context. Machiavelli's objections to mercenary armies, though he endeavors mightly to mantle it with pragmatic arguments, is based in substance on his adherence to a higher law. The use of mercenaries is a crass case of substituting material for moral incentives. The purchase of military service is a simonical practice, a traffic in what is holy. In hiring its defenders, the state both profanes itself, and corrupts its citizens and its servants.

# III

> . . . from what man ought his native land to expect greater fidelity than from that one who has promised to die for her? In whom ought there to be more love of peace than in him who can get nothing but injury from war? In whom ought there to be more fear of God than in a man who every day, being exposed to countless perils, has great need for his aid?[13]

The theme that runs throughout Machiavelli's three major works, that motivates the depraved politics of *The Prince*, the virtuous politics of *The Discourses*, and the political therapy of *The Art of War* is the fundamental role played by the people in their capacity to confer punishments and rewards. The reward of a ruler or a regime is the desire of a people to reinforce one another in their loyalty to and defense of the state. The penalty of bad government is the withdrawing of this essential support. Government whether by prince or by elected official is the art of eliciting this *fidelity*, this *love of peace*, this *fear of God* from those who though nominally inferiors possess the ultimate bond of human society in general. Fidelity, love of peace, and fear of God, invaluable as they are, can not be bought. They must be given freely.

J. G. A. Pocock has shrewdly observed that the title *L'arte della guerra* has a double meaning. It conveys the notion both of "art" as a creative profession and of *arte* as a social grouping, of a guild or confraternity, such as the *arte della lana*, the guild of the woolen trade. Every guild had its patron saint, the focal point of its civic devotions. The title *Art of War*, therefore, signifies both the acquisition and demonstration of military skills, and a body of men united in a community of craft, civic and religious interests. Inherent in the function of the guild was the notion that professional interests must not predominate but must rather be subordinated to the public good. Machiavelli's "military art" was designed to create soldiers who were primarily citizens, to dedicate them to the cult of the state.[14]

Why then did Machiavelli not come out and simply say this? And why didn't he explicitly name Polybius as the classical source of this lofty concept? The obvious answer is ironic. Machiavelli thought it safer to expose himself as a purveyor of amoral advice to would-be princes than to reveal himself as the theoretician of the moral basis of free, republican commonwealths. It is not only that the implicit paganism of Machiavelli's religiously inspired militia that would have endangered his very life—for covert paganism was then rampant among "advanced thinkers" in Italy of that day, and the authorities were well aware of it— what is more serious is his compounded felony of demonstrating with remorseless logic that political independence, military self-sufficiency, civic republicanism, and a pagan, state religion formed a seamless web.

After 1512 and the fall of the Florentine republic, in whose service he had made his career, Machiavelli lived at the forbearance of the Medici. For him to have written openly and clearly what was really on his mind would have inevitably led to his death or his exile, the latter, from the pagan point of view, the most impious of fates. Any overt reference to Polybius would have furnished his vigilant enemies with a hook on which to hang both him and his heresies.

Machiavelli is one of those intellectuals whose compensation and whose burden in life is to believe himself far cleverer than those society and fate have placed above him in the social order. He is one of those thinkers who express themselves in a manner that would be flagrantly offensive to people in power had the latter the wit to understand it, thinkers whose inner comfort it is to dwell on the intrinsic superiority of the thinker and the inherent inferiority and depravity of the audience to whom his thoughts are addressed.[15]

Nowhere is this Machiavellian mode of reference made clearer than in *The Prince* (1513), the work he wrote immediately after the fall of the Florentine republic, the collapse of his worldly ideals and his civic ambitions. *The Prince* is ostensibly a rather conventional essay. It falls in the mould of a staple genre of late medieval and early renaissance secular literature, the treatise on "The Education of a Christian Prince."[16] This is where the irony hangs. The princes directly concerned were Lodovico de Medici (1492–1519)—the nephew and secular arm of the Pope Leo X (1513–1521)—to whom the book was dedicated, and Cesare Borgia (1476–1507)—the son and secular arm of Pope Alexander VI (1492–1503)—Machiavelli's anointed model of princely behavior. It is these two princes of impeccable *Christian* pedigree who provide the purpose and the substance of Machiavelli's most celebrated book.

There is a further irony in the fact that Machiavelli decries the use of hirelings in a treatise dedicated to the Medici, a family of bankers, notorious for its wealth and for the fact that it had risen in the world through its ability to purchase the services of all who stood in its way. Furthermore, he extols the desirability of loyal citizenry to the governors of the papal states, a region whose civic disaffection was endemic to the point of being traditional. He might have been before a worshipful company of distillers and saloon keepers, preaching a sermon on the necessity of total abstinence.

But Machiavelli had not only cause to despise the Borgias and the Medicis. He had reason to hate them. It was the Borgias who had destroyed Girolamo Savonarola (1452–1498) and burnt him at the stake. It was the Medicis who had brought in the Spaniards and destroyed the republic of the Gran Consiglio. Savonarola and the republic were the two great intellectual and political passions of Machiavelli's life. Machiavelli is offering his *Prince* as a monument to those whom he had every reason to hate, fear and detest. But this monument is also his revenge. It stands as a record of the moral attitudes and political practices most suitable for princes who represent Christianity in its secular and worldly guise.

It can be objected that Savonarola, a Dominican monk and fanatical Christian, is hardly a suitable model for someone whose highest ambition was to bring about a revival of the pagan gods. But in this case the negative aspect of Savonarola, his ultimate failure, was as instructive and inspirational to Machiavelli as his positive goals. Savonarola had undertaken to reconstitute the republic of Florence on religious grounds, in this case those of primitive Christianity. He had failed because, unlike other founders of notable states, he had been, as Machiavelli pointed out, an *unarmed* prophet. This was inevitable, for Christianity is the religion of the unarmed and the meek. Savonarola had deserved a nobler faith. Under another and better religion both he and Florence would have been more successful. For the *governo civile* Savonarola had envisioned was a noble and practical project.[17]

There was still another advantage to be gained by an identification with Savonarola. The latter had denounced the corruption and immorality of the papacy in the strongest possible terms, in language which makes Machiavelli's own criticisms seem pallid and rather covert. He had called upon Florence to reconstitute itself as a new and self-redeemed holy city, and as the model of a reformed Christianity. Just as Savonarola had spoken as the prophet of renewed primitive Christianity, Machiavelli could speak as the prophet of a refined primitive Rome. Savonarola, decrying the corruption of the papacy, called upon the Florentines to create in their city a newer and purer Rome.[18] Machiavelli with deeper and more subtle reference pointed out to his fellow citizens the advantages of such a course. Under the cover of his unimpeachable pious precursor, Machiavelli could, as a Florentine patriot, attack with diminished risks the baleful influence of papal Rome and its religion. He could reaffirm the accuracy of Savonarola's accusations, and point out the moral to be drawn from Savonarola's fate. That done, he could allow the reader to draw his own conclusions.

Naked is the best disguise. It was enough to say that he was simply describing affairs as he had observed them and as they actually were.

From *The Prince* men could discover what the principles of "Christian" political behavior were. From the *Discourses* they could learn what the reasons were for the success of the Roman republic in both its military and political aspects. That the former relied on mercenaries and the latter on civic militia was obvious enough; that the princes had been practicing Christians, and the Romans ardent pagans were facts too commonplace to warrant any special attention. It was only by drawing explicit parallels between the military institutions of Renaissance Italy and its contemporary version of Christianity, and in advancing the no-tion that the military institutions of primitive Rome could be described as its public cult, that he ran the risk of detection. The publication of the *Prince*, the *Discourses*, and the *Art of War* as separate and apparently unrelated works shielded him from this risk, that and the fact that during his lifetime, at least, Book VI of the *Histories* of Polybius remained unpublished and the object only of a sort of avant garde republican curiosity.

And yet the ultimate irony belongs to his enemies. Those mercenary armies he so despised evolved through the vagaries of history and tech-nology, capitalism and firearms, into the cult object and the driving force behind a new form of political enterprise. Hired armies created a chain of kingdoms whose ever-expanding ability to raise funds and purchase ser-vices generated a degree of loyalty and sense of identity far beyond what Machiavelli had ever dared to imagine. The absolutist state openly iden-tified the ruler and his instruments with the person and cause of the almighty. The rituals of court and bureaucracy sanctified the en-trepreneurial martial spirit and made private gain a public blessing.[19] The city-state and civic humanism were wiped out. And Rome and its history became irrelevant.

## Notes

N.B. I have presumed a familiarity with the general contents of *The Prince* and the *Discourses*, and will, therefore, only cite specific references to these works.

1. See George Holmes, *The Florentine Enlightenment* (New York: Pegasus, 1969), especially pp. 36–67; Hans Baron, *The Crisis of the Early Italian Renaissance* (Princeton: Princeton University Press, 1966), pp. 404–12.

2. cf. J. H. Whitfield, "Machiavelli's Use of Livy," in T. A. Dorey, ed., *Livy* (London: Routledge and K. Paul, 1971), pp. 73–96.

3. See *Livy*, I, xxxi, V, xxi, lii.

4. Niccolò Machiavelli, "Of Francesco Valori," in *The Chief Works and Others*, trans., Allan Gilbert (Durham, N.C.: Duke University Press, 1965), 3 vols., vol. 3, p. 1438.

5. Machiavelli, *Chief Works*, Vol. 1, p. 213.

6. Machiavelli, *Chief Works*, Vol. 2, p. 571. The fact that this statement occurs in this context is particularly significant and will be discussed further on.

7. Stefan Weinstock, *Divus Julius* (Oxford: Clarendon, 1971), p. 1, passim. Horace, *Odes* III, 5, can, as my friend Wendell Clausen has pointed out, be interpreted as an exercise in this function.

8. Felix Gilbert, "Bernardo Rucellai and the Orti Oricellari: A Study on the Origin of Modern Political Thought," in *History: Choice and Commitment*, (Cambridge, Mass.: Harvard University Press, 1977), pp. 215–46.

9. Machiavelli, *Chief Works*, Vol. 1, p. 57.

10. See J. H. Whitfield, *Discourses on Machiavelli* (Cambridge: Heffer, 1969), pp. 191 ff.; Arnaldo Momigliano, "Polybius' Reappearance in Western Europe," in Emilio Gabba, ed., *Polybe* (Geneva: 1973), pp. 359 ff.

11. Machiavelli, *Chief Works*, Vol. 2, p. 690 (The guilty men punished by their comrades).

12. Momigliano, "Polybius' Reappearance," p. 359, quotes a letter of Perotti, the earliest translator of Polybius, Books I–V (1454) (Polybius) *nam et gravius fortasse scribit, et lectione eius intelliguntur apertissime multa, quae apud Livium aut nullo modo aut vix intelligebantur.* Both Perotti and Janus Lascaris, the author (see below) of the translation of Book VI used in all probability by Machiavelli, were proteges of Cardinal Bessarion. In two articles, "Constructed Letters and Illuminated Texts" *Harvard Library Bulletin*, October 1980, pp. 357–79, and "Sweynheym Pannartz, Cardinal Bessarion: Renaissance Humanism and an Early Printers' Choice of Texts," *Harvard Library Bulletin* (January 1982), I have examined some of the evidence for the assumption of neo-Platonic paganism in the circle of Cardinal Bessarion.

13. Machiavelli, *Chief Works*, Vol. 2, p. 367 (Dedication, *The Art of War*).

14. J. G. A. Pocock, *The Machiavellian Moment: Florentine Political Thought and the Atlantic Republican Tradition* (Princeton: Princeton University Press, 1975), p. 199 ff.

15. Machiavelli's evasive manner and its etiology is examined in Harvey C. Mansfield, Jr., *Machiavelli's New Modes and Orders: A Study of the Discourses on Livy* (Ithaca: Cornell University Press, 1979); his radical hostility to Christianity is made clear in Leo Strauss, *Thoughts on Machiavelli* (Seattle: University of Washington, 1969).

16. Allan Gilbert, *Machiavelli's Prince and its Forerunners* (Durham, N.C.: Duke University Press, 1938).

17. On Machiavelli and Savonarola see the illuminating essay of Whitfield, "Savonarola and the Purpose of the Prince" in Whitfield, *Discourses on Machiavelli*, pp. 87–110.

18. Donald Weinstein, *Savonarola and Florence* (Princeton: Princeton University Press, 1970) pp. 146 ff. For the tradition of Florence as the heir of republican (pagan) Rome, see Baron, *The Crisis of the Early Italian Renaissance*, pp. 61–64, 71–73.

19. M. D. Feld, "Revolution and Reaction in Early Modern Europe," *Journal of the History of Ideas* (January–March 1977), pp. 175–84.

## 5

# Professionalization in
# the Victorian Army

GWYN HARRIES-JENKINS

The genesis of the profession of arms has been variously attributed to the growth of the post-feudal military organization. The legacy of such an origin dies hard. All too commonly, the attribution "neo-feudal" to selected characteristics of the military profession within an industrialized society, is a far from flattering evaluation of contemporary armed forces. Yet it would be injudicious to equate the origins of military professionalization with any single event or historical accident. The military profession emerged as the result of a lengthy developmental process in which the nineteenth century was a period of critical importance. It was during these years—the Victorian period, as it is usually termed in the United Kingdom—that the foundations of military professionalism were expanded into a sophisticated and complex institutional structure. These were the years when newly instituted staff colleges created programs of study which anticipated by more than a century the training theories of subsequently established business schools. It was a period in which military scholars like Sylvanus Thayer of West Point introduced new dimensions of professional education to an increasingly technological society. Above all, it was a century in which a unique sense of professional ethos was engendered within the military, a sense which other occupational groups sought desperately to emulate, as they realized, in Morris Janowitz's words, that "A profession is more than a group with special skill acquired through intensive training. A professional group develops a sense of group identity and a system of internal administration. Self-administration—often supported by state intervention—implies the growth of a body of ethics and standards of performance.[1]

## The Military Ethos

Most historical studies of the development of the military profession concentrate on the analysis of "expertise," paying particular attention to the successes or failures of armed forces in combat situations as evidence of the degree of attained expertise. Alternatively, studies which have concerned themselves with the growth of professionalization in the nineteenth-century military have tended to focus on the issue of institutionalized education and training.[2] In this essay, however, the central area of concern is the way in which the sense of group identity and the system of internal administration within armed forces were furthered and developed. This reflects the belief that the distinguishing feature of military professionalization is, to reiterate Janowitz's point, something more than mere expertise or acquired skill. Essentially, it is "a way of life" in which specific attitudes and values are identified as the desired occupational norms. Moreover, the nineteenth century is of critical importance in the development of this professional socialization, for in a parent society where major social changes were affecting other occupational groups, armed forces were seemingly able to exercise their preference for the maintenance of traditional and established value-systems.

This occupational conservatism is especially well marked in the Victorian military of the United Kingdom, particularly in the way in which the role of the officer was clearly identified with an expected cluster of values. It is now something of a cliché to delineate these values as the hallmark of the "officer and gentleman," but the expression emphasizes the basic character of these values as a defining element in the inculcation of professional socialization. At the same time, the apparent persistence throughout the Victorian period of a consistently held value system among officers should not lead us to overlook the structural changes which occurred in the nineteenth century. Indeed, one of the more interesting features of the Victorian military is the way in which the profession, in adapting to required organizational change, consistently managed to perpetuate a preferred form of professionalization in the face of considerable external pressure.

The primary base of this professionalization was the degree of social control which was implemented through an initial selection process that sought to recruit aspirants who possessed an acceptable set of values and attitudes. In comparison with the highly sophisticated processes adopted by the contemporary military, nineteenth-century officer selection was crude and unimpressive. It was unashamedly elitist, for its primary function was to ensure that officer entry would be limited to those whom the center of the organization could readily identify as "fitting" into the professional group. Before 1870, the system of selection in the United Kingdom was inextricably linked to the purchase and sale of officers' commissions. The workings of this Purchase System have been analyzed in a number of studies.[3] Briefly, the aspirant, who had to be sixteen, first obtained a nomination from either the Commander-in-Chief at the Horse Guards, or, if he wanted to enter the Household Regiments of Horse and Foot Guards, from the Colonel of his selected regiment. If approved, his name was placed on the list of those eligible for commissioning and he waited for a vacancy to arise in the regiment of his choice. For many would-be officers this was an anxious period during which they sought to ensure that their claim was not overlooked and that no preference was given to an applicant with more political or family influence. Eventually, when an officer in the selected regiment decided to sell out, either by leaving the army or by obtaining a promotion which created a vacancy, the candidate's commission was gazetted and he paid the appropriate purchase price which varied from £450 in a "Marching Regiment of Foot" to £1,260 in the Life Guards.[4]

The workings of the Purchase System as an example of Weber's "appropriation of offices" were considerably criticized by Victorian reformers who argued that the personal merits of the applicants were never considered.[5] Conversely, the system was vigorously defended by those who identified selection with the maintenance of desired social values. Thus Wellington argued in 1830 in favor of the Purchase System on the grounds that: "It brings into the service men of fortune and education— men who have some connection with the interests and fortune of the country besides the commissions which they hold from his Majesty."[6] Despite this controversy, however, the process of selection, especially in the early years of the Victorian period, depended very heavily on the workings of the Purchase system, to the extent that many fewer nonpurchase commissions were gazetted than those obtained by Purchase. Between 1834 and 1838, of over a total of 1410 commissions granted in the army, 1117 were by purchase.

However, since the military elite continued to exercise a very strict control over nominations for commissions, the end result, irrespective of whether the commission was bought or not, was to bring into the organization individuals whose anticipatory socialization seemed to identify them with the desired value-system. Almost inevitably, this meant that many of these young officers initially came from the landed interest. Some were representative of the peerage; others came from the greater gentry (3,000 to 10,000 acres) or the squirearchy (1,000 to 3,000 acres). Despite variations in the size of their estates or in the income from their land holdings, the common link was the ownership of land. Underlying this linkage was the belief in the importance of a system of values which implied the existence of a common ethos. This presumed that gentlemen were to be credited with enough public spirit, probity, courage, and education to make them essential servants of the Crown. The ethos of officership was thus part of a wider and more complex pattern of social obligations and rights associated with the perceived needs of a rural society. More specifically, the paternalism of land ownership was seen to be linked with the public responsibility which such ownership entailed.

This social pattern did not go unchallenged. To the supporters of a growing middle class, such as Trevelyan and Macaulay, any attempt to maintain the exclusive social status of the military establishment could not pass unquestioned. These were the advocates of a rational, utilitarian philosophy whereby the principle of "Open Competition" would recruit candidates primarily on the basis of their academic ability. The adoption of such a policy, it was claimed, would create a military organization based on achievement. Structurally, it would develop a meritocracy. Politically, it would limit the power of an entrenched ruling class. These were important considerations in the context of the changes which were taking place in Victorian society. In other institutions, such as the Civil Service, the policy of open competition had already been adopted. Yet the military situation was particularly complex and invited specific reactions. Despite the criticisms which can be made of these "aristocratic" officers, it is nevertheless true that officers had to be men who would serve the State with loyalty. There was, it appeared, a continuing need to find men who would indicate their potential military ability, not only by virtue of their education and proven academic expertise but also by possessing the qualities of a gentleman. "The problem of army reformers," proclaimed *The Times* in 1857, "is to provide a body of officers who will not cease to be gentlemen."[7] The alternative, it was feared, was an "imperium in imperio," a military force which, separated by impassable barriers from the remainder of society, transferred its allegiance from the Head of State to its own immediate superiors.[8]

The ensuing argument between the supporters of patronage and the advocates of open competition is an interesting commentary on Victorian attitudes. It ended, however, in the apparent victory of the latter when the Cardwell reforms of 1870 abolished the Purchase System. Subsequently, a contemporary commentator writing in the *Fortnightly Review* in 1886, thought there was no question of officer recruitment following the traditional pattern any longer. He argued forcibly that: "The abolition of promotion by purchase, the institution of tests of efficiency, the shortening of the soldiers service in the ranks . . . all tend towards making the army less a class and more a popular institution standing on the broad basis of democratic goodwill."[9] But in reality this was an overly optimistic view of anticipated changes which was not endorsed by subsequent events. If the traditionalists had lost a battle, they had certainly not lost the war.

Despite the abolition of purchase, the army continued to maintain the pattern of its traditional ethos and sense of corporateness after 1871. What had been overlooked in all the arguments advanced by the supporters of reform was that commissioning as an officer had never depended solely on the ability of the individual to buy a commission. In common with other groups in society, the military had developed a corporate culture and ethos which in its own case was heavily dependent on what Cunliffe has termed the "chevalier image."[10] In the absence of a total reform which would have challenged the military self-image through the creation of an alternative structure derived from the "rifleman" or citizen-soldier image, the traditional ethos persisted. To maintain the integrity of that ethos, other criteria of selection besides the ability to pay the purchase price of a commission had always been applied. Thus acceptance into the private world of the regiment had consistently depended on the aspirant demonstrating evidence of an extramilitary lifestyle and pattern of behavior which were acceptable to the officer commanding that regiment. Consistently, this lifestyle was identified with the preferred values of the landed interest, a preference linked with an ideological and often unreal self-image. What had happened increasingly after 1870 was that the criteria of selection which had previously been informal and highly subjective, were now institutionalized under such headings as "previous educational experience" and "financial standing." The potential area of officer recruitment had been theoretically widened, but the adoption of these criteria of selection ensured that there was little expansion of the socio-economic base from which officers came.

This was particularly noticeable in the way in which social control was ensured by the belief that attendance at a particular type of school, usually the exclusive "public" school, was a prerequisite of admission to most regiments. The kinship of members of the landed interest was thus extended as a criteria of selection to embrace this peculiarly British "old school tie" relationship. As Captain Cairnes commented in 1900 in giving advice to the military aspirant: "Being a young man of discretion, and probably having friends or relations, certainly old schoolfellows in the regiment of his choice, he will put himself in communication with his corps."[11] This educational experience, moreover, was essentially irrelevant in terms of the academic attainment of the applicant. It was consistently stressed that "prominence in athletic exercises is the surest road to pre-eminence"[12] since character rather than intellect and brawn rather than brain were identified as the criteria of personal success.

The importance of this shared educational experience to the military was, therefore, in no way related to the possible development of a meritocracy within the armed forces. Its main significance was as a means of effecting social control. Its philosophy was derived from the assumption that aspiring officers had been educated to an acceptable standard of social fitness through the scholastic socialization process. This process thus usually supplemented or, more rarely, replaced the family socialization process, thereby reinforcing a sense of group cohesiveness. This reinforcement was very noticeable within the regiments.[13]

Such cohesiveness excluded outsiders. It was indicative of an ethos which depended on a curiously interrelated public school and military attitude toward such concepts as "honor" and "esprit de corps." If the initial selection process was subsequently found to have been imperfect, this group cohesiveness produced its own sanctions mechanism. Deviants, it was argued, could be safely left "to the tender mercies of their brother officers."[14] Any refusal or unwillingness to conform to the ethos of the regiment invited, at best, social ostracism; at worst, a degree of "hazing" and bullying designed to drive the non-conformist from the regiment. In this, the unofficial "subaltern's court-martial" was frequently used to punish the apparent deviant, so that any formal approach to the issue of maintaining group standards was reinforced by the informal code which was applied in practice.

The Victorian military elite's eager use of "previous educational experience" as a criterion of selection was readily rationalized. Officers whose educational experience could be acquired in the major public schools had joined the British elite in receiving a common education which posited a connection between the defence of classicism and social leadership. The emphasis placed within such schools on the develop- ment of "character" was a very attractive criterion of selection. "Intel- lect," conversely, was usually identified as a concomitant of social illit- eracy. It was frequently equated with undesirable attributes which implied that the intellectual was the boor and the prig who knew his books better than his men and who preferred work at the desk to delights in the saddle. Consequently, any "decent" regiment during the Vic- torian period could readily justify to itself its reluctance to accept officers of an inferior social standing whose only claim of entry into the exclusive circle of the officers' mess was their academic attainment. It preferred to recruit officers whose "character" traits could be expected to predispose them to accept an established behavioral pattern and who would "fit" in with existing group members.

Such a preference, it appeared, could also be implemented by insist- ing that aspirants enjoyed a sufficiently high private income to enable them to live up to the group expectations which accompanied this be- havioral pattern. Since remuneration in the Victorian military was al- ways an *honorarium* rather than *merces*, officers persistently needed a private income to survive. After 1870, however, this requirement was increasingly formalized so that it could be used as a quasi-objective selec- tion criterion. Many regiments thus laid down a recommended scale of private incomes which young officers were to possess. In the more exclu- sive regiments of the cavalry, £600–700 a year was thought to be neces- sary.[15] Line regiments reduced this to an annual income of £100, but such a rate was the mandatory minimum and the recommended rate was often more than this. As Baynes comments, "The average officer in the 2nd Scottish Rifles had a private income of about £250 a year. The regiment itself only insisted upon £100 a year. This needs to be seen in perspective. The Coldstream Guards at this time considered £400 a year to be the minimum for an ensign on joining."[16] It was possible for an officer to manage on less than this, but most officers would have agreed with the general belief of the Victorian middle class that individuals needed at least "seven hundred or a thousand golden sovereigns a year" to maintain a solid standard of living.[17] The regiment's insistence on officers possessing a private income of this kind could thus be easily rationalized since without such an income, it would be impossible for officers to enjoy the normal standard of living for their social class. Certainly, all officers were expected to live up to the standard of their regimental mess and to bear a due share of expenses involved by the entertainment of mess guests, balls, race-meetings, and so forth as the group responded to its perceived social obligations. Selection based partly on the criterion of financial standing was consequently seen to be an essential element of social control if group cohesiveness were to be maintained within the military organization.

Both Victorian and contemporary critics of the level of attained professionalism within the nineteenth-century British army have reacted with considerable asperity to these features of military professionalization. A common reaction is that the ethos of, and the expected pattern of behavior within, these regiments were anachronistic in a century of considerable technological and social change. The contrast, it would seem, was between a utilitarian philosophy exemplified in the activities of men such as Samuel Smiles (1824–1904), retired secretary of the South-Eastern Railway, whose attitudes were reflected in the titles of his books, *Self-Help, Character, Life and Labour,* and with the apparent indolence of the military establishment. What other interpretation of military life could be placed on officers' expectation that they would be allowed two days each week for hunting?[18] How could an articulate middle class, excluded from these regiments by the selection policy which was adopted, accept that the military ethos and desired pattern of behavior were relevant and desirable aspects of professionalization?

Given, however, that the creation of a sense of corporateness was, and is, an essential facet of such professionalization, a critical question is whether there was any other rational alternative to the employment of these aspects of social control as a means of ensuring this cohesive sense in the Victorian period. In contemporary professions, institutionalized educational and training programs have become a most significant part of the socialization process. Equally, in the Victorian period such programs were of more than passing importance. These were, for example, a major means of socialization at West Point and Saint-Cyr. Yet although the Royal Military College at Sandhurst had been set up in 1802, it nevertheless played little part for much of the Victorian period as an institution of socialization. In the four years 1834–1838, for example, the College provided less than one-fifth of all new entrants into the army. Until the 1870 reforms, a comparably low number of graduates, although the total varied in subsequent years, meant that Sandhurst graduates were always a small minority of officer recruits. It was, moreover, very noticeable that when the army suddenly expanded in size, as in the Crimean Wars and after, an increasing number of officers were commissioned directly from civilian life.

The limited use which was made of Sandhurst as a means of socialization until the 1890s reflects very complex attitudes toward the function and role of a military academy. One part of public reaction was derived from a realistic appreciation of the cost of maintaining the RMC. In the same way that critics of the costs of a standing army persistently argued that there was nothing done by regular armed forces which could not be carried out more cheaply—and more effectively—by volunteer and auxiliary forces, so did critics of Sandhurst compare it unfavorably with the public schools. The net charge of £17,000 a year to maintain Sandhurst was seen as an excessive and unwarranted expenditure of public funds, particularly when military cadets were considered to be generally idle.[19] Nothing was done there, it was argued, which could not be better carried out at one of the major public schools.[20]

Underlying such a reaction were very definite attitudes toward the whole issue of professional education. To many British educationalists of this period, the primary purpose of an institutionalized educational program was to provide a general education. The "generalists" who were turned out by these programs were considered capable of carrying out the specialist tasks implicit in the concept of a profession without further specific training. Such a reliance on the efficacy of a general school education as the primary base of professionalism was endorsed by many commentators. W. J. Cowthorpe, Senior Civil Service Commissioner, for example, declared in his evidence to the *Dufferin Commission* in 1902 that "Our public schools, as at present constituted, furnish the very best material for the officering of our army."[21] While it was, perhaps, natural that the Headmaster of these public schools should equally argue that their schools could provide the most effective educational base, it was also noticeable that many senior Army officers agreed with this comment. Thus Lieutenant-General Lord Paulet made his views very clear to the 1868 *Military Education Commission:* "I know that when I commanded a regiment, I would rather have taken an Eton Boy, from choice, than a Sandhurst Boy, to make an officer."[22]

These views reflected the conviction that the "moral tone" of the military college was inferior to that of the public school. In the latter, it appeared, education carried out in a closed community encouraged cohesiveness and morale, thereby developing a "good tone." Public schools in short, produced: "A thorough English gentleman—Christian ready and enlightened—a finer sentiment of human nature than any other country, I believe could furnish."[23] Since the characteristics of the gentleman were the foundation of the ethos which was identified with the Victorian officer, the anticipatory socialization of the public school program was seen to be very important. Accordingly, such a program was seen as preferable to in-service institutionalized education at Sandhurst, where the development of character could not be so readily achieved because the program was "tainted" by training requirements.[24]

Toward the end of the century, the emphasis placed on education for leadership in the public schools was increasingly subject to criticism. In common with complaints in other professional groups that entrants to the profession were inadequately educated in those subjects suitable for an increasingly technological society, criticism of the pre-entry education of army officers was very marked. More of this criticism emerged from the inevitable committees and commissions which followed the Boer War. A *Times* leader which commented on the level of expertise exhibited by officers during this war argued that there was an over-simple belief in the public school curriculum, and too great a readiness to be guided by public school masters.[25] The committee appointed to consider the *Education and Training of the Officers of the Army* (the Akers-Douglas Committee) in 1902 not only drew attention to the lack of professional knowledge and skill among officers but also sought an explanation for the low standard of professionalization. One of the comments made by the Committee was that the initial recruitment of officers was defective.[26]

But this situation was not peculiar to the military organization; it reflected a national preference for the perpetuation of the "gentlemanideal" which preferred amateurs and gentlemen to professionals and cads.[27] As long as this remained a national preference, organizations sought ways to ensure that recruited members fit in with the characteristics of the gentleman ideal. For many newly emerging professions, institutionalized professional associations were created to develop an ethos which relied heavily on these characteristics. In the Victorian army, however, a recruitment policy was continued whereby selection as a form of control used previous educational experience as a critical criterion. As long as public school education was identified with character development and a grounding in those subjects which were needed by a gentleman, it remained of major importance in the selection process.

In this situation, the significance of academy education as part of a complex socialization process tended to be pushed to one side. It was difficult, if not impossible, to counter the argument that a good general education in a public school was the best means of developing that behavioral pattern which was seen to be a necessary concomitant of leadership. Practical training, it appeared, was a plebian activity and an infringement of the status of the gentleman all-rounder whose pre-entry experience reflected the expressed preference for the educated amateur.

This perhaps was indicative of the conclusion that "England, at heart, hates the expert: Germany rejoices in him."[28]

The identification of professionalization with the internalization of certain attitudes, values, and norms was thus exemplified in the Victorian army by a selection policy based on the belief that such internalization was primarily achieved outside the organization. Complex kinship patterns, a network of social relationships, and, above all, a shared educational experience were seen as evidence of anticipatory socialization which, in association with family experience, reduced the need for formal internalization programs within the military organization itself. The consequent professional ethos was essentially that associated with the concept of the officer and gentleman, an ethos in which the gentleman ideal was of paramount importance.

## The Organizational Setting

The premise that character was more important than intellect as a criterion of appointment can, with hindsight, be rigorously criticized. The Crimean War, the campaigns of the American Civil War, and the Franco-Prussian conflict of 1870 provided ample evidence of the changing dimensions of the profession of arms. Yet the Victorian military, as the *Royal Commission on the War in South Africa* morosely concluded, have revealed causes of failure which suggested that few lessons had been learned.[29] The conservatism of this armed force was, however, in itself an important aspect of the military ethos of this period. The wish to maintain the status quo was part of the desired gentleman ideal. Nevertheless, the attitudes of the Victorian army seem to contrast most markedly with those of other military organizations. On the continent of Europe, for example, armed forces were already becoming worlds in themselves, characterized by the emphasis placed on expertise as the basis of their professionalization, their closed organization, a special technology, and their own value system and norms. In short, these were the armies of an industrialized society, armies which apparently were able to exploit the advantages of mobility, fire power, and concentration which a technological age had conferred upon them.

The Queen's army, in contrast, continued to operate as a heterogeneous collection of individual regiments and corps, each of which sought to maintain its identity and preserve its specific ethos. They were linked not by any universally accepted sense of military professionalism but by the civilian interests of their members as part of the landed interest. A common acceptance of the norms and standards of the English ruling class from which the majority of their officers were recruited formed the basis of regimental attitudes toward many critical aspects of military life such as training, technological innovation, and tactics. Moreover, the army was held together socially by a complex pattern of individual relationships, in which the claim to hereditary authority on the part of officers reflected the belief of the gentleman that he had an inborn right and duty to lead others.

The professional ethos of these officers was, as has been noted, increasingly challenged by an expanding middle class. Time and again, these critics discovered ample evidence of the way in which the army perpetuated a set of values and norms that were anachronistic in a changing society. The courage, recklessness, and physical toughness of many officers, for example, reflected qualities which in the Regency period had been cultivated for their own sake and which in the early Victorian era had been accepted as the eccentricities of the fox hunting squire. But as the nineteenth century developed, qualities such as these, in which brawn was apparently preferred to brain, and character to intellect, compared unfavorably with the cool, detached professionalism of other occupational groups.

Yet there was apparently very little which these critics could do to change the ethos of the Victorian military. In the absence of conscription or a mass army, members of the middle class had no obligation to serve in this military. Consequently, the alternative and more utilitarian value system which they might have brought with them into the armed forces at no time replaced the traditional set of norms and values. Nor did this position change much during the Victorian period. Officers were always a numerically small group. Even after 1870 when the employment of troops in an expanding empire led Cardwell, the secretary of state for war, to introduce an ambitious program of military reform, the regular army numbered no more than 135,000 officers and men. In contrast, the Prussian field army alone in the 1870 War comprised 462,300 infantry and 56,000 cavalry, while the total effective strength of the military establishment was well over a million men. Shortly before the war in South Africa, the numerical strength of the British army compared very unfavorably with that of her Continental neighbors. In the German Empire, with a total population of 61,479,901, the peace-time establishment of the army, exclusive of troops serving in the African protectorates, was a cadre of 591,507 officers and men. France supported a comparable cadre of 573,743, but the United Kingdom consistently found it difficult to meet the target of 130,000 regular officers and men.

Since the "man on the Clapham omnibus" was rarely part of this total, it is not surprising that the norms of the Victorian officer were those of an unrepresentative group. Military service was an alien experience for almost all British citizens.

Although pressure to change this military ethos surfaced periodically, it was always extremely difficult to implement innovation. The changes which were taking place outside the army seemed to have consistently passed by the Victorian military. For example, the demand for institutionalized professionalization, with its emphasis on academic ability, increasingly affected other occupational grounds but did not alter the armed forces. One often overlooked explanation of this is that the Victorian army was regularly engaged in colonial campaigns which encouraged the persistence of a small-war mentality. In these campaigns, intellectual ability, technical skills, and technological developments were considered to be disabilities. The traits of the gentleman ideal marked the successful leader. The form of this "character" was brought out clearly in a description by Steevens, one of the most jingoistic of Victorian war correspondents, of Major-General Archibald Hunter, Kitchener's "sword-arm" in the Sudan: "Reconnoitering almost alone up to the muzzle of the enemy's rifles, charging bare-headed and leading on the blacks, going without rest to watch over the comforts of the wounded, he is always the same—always the same impossible hero of a book of chivalry. He is reckoned as a brave man, even among British officers; you know what that means."[30]

This would have been a generous evaluation of the actions of a young subaltern, tasked with looking after his men and expected to show evidence of personal bravery. But Hunter was no junior officer. He was responsible for three brigades of Egyptian troops, each of which was commanded by a perfectly competent brigadier. His style as a commanding general, however, epitomized the core traits of the Victorian military ethos: a preference for action rather than administration, an almost total disregard for personal safety, a paternalistic concern for subordinates, and a display of charismatic leadership. Colonial campaigns with their emphasis on individualism and improvisation thus encouraged the retention of these traits. Moreover, they fostered the homogeneity of the small group in which an informal camaraderie recognized the "character" of individuals and facilitated the perpetuation of the military ethos. The organizational setting, in short, justified the retention of a selection policy which laid great stress on the applicant's internalized values, norms, and attitudes. It vindicated the preference that aspiring officers possess core traits of character developed in the family and scholastic socialization process, rather than evidence of intellectual ability which could be furthered in specific military training courses.


## The Military Elite

The considerable emphasis placed on the gentleman ideal as the epitome of a desired set of social values within the Victorian army was also reinforced by the example of the military elite. In the absence of a deliberately structured professional association (found increasingly in other occupational groups), new entrants to the military establishment were quick to identify with the norms of senior officers. The wish to conform, to imitate, and to identify with the traditional holders of power was thus a common phenomenon among army officers. The attitude of occupational novitiates in the military reflected a widely prevalent Victorian situation in which individuals sought to confirm their claim to status by imitating the norms of the landed interest. Essentially, the dominance of such norms suggested that only through imitation would individuals be accepted by the relevant "in-group." Officers were as quick as many other members of society to take on such attitudes.

Within the Victorian military, such imitation meant internalizing the values of the military elite, for the connection between that elite and the landed interest was a persistent feature of the military ethos. In 1838, for example, 496 of the 507 general officers were members of major landed families. In 1870, when there were seventy-six generals in the army, 43 percent could be identified as the sons of major landowners, while in 1897, as the Victorian period was coming to an end, 40 percent of the generals and lieutenant generals were from this group. As Razell comments, "There are 2-1/2 times as many aristocrats in the ranks of Major General and above than one would expect from the proportion of aristocrats in the whole corps. . . . This means that the aristocracy maintained their relative monopoly of top ranks, although they lost an absolute monopoly throughout the nineteenth and early twentieth centuries."[31] It is little wonder that the lay critic often saw the military elite as the last bastion of neo-feudal attitudes and characteristics.[32]

The landed interest's quantitative dominance of the military elite was, however, much less important than the qualitative dominance of their values and interests. The influence of these officers permeated the military establishment. At one level, they were the social leaders of the regimental, perpetuating within the army the attitudes which they had internalized in their formative years. Cairnes makes this very clear: "In most districts the General is the leading light in a social sense . . . the presence of any individual at the General's dinner table is generally accepted as a guarantee of his fitness for any ordinary society."[33]

More important, as social leaders they encouraged the perpetuation of an amateur tradition, frequently preferring the recreations of a country gentleman to the responsibilities of a soldier. General Sir George Higginson (1826–1915) who had served with the Grenadier Guards for thirty years summed up their ethical sense very clearly:

> Our commanding officers were men of the world, thoroughly conversant with social and political life; if they preferred life in a wider community to the somewhat narrow sphere of regimental command, they took the most high minded view of the work of their subordinates, holding themselves absolutely responsible for any error of judgment which they might betray and were generous in their praise of duties well performed.[34]

This was the translation of the social philosophy of the landed interest into the life of the military establishment. Relationships within the officers' mess were expected to resemble behavior consistent with the notions of the gentleman ideal. Selection, based on criteria derived from these expectations ensured that new entrants to the occupational groups would be individuals who were predisposed toward the unquestioned acceptance of the postulated norms and values. A structured socialization process was thus deemed of less importance in formulating a sense of professional ethos than initial selection procedures. Individuals were gentlemen first and officers second.

## The Victorian Legacy

The development of professionalization within the Victorian military is in itself interesting. It has, however, a wider and more important relevance as an example of the manner in which an occupational group in the nineteenth century created barriers against attempts to introduce recruitment on the basis of universality. In the French revolutionary forces, the explicit ideal was open recruitment into the officer corps. This strategy was more than a tacit assumption in the American Revolutionary forces, despite occasional pronouncements by individual military figures about the desirability of gentleman officers. In other instances, the prevalence of the militia and the militia officer undermined the ideal of the aristocratic model. Yet in the United Kingdom social control over entry to the army was rigidly maintained despite public criticism of the

limits which this placed on policies of open recruitment. Selection criteria took into account the anticipatory socialization of aspirants in the
belief that this was the most important means of creating a desired and
internalized value system.

The concomitant set of norms constituted a persistent professional
ethos which generated its own characteristics of professionalization. The
existence of group cohesiveness was neither questioned nor doubted.
What this meant in practice was that military professionalization was not
oriented to the creation of a meritocracy. One effect of this was that
major problems subsequently arose when a changing technology demanded the narrowing of the skill differential between armed forces and
other professions. To meet these demands, the military—particularly
after the Boer War—began the search for officer aspirants who would
provide a suitable mix of intellectual and character traits. The structural
advantage of such a move was that the weighting given to the respective
component parts of this mix could be readily adjusted in response to
situational changes. There were, however, two major disadvantages.
First, over-frequent adjustment of this weighting to meet manpower
needs created uncertainty about the direct relevance of any postulated
selection criteria. Second, the emphasis still placed on the importance of
"character" as a core-trait of officership, encouraged subjective selection.

In short, although educational criteria were becoming increasingly
important in other occupational groups seeking professional status, they
were not of primary importance to the military before 1914. Guards,
cavalry, and infantry units recruited largely along prestige lines since
organizational commitment and esprit de corps continued to be identified as major professional characteristics. Even in the old Scientific
Corps—the Artillery and the Engineers—where the possession of technical qualifications was an essential criterion of recruitment, the traditional traits were also required. From time to time the perpetuation of
this policy created its own problems, as in 1901, when, to meet an
annual intake requirement of 795 officers, 355 officers had to be commissioned directly from militia regiments because of the shortage of academy
graduates. Yet for as long as society was prepared to accept that a preferred level of professionalization could be equated with a professional
ethos dependent on specific selection criteria, the military was able to
perpetuate a traditional recruitment policy. The effect of this policy upon
the development of expertise and on the limiting of the socio-economic
base of recruitment was acknowledged. But in a deferential and elitist
society the identification of the professional officer with the gentleman
ideal ensured its continuance.

Any evaluation of the merits and demerits of this form of military professionalization must perforce be subjective and partial. It is significant that most critical analysis has concentrated on the relationship of professionalization within the Victorian army and the attained level of expertise. While such analysis extends our understanding of the historical effects of such professionalization, it has tended to overlook the most important consequence of the adopted policies. This was the effect of such professionalization upon the linkages between armed forces and the parent society when the Victorian officer was unashamedly elitist and officership was a closed profession.

But the selection policies, the organizational setting, the role of the armed forces, and the isolation of the Victorian army seemed to justify a public reluctance to accept the general burdens of the military obligations. In other industrialized societies the citizen soldier concept, as applied to the militia and the conscript force, implied a strong emphasis on universal service; at no time was such a service acceptable to British society. On the Continent of Europe, the symbolism of the French Revolution, drawing heavily on the political appeals and experiences of the American War of Independence, emphasized the theme of the "nation in arms." Applying universality to officers implied that entry into the private world of the regiment be no longer defined as the monopoly of the landed interest. But a broadening of the base for officer recruitment could only be achieved when the average citizen accepted his eligibility for military service. However, this presumption was steadfastly rejected by the bulk of an emerging middle class. Some joined the Militia, yet there was a repeated shortage of officers in the Militia establishment. Thus, in the *Report of the Military Education Committee* (1902), at a time when there was an annual deficit of 500–550 officers against an establishment of 3,385 officers, Major-General A. E. Turner, the Inspector-General of Auxiliary Forces, commented morosely that "The War Office cannot afford to pick and choose to any great extent, but must take in candidates that appear suitable, in the opinion of the Commanding Officer of the Regiment, to hold a Militia Commission." Since most of these candidates had, in any event, failed to gain entrance to Sandhurst and joined the Militia for subsequent transfer to the regular army, it is evident that few members of the parent society were prepared to accept the responsibilities and obligations of military service.

Consequently, professionalization within the Victorian army continued to reflect an ethos in which the social value of the landed interest became enshrined and unchangeable. The projected military image was that of an elitist group which was the guardian of traditional values in a changing world. Officers, like the other members of the ruling elite, were men who during their formative years had been subjected to a prolonged molding of character, personality, and outlook. The critics of the army argued that this socialization process ignored the forces of technological and social change for the secure world of the Victorian public school, the undue emphasis placed on the study of classics, on the acquisition of manly Christian virtues, and on the idea of public service, produced an army of officers endowed with a complacent appreciation of their role in society.

Yet such a socialization process concomitantly engendered a set of values in which a belief in the importance of group membership was governed by an intricate behavioral code. Such a code preferred honorable defeat to dishonest victory and favored gentlemanly qualities of character over the competitive attitudes of a profit-conscious mercantile interest. Whether this sense of group identity and set of values was appropriate for an army in a changing technological environment remains a contentious question, but what is certain is that the process of professionalization still permeates the contemporary British armed forces.

## Notes

1. Morris Janowitz, *The Professional Soldier* (New York: Free Press, 1960), p. 6.
2. See, for example, Jay Luvaas, *The Education of an Army* (London, 1965); E. C. Masland and M. Radway, *Soldiers and Scholars* (Princeton, N.J.: Princeton University Press, 1957).
3. See Gwyn Harries-Jenkins, *The Army in Victorian Society* (London: 1977), esp. chap. 3, "The Purchase System."
4. These prices were laid down in a *Royal Warrant of 1821* which fixed both the price of initial commissions and the price of subsequent promotions. The latter were frequently affected by market forces; it was alleged in the 1850s that as much as £14,000 had to be paid for the lieutenant-colonelcy of a cavalry regiment in comparison with the regulation price of £6,175. The Earl of Cardigan, it has been alleged, paid between £35,000 and £40,000 for the Lieutenant-Colonelcy of the 15th Hussars in 1832.
5. Sir Charles Trevelyan, *The Purchase System in the British Army* (London, 1867), pp. 1–2.
6. *Memorandum of the Duke of Wellington*, 1830, cited in J. H. Stocqueler, *A Personal History of the Horse-Guards* (London, 1837), p. 153.
7. *The Times*, August 20, 1857.
8. *The Times*, March 5, 1858.

9. Anonymous, "The Army and Democracy," *Fortnightly Review* (March 1886): 340.

10. Marcus Cunliffe, *Soldiers and Citizens* (London, 1969), pp. 417–23.

11. W. E. Cairns, *Social Life in the British Army* (London, 1900), p. 14.

12. Cairns, *Social Life in the British Army* p. 7.

13. John Baynes, *Morale* (London, 1867), p. 29.

14. Cairns, *Social Life in the British Army*, pp. xviii–xix. In the 1850s the effects of "hazing" within the world of the officers' mess received very unfavorable publicity. In 1896, the case of two young officers of the fourth Hussars who were bullied and hazed because they were unable to live in the manner their fellow officers expected was brought before Parliament. *Hansard* 38 (June 19, 1896): 1481–84.

15. *Report of the Committee to Inquire into the Nature of the Expenses Incurred by Officers of the Army.* Cd. 1421 (London, 1903): X, 7–8.

16. Baynes, *Morale*, p. 29.

17. See Peter Laslett, *The World We Have Lost* (London, 1971), p. 227ff. Since at this time, fewer than 280,000 households from a total of 7,000,000 enjoyed such an income level, the life-style of the officer was perforce atypical of the poulation as a whole.

18. R. A. L. Pennington, "Army Reform from a Battalion Point of View," *Fortnightly Review* (February 1901): 326.

19. *First Report of the Royal Commission on Military Education Parliamentary Papers* (1886–1889) XXII, p. 18.

20. *First Report of the Royal Commission on Military Education Parliamentary Papers Minutes of Evidence* (1870) XXIX. Evidence of Reverend R. A. Southwood, Headmaster, Modern Department, Cheltenham College.

21. *The Times*, June 12, 1902.

22. *Minutes of Evidence*, p. 230.

23. A. R. Stanley, *The Life and Correspondence of Thomas Arnold, DD* (London, 1890), p. 198.

24. *Minutes of Evidence*, Evidence of Major-General Herbert, MP.

25. *The Times*, June 20, 1902.

26. *Report of the Committee Appointed to Consider the Education and Training of the Officers of the Army* (1903), p. 2.

27. "Gentlemanideal" was a portmanteau word coined by the German writer Dibelius to describe the English veneration for the specific lifestyle and its associated attitudes which characterized the gentleman.

28. M. E. Sadler, "The Unrest in Secondary Education in Germany and Elsewhere," *Special Reports on Education Subjects* 9 (1902): 50.

29. See *Report of His Majesty's Commissioners Appointed to Inquire into the Military Preparations and Other Matters Connected with the War in South Africa*

Cd. 1789 (London, 1903): XL; *Minutes of Evidence* (1903), Vol. I: Cd. 1790 and Vol. II: Cd. 1791; *Appendices* (1903), XLIII, Cd. 1792.

30. G. W. Steevens, *With Kitchener to Khartoum* (Edinburgh, 1898), p. 56.
31. P. E. Razzell, "Social Originas of Officers in the Indian and British Home Army," *British Journal of Sociology* XIV (September 1963): 248–56.
32. R. Cunningham, *Conditions of Social Well-Being* (London, 1878), p. 328.
33. Cairns, *Social Life in the British Army*, p. 26.
34. General Sir John Higginson, *Seventy-One Years of a Guardsman's Life* (London, 1916), p. 74.

# 6

# The Dissolution of Armies in the Vietnam Perspective

KURT LANG

A Russian archduke is reported to have said that he hated war because "it spoiled armies." His observation fits, most uncomfortably, the American experience in Vietnam, where signs of partial dissolution coincided with increasingly strident opposition at home, particularly after the Tet offensive in January 1968. That the American military faced problems in Vietnam is clear, though their exact nature and extent remain in dispute. Although some maintain that the home front managed to lose a war the troops were on the verge of winning, no one disputes that there was also a good deal "unsoldierly" conduct. Responsibility for these problems has alternately been assigned to the permissiveness of American society, poor leadership, and the professional climate within the military. Opponents of the war, on the other hand, have argued that Vietnam drove home to many soldiers the immorality and illegitimacy of U.S. intervention there.[1]

When examined in the light of other twentieth century wars, many aspects of the Vietnam experience take on a familiar appearance. For example, in both the South African War by the British against the Boer Republic (1899–1903) and the French effort against the Algerian National Liberation Front (1954–1961),[2] a major power tried, with modern weapons, to subdue what was essentially a guerrilla force. The major powers' advantages in strictly numerical terms were even greater in these wars than the Americans' in Vietnam. The British did crush the Boers, but the victory proved unexpectedly costly, especially in terms of lives lost. The French effort ended with full independence for Algeria. Atrocities were charged in both wars. The British forced resettlement on the Boers in order to separate the resisters from their supply bases and, in this, anticipated a major element of American Vietnam strategy. So did the French measurement of their progress against an invisible enemy by body counts, strict inventories of weapons and ammunition captured, and the mapping of "pacified" areas.

These "little wars" had, when they began, considerable popular support. A large number of middle class volunteers rallied around the British flag to fight the Boers.[3] The Algerian campaign attracted little attention at first, but had a natural constituency among both settlers and nationalists, who were determined to keep the colony French at any cost. In each case, early opposition was muted but became more vocal as the war bogged down. The troops who ultimately brought victory in South Africa were not the original volunteers, most of whom had been repatriated after the first year, but mercenaries who, having been recruited from among the poor, were expendable.[4] In Algeria, the elite paratroop units did most of the fighting, with draftees pretty much limited to garrison duty. When irredentist officers revolted to keep the government from making peace, the coup was foiled because these draftees refused to heed them.

One must not, of course, overlook such differences as the extent to which the fighting in Vietnam during the critical period came to approximate conventional warfare and how this change affected the experiences of combat soldiers. The more meaningful comparison here is between Vietnam and the world conflicts of 1914–1918 and 1939–1945 and the American involvement in Korea.

This chapter reviews how what we have learned about the effect of four factors on performance—combat stress, group cohesion, strategic situation, and political commitment—and applies these lessons to Vietnam.

## The Stress Factor

*Combat performance normally falls short of the prescribed optimum.* Not until recently has the vast output by military historians included much information about the battle experience of troops at the tactical level. S. L. A. Marshall's demonstration[5] that a large number of soldiers in the typical combat encounter of World War II had failed to direct fire against the enemy even when clearly in a position to do so was initially greeted with dismay. Reports of this "performance gap" were soon followed by other disquieting news about the behavior of American POWs held in North Korean and Chinese camps. Though only about a score among the many thousands had refused repatriation, many more, including officers, had falsely confessed to germ warfare or engaged in what was defined as collaboration with their captors.[6] In the soul searching that followed, the far larger number of Chinese and North Koreans who chose not to be returned and the units of ex-Soviet soldiers who fought alongside the World War II *Wehrmacht* were often overlooked.[7]

Nor was this the first time that the idea that citizen soldiers were not totally committed had arisen. In the first world war, there was controversy over the many men who appeared uninjured, yet were granted casualty privileges because they were too distraught to carry on. Was "shell shock" caused by repeated near-misses a legitimate injury? Many, especially in Great Britain, had insisted that it amounted to nothing more than a "recategorization of behavior that had traditionally been filed under 'cowardice,' 'indiscipline,' or neurological wounds with unexplained causes."[8] As the war progressed the notion of psychiatric breakdown gained acceptance, but the British army persisted in the disciplinary approach and had, by the end of the war, executed more deserters than other belligerents.[9]

The official acknowledgment that anxiety is natural and to be treated as a medical rather than a disciplinary problem has side effects. No one really wants to be killed, and the psychiatric way is an acceptable escape route. It also allows unit commanders to rid themselves of misfits without time-consuming disciplinary action that might, in the long run, jeopardize their own standing with troops as well as superiors.[10]

*The effects of stress are both traumatic and cumulative.* The logistic revolution brought on by the military exploitation of the railroad, of motor transport, and of aircraft has promoted a *Blitzkrieg* image, but has actually had the reverse effect. Assured of an uninterrupted flow of replacements, armies can now carry on where heavy losses would once have meant an end to hostilities.[11] Until World I, there had always been fewer deaths due to enemy action than to disease.[12] Better support and more lethal weapons have reversed this rule. Although a disproportionate number of neuropsychiatric cases have occurred during the first exposure to combat, after a time, even the most effective fighting men grow indifferent—many of them ending up on the neuropsychiatric casualty list.[13]

The period of combat effectiveness can be extended by frequent breaks—as in World War I, when units were routinely rotated between front-line positions, a rest period, and a period of reserve. Ahrenfeldt, comparing British and American troops in World War II, noted both the positive effect of more frequent rest periods on the British and that the American belief that every man had a "breaking point" may have had self-fulfilling consequences.[14] The potentially adverse effects of a strictly delimited tour of duty have also been noted. Many American fliers in World War II would exhibit a marked increase in anxiety as they approached the twenty-five missions that made a man eligible for relief. But when military necessity caused that magic number to be increased, the onset of these symptoms was also delayed.[15]

The stress reactions of troops in Vietnam were affected by similar factors, one of which was the nature of the warfare there. Intermittent but usually brief periods of contact with the enemy, fairly large and generally comfortable base camps that, while not so secure as rear echelons in previous wars, nevertheless afforded rest and time for clean up and equipment care between the forays, together with a precisely delimited tour of overseas duty, where each man knew in advance the date on which he might return to the States, and prior screening to weed out the unfit helped depress neuropsychiatric rates far below those of World War II and Korea. Moreover, psychiatric facilities in Vietnam were brought close to the battle zone and designed to speed the return to duty of those with less serious symptoms. As a result, through much of the war, neuropsychiatric casualty rates among American troops were fairly uniform, regardless of whether they were stationed in the United States, Europe, or Vietnam, and there was general satisfaction with the morale and good health of troops in the combat zone.[16] Yet one familiar problem resurfaced: the so-called short-termer's syndrome, characterized by a decline in effectiveness as men approached the end of their prescribed tour was so marked that, I have been told, some veterans were allowed to mark time in anticipation of their near-departure.[17] This relaxation of pressure may explain why the lowest incidence of neuropsychiatric casualties occurred within the last two months of a Vietnam tour.

In one respect at least, the Vietnam pattern was unique: where battlefield and psychiatric casualties had always been strongly correlated, the latter rose unambiguously in the second half of 1968 when losses had begun to decline and fighting was slowly winding down. The increase was in behavioral and character disorders, not in the psychotic or neurotic disorders more often associated with a prior psychiatric history. There does not seem to have been any relaxation of standards to account for such a rise, especially as the esprit of draftees, large numbers of whom had begun to reach Vietnam in 1967, was if anything better than that of the "regulars."[18]

It is possible that, although the absolute risk of injury may have lessened, anxiety over fragments from exploding mines and booby traps, which by 1970 accounted for 80 percent of all battle wounds, may have been more debilitating than fear of actual combat (against which solidarity afforded at least some protection). Alternatively, as some reports suggest, soldiers in Vietnam occasionally behaved so as to provoke an early return from overseas on psychiatric grounds, while others sought undesirable, even punitive, discharges in the belief, or hope, that the type of discharge could later be changed. Whatever the case, it was during this period that increases in the number of attacks on officers ("fraggings") and collective refusals to obey an order were noted and that drugs were identified as either a cause or a symptom of disintegration.[19]

## Group Cohesion

*Peer cohesion assures mutual help in stressful situations.* Nineteenth-century writers like Ardant du Picq and commentators on World War I like Kurt Hesse insisted that the bonds of comradeship, now called peer cohesion, were a pre-condition for effective performance at the tactical level. They sensed their importance as motivational supports for soldiers in combat. But it took the more systematic psychological warfare and morale studies of World War II to raise what had been a folk theorem to a sociological principle. Surveys of German POWs led Shils and Janowitz to conclude that the strength of national socialist convictions contributed little to the Wehrmacht's ability to resist disintegration in the face of defeat. The cement that held it together was the military group, which was built around an experienced cadre of non-commisioned officers.[20]

Studies of American troops provide further evidence.[21] Thus, a replacement going into the line as an individual replacement was usually less effective than one who was sent in with a familiar group. The World War II experience also showed that stragglers lost from their unit during an operation and picked up by groups who were strangers to them tended to be militarily useless. Some "straggling" is of course a deliberate avoidance of danger, to which those less well-integrated were more prone to resort. However, stragglers who remained part of a group often continued to function.

These interpersonal ties must be viewed as an adaptation to the exigencies of military life, such as the separation from family and familiar surroundings and frequent reassignment, often on short notice. In combat, the need for group support is even greater. There survival is a joint undertaking, and the solidarity that results usually overrides the traditional social barriers of class, race, and religion. Although such ties develop spontaneously, their formation is facilitated by certain forms of leader behavior, by practices that encourage participation, by weapons whose operations require team work, by shared pride in one's unit or branch of service or in just being a soldier, by a cultural norm of comradeliness, and—last but not least—by a common background and allegiance to secondary symbols. At the same time, these ties are inevitably ruptured by the turnover to which every unit is subject, changes which are a perpetual source of strain. Casualties, which increase anxiety among survivors and cause them to mourn lost "buddies," undermines their ability to form new relationships.

In Vietnam, as elsewhere, every "new guy" had first to be integrated. Nevertheless, the negative consequences of the rotation policy have probably been exaggerated. Similar policies have long governed assignment to isolated posts and other hazardous duty. Their existence in Korea prompted no claims that the solidarity of the military group was thereby destroyed. Moreover, the yearly casualties in some combat units have greatly exceeded 100 per cent of allocated strength, making rotation seem rather benign by comparison. Moskos confirms that, rotation notwithstanding, military units in Vietnam were indeed held together by a "granular" network of primary ties built on mutual interest and characterized by a detachment,[22] ties consistent with the idea that overseas service is an individual contract between each man and the military. There was less reason to identify with one's unit or to perceive a link between one's own fate and victory. In the last analysis, rotation probably had a greater effect on the quality of the leadership than it had on troops. An average tenure in officer commands of under six months hardly allowed time for the establishment of trust and close working relationships between leaders and subordinates, who were themselves being rotated.[23]

*Cohesion contributes to military effectiveness but only if military groups transmit the appropriate norms of conduct.* The understanding within the informal group that they will avoid needless danger, even if doing so means going against some directive, graphically illustrates how the endemic tension between the work group and official authority (a major focus of organization research) is heightened by the specifically military cleavages around risk and rank. The dangers of combat are not shared equally; they fall heavily on a small minority. Many privileges are monopolized by officers, although there is a great difference between the highly visible caste system in rear areas and the relative egalitarianism in combat zones. Because combat soldiers are forced to improvise, certain deviations are widely tolerated, even condoned. Some regulations are simply discarded as unnecessary; others are seen as interfering with getting the job done.

The havoc front-line norms play with discipline is expressed in the subterfuges military groups use to protect themselves. In Vietnam these tactics fell short of outright refusals of orders to attack, as happened on such a massive scale in the French army in 1917 that the country was, for all practical purposes, defenseless for several months.[24] More benign examples of "indiscipline" were the unofficial "truces," when occupants of opposing trenches in World War I withheld fire to allow the rescue of a man lying wounded in no man's land or simply to exchange Christmas greetings.[25] These truces fell short of fraternization across the lines and did not interfere with operational plans. Other examples are the use of intoxicants (and drugs), the occasional harsher treatment of prisoners than regulations allowed, and various traffic with civilians, such as the wholesale violation of General Eisenhower's order against fraternization with German women, an order soon rescinded when it proved impossible to enforce.

Such deviations have always occurred, and most have had only a marginal bearing on military effectiveness. Yet they can interfere with operations. For example, the overriding obligation World War II American infantry men felt to care for wounded comrades[26] and the careless expenditure of property in combat[27] did not have official sanction, but higher authorities may have felt it imprudent to try to stop such practices. In addition, combat offers multitudinous opportunities for subtle sabotage, particularly against a superior who, through ineptness or overeagerness, shows himself indifferent to the lives of his men. Such an officer may not be warned of impending danger, or he may just happen to meet with an "accident." Enlisted lore is full of such stories, and, although many are exaggerations or just plain lies, the fact that they circulate in every army indicates that they contain some truth.

By the same token, it should be recognized that a collective refusal to obey is a symptom, not of weak peer cohesion, but of the endemic conflict between those who issue orders and those who see themselves as taking the risks. Evidencing this conflict are wartime mutinies, such as the one reported at a replacement depot near Salerno, Italy, during World War II, when recently recuperated British wounded were counting on rejoining the units they left. Having heard through the grapevine of their pending reassignment, some hundred soldiers were so intent on rejoining their outfits that they refused to comply with their marching orders. Facing a clear conflict, they chose to disobey orders and brought severe punishment upon themselves.[28] This "mutiny" was mild compared to the behavior during the French mutinies of 1917, which involved some violence, mostly against staff officers, who were denounced as *buveurs du sang*.[29] But here, too, many of those singled out for punishment had been good soldiers and without any prior history of maladjustment either inside or outside the army. They had acted with the approval of their group.

This cleavage stands out starkly in the German naval mutiny of 1918. Here the chief targets were the deck officers who, convinced of their social superiority, wined and dined while sailors were fed on what they called "slop." The officers looked down even upon the technical officers, who did most of the work to keep the ships seaworthy. Similarly, in the Russian army of World War I, the officers first singled out for assault were the ones whose background made them suspect of harboring pro-German sympathies; then in the epidemic of assaults after the February revolution, they were directed against those who refused to accept the new directives which abolished the worst disciplinary abuses.[30]

Combat refusals in Vietnam resemble those in World War I. For example, in August 1969 the men of A Company in the 196th Light Brigade, a unit that had experienced unusually high casualties, refused to mount an attack in the area north of Danang.[31] In this instance, the usual disjunction between informal norms and official directives was aggravated by what has been described as a "commander's war."[32] Division headquarters was able to maintain direct radio supervision of all operations down to the level of platoon. As a result, unit leadership in its traditional sense became superfluous. When troops out on a mission made enemy contact, their immediate response was to call on the division for concentrated fire. Massive amounts of ammunition would be expended on objectives whose importance later turned out to be trivial. Another problem was the level of the success all echelons became geared to. As troops learned how easily counts could be faked and how readily their numbers were accepted, the inflation of enemy casualty figures, of number of weapons captured, of areas pacified, etc., became another form of the self-protection practiced by nearly everyone, including superiors who had nothing to gain from questioning such claims, since to do so might only depress their own performance rating. The long-term effect of these widely practiced circumventions was the discrediting of organizational authority.

Three other cleavages further complicated the situation in Vietnam: the existence of two mutually hostile sub-cultures, official attitudes toward drug use, and race.

The way "lifers" and "grunts" sorted themselves out is too well known to merit much comment.[33] This cleavage had a generational basis. Many old-timers, who had made the army their life, did not fit the conventional role of the NCO leader who, because he was both respected and feared, was able to insist that every order be punctiliously carried out. Enjoying limited, or very little, respect, many felt it was in their own interest to let things go so long as they did not jeopardize their positions vis-à-vis their own superiors.

The extent to which troops used drugs touched off something close to a national scandal. Alcoholic beverages were available through military supply channels, while drugs were outlawed. Users were therefore pushed into illicit networks. The conflict that arose over drug laws easily generalized to include other issues.

Race had little effect on relations in combat, but outside combat there were clear signs of cleavage along racial lines. Conflict over orders where one party was black and the other white was apt to have racial overtones. Race undoubtedly played a role in some "fraggings" (the use of fragmentation grenades to attack leaders), but in the majority of cases both perpetrator and victim were of the same race.

## Military Factors

*Troops are responsive to the strategic situation.* The control the military group exercises over its members is highly contingent on its ability to provide minimal comfort and security and the best chance of survival under the circumstances. This ability varies with the military situation.

Specifically, the neuropsychiatric casualty rate, which we have taken as one of the indicators of stress, has typically been lower during combat involving movement than during action along a more or less stable front. When troops are in retreat, evacuation facilities are apt to be scarce and anyone unable to keep up is in danger of falling into enemy hands. A rapid advance reduces the neuropsychiatric casualty rate because of the temporary autonomy with which small units operate. Troops manage to get "lost," but then rejoin their unit.[34] Similarly, Kalinowsky noted that few of the French taken prisoner at Verdun exhibited the psychiatric symptoms so prevalent among their German counterparts for whom the war was not yet over.[35]

That soldiers also view their own fate in a larger context is very much in evidence in the French mutinies, which Pedroncini, their main chronicler, has characterized as essentially "military," a "protest, more or less violent, on the part of the army against the form of warfare it has been required to conduct up to then."[36] These mutinous incidents were concentrated in units that had seen the heaviest and most fruitless fighting. The typical refusal to attack or to move up to attack, as Pedroncini recounts, would be "triggered when the regiment had been out of the line for a short period and then was ordered back to the front,"[37] especially if the men felt that they had not had enough rest or that the unit to be relieved had done less than its share of fighting. The common theme was the troops' unwillingness to sacrifice themselves in an attack they saw as having little chance of success and absolutely none of bringing the war to a speedy end. Many of these units fought bravely only days after the mutiny. Wildman points to a similar attitude on the part of Russian troops. They were willing to man defensive positions, but not to be slaughtered in a senseless attack because of an officer's order.[38] This "military" element is also to be found in the 1918 revolt of the German fleet at Kiel. Sailors resisted the final suicidal foray that could have only served to preserve the honor of the officer corps since it would have delayed the certain Allied victory at most by weeks.[39]

Military reverses spur desertions.[40] By the fall of 1916, desertions in the Russian army showed a steep increase by the following spring, they had reached staggering proportions. In Italy, after the defeat at Carporetto, parts of the army just melted away, many onto the sick lists. The Wehrmacht is perhaps an exception. Despite the Allied successes after the landing in Normandy, few soldiers gave themselves up until after their positions had been overrun. One explanation is to be found in the apparent indifference of the prisoners that fell into Allied hands to the larger strategic picture, about which they had deliberately been kept ignorant.[41] But German authorities viewed desertion as a problem, as the harsh punitive measures they ordered against any unauthorized absence of more than twenty-four hours and the greater use of death sentences for anyone caught make clear. For each month in 1944, the number of convicted deserters was six times that in 1940. In view of the many who were never convicted because they could not be found, we can assume that the real increase was even greater.[42]

Desertion to the rear, always more common than the reverse, was discouraged by constant and meticulous checks of leave papers, by the non-replacement of "lost" ration books that might have been given to deserters, and by the increasingly harsh penalties for being without an identity card or for sheltering or giving any kind of aid to an AWOL. Furthermore, a deserter to the enemy, if caught, not only risked his own life, but also chanced retaliation against his family. Reminders of these perils included references to Nazi agents said to be operating in enemy POW camps. These measures, together with the fear of Russian captivity (many believed that Russians did not take prisoners), were disincentives as long as the army system managed to minister at least minimally to soldiers' personal needs and held out the prospect of eventual reunion with their families.

It should be evident that desertion in Vietnam was discouraged less by punitive measures than by the limited attraction of civilian life there. In addition, soldiers were dependent on military transport home. Escape to a Westernized country was difficult to negotiate, given the distances and language barriers to be crossed. The strategic situation was desperate compared to the strategic collapse suffered by some belligerents in two world wars. In strictly military terms, the Tet offensive was actually an American victory. Only when judged against previous claims was it a serious setback.[43] In terms of what troops must have experienced, the strength of the enemy attack further called into question the credibility of the command, and criticism was inevitably communicated down the line. It was after Tet that certain deviance rates began their climb. Desertions also increased, not so much among those in Vietnam as among soldiers intent to avoid going there. For those already caught in the net, the preferred solution was to limit risks by routine performance until it was time to return to the "land of the great PX." In addition, at this point a variety of political factors came into play, among them President Johnson's offer of negotiations. Its effect on the strategic perspectives of troops is not to be discounted.

## Political Influences

*Political opposition to war derives from civilian, not military perspectives.* The thrust of the argument so far has been that combat is a world apart, a temporary stay away from the normal world to which the soldier will ultimately return. Leed has highlighted what he calls the "liminal" aspects of this experience.[44] Although the separation from civilian life is very real, troops are not totally removed from its influence or immune to the currents of public opinion.

A perceived threat to the nation when war is declared gives meaning to patriotic appeals. Potentially divisive issues are temporarily shelved, and the new solidarity may last as long as the war. But, as costs mount, old conflicts are reactivated. The burden is never distributed evenly, and some politicians cannot refrain from trying to capitalize on what may appear to be inefficiency and unnecessary military setbacks.

Also, the longer a war drags on, the greater the war-weariness. Thus in World War I, every major European belligerent experienced a rise in the number of strikes.[45] Nothing comparable happened in World War II, because that war was not—at least not to the same degree—a war of attrition. Polls nevertheless reveal a clear downward trend in American support for that war effort, and, similarly, for Korea and Vietnam.[46]

Homefront opinion inevitably makes its way to the front. The influence of the pre-service socialization of recruits is renewed with the arrival of every new contingent of replacements. To the extent that those in uniform are self-selected, their attitude toward soldiering will be more positive and less affected by changes in the political climate, including news of war-weariness. But even those who are young, apolitical, and highly patriotic will pay heed to charges of military ineptness against their government and to demands that the war be brought to a quick end. Such civilian views, if current, will reach combat troops through mail and other communication with home, through observations relayed by soldiers on home leave, and through whatever mass media are made available to them.

In a war that has enthusiastic support, appeals to flag and country (or some political ideology) bring forth volunteers of a higher quality— physically, mentally, and what is called morally—than the regulars on which peacetime armies in countries without conscription are forced to rely. Thus, British middle class citizens volunteered in droves to fight the Boers; then, as the war fever subsided, the cadre of professionals was left with the residue of what was essentially a mercenary force, recruited from the population that the labor market could not absorb.[47]

Replacements always bring changes. In World War I, staggering manpower losses forced the belligerents to call up older men and to take away the exemptions many had enjoyed as heads of families. These men, more established in careers and more integrated into their communities than the ones they replaced, were also more attuned to developments on the home front. Another untapped pool consisted of workers in the munitions factories, a milieu in which the anti-war left had been active. With their deferments terminated, some workers would carry their radical pacifist views with them into the military. In Russia, where heavy losses had created an unusual number of vacancies, they were filled by granting reserve commissions to persons with certain educational qualifications, few of whom shared the traditional attitudes of the regulars, and most of whom were likely, as students at university, to have had exposure to socialist and revolutionary ideas.[48] As a last resort, armies can fall back on men whose criminal, ethnic, or political background had previously disqualified them from service in the armed forces. The Nazis, when forced to draw on non-Germans and others with high subversion potential, placed them in separate units and under special supervision, where they presumably could not contaminate the rest.

In Vietnam, so far as I have been able to determine, manpower changes were insufficient to explain the change in atmosphere during the later years. To be sure, the Special Forces, very much in evidence during the early phase of American involvement, had disappeared from the scene as missions changed and the Marine Corps and Army took over. No adverse effects have been attributed to the influx of draftees, whose overall performance was said to have been more than equal to the regular army personnel they replaced.[49] Like young men generally, they cared little about the politics of the conflict. Increasingly, however, they turned out to have been affected by the anti-authoritarian elements of the youth culture of the 1960s. In addition, the way America had drifted into the Vietnam war without a sense of national emergency suggests that few were eager to serve. As the anti-war protests gained strength, the feeling that theirs was a citizen obligation must have been weakened. Finally, the ease with which deferments could be obtained—not only by students but also on a variety of occupational, medical, religious, and other grounds—resulted in a military force consisting disproportionately of persons who either had been driven into the army by poor job prospects, were unwilling, or had actually tried but failed in their effort to avoid the draft.[50]

Perceived inequities in the application of the draft law could hardly enhance motivation. Then, as the peace protests back home gained momentum and public opinion began to turn against the war, each newly arriving cohort came to resent more deeply the injustice of a system that afforded others the freedom to protest but pushed them into the least desirable of military assignments.

Barring those few who welcome war as a release from the prosaic existence of bourgeois society, civilians require some moral or ideological justification before donning a uniform. The extent to which European youth was enthralled by the opportunity for heroic sacrifice afforded by the outbreak of the first world war is incomprehensible today, when patriotic appeals of the flag-waving variety usually fall on deaf ears. For the members of the anti-Franco Abraham Lincoln Brigade in the Spanish civil war, horror of the world the enemy intended to create was a more effective antidote to fear than the more traditional means, such as leadership, training, and unit pride.[51] Convictions of such strength were rarely encountered among American troops in World War II. Yet, although their patriotism was hardly demonstrative, few questioned that this was a "just" war, forced upon us by the enemy.[52]

Military groups will function as long as orders are issued within a context of fundamental legitimacy. "The American Soldier" studies, which generally emphasize group ties as the key to motivation in combat, do not ignore and actually go out of their way to acknowledge the importance of this moral consensus.[53] Even when the *Wehrmacht* faced defeat, faith in Hitler as the *Führer* of Germany proved remarkably resilient, while other secondary symbols evoked little loyalty. Of course, nearly every unit had a hard core of fanatical Nazis, ready to denounce any expressions of pessimism as defeatist and traitorous in order to keep them from spreading.[54] Recognizing the morale-sustaining value of ideology, all armies have "orientations," and some have gone so far as to appoint political commissars to monitor all subversion, from behavior to even the mildest expression of dissent.[55]

Of the other routes by which civilian political attitudes infiltrate to the front, home leave is potentially the most disruptive. It affords an escape, if only a temporary one, from the control of military discipline. There are many World War I reports of ever more unmanageable disorder on leave trains, at railway depots, and at other places where soldiers in transit would naturally congregate. In France, such incidents peaked just before the cancellation of leaves in preparation for the 1917 spring offensive, a cancellation that was to set off the mutinies. In addition, being back home opened a man to persuasion from family, friends, long-standing associates, and even strangers, and to the temptation to overstay his leave. A unique manifestation of the effect of proximity to civilians was revealed in Italy where a study demonstrated a direct quantitative connection between the amount of left-wing activity in the different parts of the Genzano district and the number of soldiers there on the army sick lists.[56] The mutinous behavior of sailors at Kronstadt, and later at Kiel, was likewise influenced by the ease with which they could mingle with workers at the shore installations, and the anatagonism of soldiers to their officers after the March revolution in Russia did not begin at the front, but in units closer to the industrial centers.[57]

The importance of mail to morale is everywhere appreciated. But the Nazis went farther than most: Aware that not all news is good news, they pressured the civilian kin of soldiers to omit the less cheerful items about shortages and bomb damage. This was an effective technique when coupled with strict control over what news the media could disseminate, although the direct impact of "subversive" media messages is limited in comparison with that of personal pleas. German soldiers were found to have paid little attention to anything but the "safe conduct" pass in Allied propaganda leaflets dropped on them during the fighting in the last year.[58] Much depends, of course, on whether the situation is such that troops are ready for "subversive" messages. There is no question, for example, that the publicity given to calls for a negotiated end to the stalemate that had developed by 1917, such as the plea issued by the congress of socialist parties held in Stockholm, had some resonance even outside Russia. There the Bolsheviks had managed to use the desire for peace to turn Russian soldiers against their officers and, ultimately, against the new provisional government for its continuation of the war. The Bolsheviks succeeded because, after an unbroken series of defeats, the army already was in a state of advanced decomposition. Again, German sailors' attempt to foil the final naval sortie against the British was sparked by news about changes in the German government that indicated that peace initiatives were now in the offing.[59]

In "mutinies" led by officers the media are crucial. Plotters against Hitler had to gain access to the media in order to justify their attempt on his life as the first step toward a negotiated peace. Failing in this, they soon found themselves discredited by mass media portrayals of this action as a betrayal of German soldiers who were shedding their blood for the fatherland. By contrast, De Gaulle's urgings to French troops to disobey their rebellious officers were crucial in crushing this last-ditch effort to sabotage the peace that created an independent Algeria. General De Gaulle's appeal met with instantaneous success,[60] not only because he was the legitimate head of state, but also because this seemed the most direct route home for the many conscripts reluctant to risk life and limb for French colonial interests.

Vietnam was different in that one could count on home leave only at the end of one's tour. The main contact was by mail and by the direct telephone circuits the military had made available. There was no effort to monitor the mail, so that a tract, a song, or a poem of the peace movement could be sent by a civilian friend to a sympathetic soldier for circulation. But most mail was concerned with personal matters. Vietnam was simply too remote to allow for political links to the peace movement or even for an effective political dialogue. Troops were understandably ambivalent about the motives of peace protesters but found their demands consistent with their own nostalgia for home. In this way the elements of what Moskos has called "latent ideology"[61] worked against, rather than for, the goals of military organization. The decline in American soldiers' will to fight after President Johnson's decision to shift course and seek a negotiated settlement is no less understandable than the mobilization riots at the end of World War II.

It is my contention that the main cause of disaffection in Vietnam was neither ideological opposition to the United States presence there or moral revulsion against military policies. Although some Vietnam veterans with no previous political interest played a role in the anti-war movement, this change of heart rarely occurred before their return to the States and their exposure to changed civilian attitudes. The few "conversions" during the Vietnam tour seems to have come about under the tutelage of a local person, usually a woman with whom the soldier had formed a stable relationship.[62]

## The Process of Politicization

*The usual forms of military deviance become politicized.* The proposition that the cohesion of an army in the field depends only to a very limited degree on the soldiers' allegiance to secondary symbols has almost become a truism. Cohesion is affected more by such organizational factors as group solidarity, the quality of leadership, and the adequacy of command and supply channels than by ideology. The effect of ideological convictions is not to be discounted, however. Though inadequate as a defense against the disorientation attributable to stress, ideology remains the foundation on which a citizen army is built. Furthermore, controversy over a war coupled with open expressions of defeatism have their effect on the

deviance always present in military organization. Such deviance, whatever its original cause, will seek justification in political terms. When the
deviants come to be seen as victims, even heroes, this limits the military
options available for dealing with it.

To repeat, most infractions of discipline or refusals to fight lack the
political content that others, for various reasons, may later read into
them. This was true even in Vietnam, which in its later years had
become an unpopular war. Nothwithstanding all the publicity, the typical Vietnam era deserter was no different from that of other wars. Most
were individuals beset by multiple personal problems having nothing to
do with their belief about American conduct in Vietnam,[63] although
some were later to adopt the rhetoric of the anti-war protest.

Caution is in order when seeking to generalize from the characteristics of individuals to social processes. Increases in psychiatric malaise,
indiscipline, and other indicators of disaffection are the inevitable result
of attrition. And, as rates rise, some predictors lose their power to dis-
criminate. This is particularly true of descriptions of mutinous group
protests which are talked out and compromised on the spot. The profile
of these "mutineers" is closer to that of the typical soldier (or sailor) than
is that of the deserter. Despite the few chronic troublemakers always to
be found among them, most were without a disciplinary history; some
had even been decorated.[64] Their main distinction was exposure to
unusually heavy stress and/or a perception that what was being demanded of them was strategically useless.

Declining support for war contributes to the dissolution of armies,
then, in a number of ways. The first factor is contact with the home
front. In previous wars, revolutionary pacifist slogans surfaced more often
among troops near centers of anti-war activity than among units most
exposed to danger.

A second factor is the catalytic effect of persons who openly voice
dissent and extreme deprecatory attitudes. Whether or not these dissen-
ters themselves get into trouble, their presence in sufficiently large numbers may trigger the delinquency of others who depend on firm authority
to keep their own delinquent dispositions in check. Such a phenomenon
was documented with the reinstitution of the draft in response to Korea,
and the military had to absorb many persons with considerably more
education, and correspondingly more negative attitudes toward the military, than the regular army personnel. Units with large numbers of draftees had higher delinquency rates than units where the number was
small.[65] But it was not because the draftees committed more offenses;
rather, the derogatory attitudes toward the army expressed by the many

conscripted against their will seem to have changed the atmosphere enough to incite the previously well-behaved to delinquency.

Third, civilian disapproval of certain "military" sanctions to uphold discipline. Pressure is exerted by way of legislative hearings, such as the inquiry in the *Kitty Hawk* incident (where racial tension led to a near-mutiny during the Vietnam war), or public expressions of concern, in and out of Congress, about protecting the right of free expression against incursion by overly zealous commanders. There are other, more subtle, encouragements to deviance. In a study of AWOLs from the Bundeswehr, many respondents claimed that they almost never had to justify their behavior to civilians. Deserters often managed to find employment, even without the required papers, and in only 14 percent of the cases did the parents urge their sons to return to units voluntarily.[66] Such sympathetic treatment of military delinquents borders on subversion.

Fourth, certain policies, such as prescribed rotation after a twelve-month tour, must be understood as *concessions* to make military requirements more acceptable to civilians. This individualization of war may have some adverse effects, but it helps to distribute the burden of active service and to lessen the chance that discontent might coalesce. Similarly, the therapeutic treatment of some forms of indiscipline, whatever its justification on medical grounds, functions as an additional safety valve.

Finally, we note that when disaffection is rife, soldiers will embrace a rhetoric to make their behavior acceptable, be it the rhetoric of class, of race, or simply of anti-militarism.

Because combat perspectives are too parochial, too pragmatic, and too preoccupied with personal survival to generate more than sporadic protest, the politicization of deviance requires a link-up with civilian political organizations ready to contest the claims of command authority with their own claims to legitimacy. What happened in World War I on a fairly large scale was inhibited in Vietnam by the intermittent nature of warfare, by internal policies (such as rotation), and even more perhaps by the sheer physical distance of that theater of war from American civilian life. There is no question, on the other hand, that many returning troops were shocked by how little their ordeal, which was outside the normal categories of civilian experience, was understood. The shock was the greater because of the change of mood in the country; they found themselves, not heroes, but pariahs.[67]

## Conclusion

The American government was able to absorb the anti-war protest with a minimal loss of legitimacy. Although the anti-war movement did not succeed in capitalizing on the widespread desire for peace—inside and outside the military—as a first step in mobilizing a more general social movement directed at broader and equally pressing domestic problems, the effect on the military may have been less benign. Concerned over the loss of popular support, it can try to insulate itself from the political cross-currents of civilian society by a renewed emphasis on professionalism and reliance on long-term volunteers. This may reduce some problems only by creating others. Experience since Vietnam has demonstrated that the manpower obtainable through the volunteer mechanism may not be adequate and that the creation of a force that is socially unrepresentative may be undesirable on other grounds. The fact that what appeared to be disproportionately high black casualty rates in Vietnam became a political issue shows that, given modern means of communication, no military—in peace or in war—can realistically expect to escape the infiltration of public dissatisfaction, especially when it assumes epidemic proportions. All this points to limits on the effective use of military force, except for small ventures, without significant popular support. The relation between armed forces and society is after all an organic one.

A further lesson to be drawn from historical comparison relates to the inadequacy of single-factor explanations. In every instance, the decomposition of armed forces was a joint effect of narrowly military factors, of organizational deficiencies, and of just plain human failings and defects. These factors typically interact. They exert their influence within a context of beliefs that are political, not necessarily in the conventional meaning of the term, but in the deeper and more profound sense that they relate to the legitimacy of the demands being made on soldiers. It is in this sense that political factors contributed to the military outcome in Vietnam.

## Notes

1. U.S. Army War College, Carlisle Barracks, Carlisle, Pa. *Study on Military Professionalism*, 30 June 1970, ". . . transitory ingredients of societal change, such as the anti-war, anti-establishment movements did not appear to be primary causative factors . . . of the professional climate" of the Vietnam era (p. 27). For other views, see W. L. Hauser, *America's Army in Crisis: A Study in Civil-Military Relations* (Baltimore: Johns Hopkins University Press, 1973) and P. L. Savage and R. A. Gabriel, "Cohesion and Disintegration in the American Army: an Alternative Perspective," *Armed Forces and Society*, 2(1976):340–376. The elaboration of their argument in *Crisis in Command* (New York: Hill and Wang, 1978), pp. 33, 40, does refer to the lack of political support for Vietnam. J. Helmer, *Bringing the War*

*Home* (New York: Free Press, 1974), sees the spontaneous revulsion against the war as a first step toward politicization.

2. For historical accounts, see Pakenham, *The Boer War* (New York: Random House, 1979) and A. Horne, *A Savage War for Peace* (London: Macmillan and Co., 1977).

3. R. Price, *An Imperial War and the British Working Class* (London: Routledge & Kegan Paul, 1972).

4. Price, 1972.

5. S. L. A. Marshall, *Men Against Fire* (Washington, D.C.: Infantry Journal, 1947).

6. A. D. Biderman, *March to Calumny* (New York: Macmillan Co., 1963).

7. S. M. Meyers and A. D. Biderman, eds., *Mass Behavior in Battle and Captivity: the Communist Soldier in the Korean War* (Chicago: University of Chicago Press, 1968); G. Fischer, *Soviet Opposition to Stalin in World War II* (Cambridge, Mass: Harvard University Press, 1952); A. Dallin, *German Rule in Russia, 1941–1945: A Study of Occupation Policies* (New York: St. Martin's Press, 1957).

8. E. J. Leed, *No Man's Land: Combat and Identity in World War I* (Cambridge: At the University Press, 1979). See also Great Britain, Army, *Report of the War Office Committee into "Shell Shock"* (1922) and *Statistics of the Military Effort of the British Empire during the Great War 1914–1918* (1922), p. 648. Total British death sentences, not all for desertion and not necessarily carried out, were 3,080 for four and one quarter years of war. The French total, according to G. Pedroncini, *Les mutineries de 1917* (Paris: Presses Universitaires, 1967), was roughly 700 until May 1917, 629 for the remainder of that year, and 250 to 300 for the last year of war. These figures omit an unknown number of "executions sommaires sans jugement."

9. G. J. Tischler, "Patterns of Psychiatric Attrition and Behavior in a Combat Zone," in P. G. Bourne, ed., *The Psychology and Physiology of Stress* (New York: Academic Press, 1969), pp. 19–44; R. E. Strange and R. J. Arthur, "Hospital Ship Psychiatry in a War Zone," *American Journal of Psychiatry* 124 (1967): 281–286.

10. See A. J. Glass, "Conclusion and Summary," in W. S. Mullins, ed. *Overseas Theatres*, Vol. 2 of *Neuropsychiatry in World War II* (Washington, D.C.: Government Printing Office, 1973), and "Observations upon the Epidemiology of Mental Illness in Troops during Warfare," in *Symposium on Preventive and Social Psychiatry* (Washington, D.C.: Walter Reed Army Institute of Research, 1957), pp. 185–197; also R. L. Pettera, et al., "Psychiatric Management of Combat Reactions with Emphasis on Vietnam," *Military Medicine* 134 (1969): 673–679.

11. J. Keegan, *The Face of Battle* (New York: Viking Press, 1976).

12. S. Dumas and K. O. Wedel-Peterson, *Losses of Life Caused by War* (Oxford: Clarendon Press, 1923).

13. S. A. Stouffer, et al., *The American Soldier: Combat and its Aftermath* (Princeton, N.J.: Princeton University Press, 1949). See also R. Sobel, "The Old Sergeant Syndrome," *Psychiatry* 10 (1947): 315–321; and E. Z. Weinstein, "The Function of Interpersonal Relations in the Neurosis of Combat," *Psychiatry* 10 (1947): 307–314.

14. R. H. Ahrenfeldt, *Psychiatry in the British Army in the Second World War* (New York: Columbia University Press, 1958).

15. Stouffer, et al., *The American Soldier*.

16. E. M. Colbach and M. D. Parrish, "Army Mental Health Activities in Vietnam: 1965–1970," *Bulletin of the Menninger Clinic* 34 (1970): 333–342. Also W. S. Allerton, "Army Psychiatry in Vietnam," in Bourne, *Psychology and Physiology of Stress*, pp. 1–18. "Vietnam [neuropsychiatric] incidence rates were one-tenth of the highest rate ever reported in World War II and less than one-third of rates reported during stressful periods in the Korean conflict" (p. 14). According to U.S. Army Surgeon General's Office, combat deaths per 1,000 of average yearly troop strength were 51.9 in World War II, 43.2 in Korea, and 18.0 in Vietnam. This was coupled with a remarkably low percentage of all medical evacuations represented by neuropsychiatrics.

17. This "lying low" is not very different from what has been reported about French conscripts in Algeria.

18. U.S. Department of the Army, "Medical Support of the U.S. Army in Vietnam," *Vietnam Studies* (Washington, D.C.: Government Printing Office, 1973); R. E. Huffman, "Which Soldiers Break Down," *Bulletin of the Menninger Clinic* (1970): 343–351.

19. Statistics on "fragging" are bound to be unreliable. The generally accepted Department of Defense figure is "about 800" between 1969 and 1972, with a steady increase each year through 1971, by which time troop strength had been sharply reduced. This figure compares with 370 cases of "violence against superiors" brought to court martial during 18 months of World War I, which involved over 4.7 million troops. No statistics on "refusal to fight" have come to this author's attention. Drug abuse was first officially recognized as a problem when the Army established its first amnesty program in October 1969. It was not unique to Vietnam, although heroin use there seems to have been higher than elsewhere. See L. N. Robins, *The Vietnam Drug User Returns. Special Action Office Monograph*, Series A, No. 2. (Washington, D.C: Government Printing Office, 1973), chapter six. See also P. Starr, *The Discarded Army* (New York: Charterhouse, 1973) and Helmer, *Bringing the War Home*.

22. E. A. Shils and M. Janowitz, "Cohesion and Disintegration of the German *Wermacht* in World War II," *Public Opinion Quarterly* 12 (1948): 280–315; Stouffer, *et al.*, *The American Soldier*; E. A. Shils, "Primary Groups in the American Army," in R. K. Merton and P. F. Lazarsfeld, eds., *Continuities in Social Research: Studies in the Scope and Methods of "The American Soldier"*

(Glencoe: Free Press, 1950); R. W. Little "Buddy Relations and Combat Performance," in M. Janowitz, ed., *The New Military* (New York: Russell Sage, 1964); A. L. George, *The Chinese Communist Army in Action* (New York: Columbia University Press, 1967); C. C. Moskos, "The Military," *Annual Review of Sociology* 2 (1976): 55–77.

21. A. L. George, "Primary groups, Organization, and Military Performance," in R. W. Little, ed., *Handbook of Military Institutions* (Beverly Hills, Calif.: Sage Publications, 1971).

22. C. C. Moskos, *The American Enlisted Man* (New York: Russell Sage, 1970).

23. This is the thrust of the argument by Gabriel and Savage, *Crisis and Command*.

24. Pedroncini, *Les mutineries de 1917*.

25. A. E. Ashworth, "The sociology of trench warfare," *British Journal of Sociology* 19 (1968): 407–423.

26. Shils, "Primary Groups."

27. Little, "Buddy Relations."

28. Ahrenfeldt, *Psychiatry in the British Army*.

29. Pedroncini, *Les mutineries de 1917*, p. 89.

30. D. Horn, *The German Naval Mutinies of World War I* (New Brunswick, N.J.: Rutgers University Press, 1969); A. K. Wildman, *The End of the Russian Imperial Army; the Old Army and the Soldier's Revolt, March to April, 1917* (Princeton, N.J.: Princeton University Press, 1979).

31. R. Boyle, *The Flower and the Dragon* (San Francisco, Calif.: Ramparts Press, 1972). See also AP reports in the press.

32. U.S. Department of the Army, "Tactical and material innovations," *Vietnam Studies* (Washington, D.C.: Government Printing Office, 1974).

33. C. C. Moskos, "The American Combat Soldier in Vietnam," *Journal of Social Issues*, 31, no. 4 (1975): 25–37; also subject of many popular accounts.

34. G. W. Beebe and M. E. DeBakey, *Battle Casualties: Incidence, Mortality, and Logistic Considerations* (Springfield, Ill.: Charles C. Thomas, 1952).

35. L. B. Kalinowski, "Problems of War Neuroses in the Light of Experiences in Other Countries," *American Journal of Psychiatry* 107 (1950): 340–346.

36. Pedroncini, *Les mutineries de 1917*, p. 89.

37. Pedroncini, *Les mutineries de 1917*, p. 106; R. M. Watt, *None Dare Call It Treason* (New York: Simon and Schuster, 1963).

38. Wildman, *The End of the Russian Imperial Army*.

39. D. Woodward, *The Collapse of Power; Mutiny in the High Seas Fleet* (London: Arthur Burke, 1973) and W. Deist, "Die Politik der Seekriegsleitung und die Rebellion der Flotte Ende Oktober 1918," *Vierteljahreshefte fuer Zeitgeschichte* 14, no. 4 (1973): 341–368.

40. F. L. Klingberg, "Predicting the Termination of War: Battle Casualties and Population Losses," *Journal of Conflict Resolution* 10 (1966): 129–171.

41. Shils and Janowitz, "Cohesion and Disintegration."

42. F. W. Seidler, "Die Fahnenflucht in der deutschen Wehrmach waehrend des Zweiten Weltkrieges," *Militärgeschichtliche Mitteilungen* 22 (1977): 17–22; O. P. Schweling states that the number of desertions and AWOLs increased over the war but that *military* courts resisted pressure for harsh treatment, *Die deutsche Militärjustiz in der Zeit des Nationalsozialismus* (Marburg: Elvert, 1978), pp. 159 and 249ff.

43. D. Oberdorfer, *Tet* (New York: Doubleday 1971); and P. Braestrup and B. Roper, *Big Story: How the Press and Television Reported and Interpreted the Crisis of Tet in Vietnam and Washington* (Boulder, Col.: Westview Press, 1977).

44. Leed, *No Man's Land.*

45. M. Ferro, *La grande guerre 1914–1918* (Paris: Gallimard, 1969).

46. J. E. Mueller, *War, Presidents and Public Opinion* (New York: John Wiley and Sons, 1973). An interesting assessment of opinion during World War I based on reports of monitored mail and other indicators can be found in *Revue d'Histoire moderne et contemporaine* 15, entitled "Collogue sur l'annee 1917."

47. B. Farwell, *The Great Boer War* (London: Allen Lane, 1977). Price, *An Imperial War*, notes that volunteers had not only been paid more than the "regulars" but were also allowed to serve in groups.

48. On officer losses, see F. D. White, *The Growth of the Red Army* (Princeton, N.J.: Princeton University Press, 1944) and Wildman, *The End of the Russian Imperial Army.*

49. For example, F. T. Hartnagel, "Absent Without Leave—A Study of the Military Offender," *Journal of Political and Military Sociology* 2 (1974): 205–220, notes that more "volunteers" went AWOL than draftees. According to Robins, *The Vietnam Drug User*, 65 per cent of the drug users but only 44 per cent of the non-users were "regular army."

50. L. M. Baskir and W. A. Strauss, *Chance and Circumstance* (New York: Alfred A. Knopf, 1978).

51. J. Dollard, *Fear in Battle* (New York: Infantry Journal, 1943).

52. R. Tucker, *The Just War: a Study in Contemporary American Doctrine* (Baltimore: Johns Hopkins University Press, 1960).

53. Stouffer, *The American Soldier;* Shils, "Primary groups."

54. Shils and Janowitz, "Cohesion and Disintegration."

55. E. A. Shils et al., *Service Conditions and Morale in the Soviet Armed Forces: a Pilot Study* (Santa Monica: Rand Corp., 1951) and H. Goldhamer *The Soviet Soldier; Soviet Military Management at the Troop Level* (New York: Crane, Russak, 1975).

56. Ferro, *La grande guerre.*

57. White, *The Growth of the Red Army;* and A. I. Denikine, *La decomposition de l'armee et du pouvoir* (Paris: Povolozky, 1921).

58. Shils and Janowitz, "Cohesion and Disintegration"; also H. Speier, Psychological Warfare Reconsidered," in D. Lerner and H. D. Lasswell, eds., *The Policy Sciences* (Stanford: Stanford University Press, 1951).

59. Wildman, *The End of the Russian Imperial Army.*

60. A. Horne, *A Savage War for Peace.*

61. Moskos, *American Enlisted Man.*

62. Helmer, *Bringing the War Home.*

63. D. B. Bell and B. W. Bell, "Desertion and Anti-war Protest; Findings from the Ford Clemency Program," *Armed Forces and Society,* 3 (1977): 433–444; and E. A. Shils, "A Profile of the Military Deserter," *Armed Forces and Society* 3 (1977): 427–432.

64. Pedroncini, *Les mutineries de 1917;* Horn, *The German Naval Mutinies.*

65. H. G. Osborn, et al., "A Preliminary Investigation of Delinquency in the Army," *Human Resources Research Organization Technical Report,* No. 5 (1954) and K. Crawford and E. D. Thomas "Organizational Climate and Disciplinary Rates on Navy Ships," *Armed Forces and Society* 3 (1977): 165–182.

66. H. Feser and J. Schenk, *Wehrpflicht und Abweichung* (Boppard/Rhein: Boldt, 1974).

67. J. D. Retzer, "War and Political Ideology; the Roots of Radicalism among Vietnam Veterans," Unpublished Ph.D. dissertation, Yale University, 1976.

# *Part III*

# American and World Contemporary Perspectives

# 7

# The Citizen-Soldier and the All-Volunteer Force

CHARLES C. MOSKOS

The conventional wisdom holds that the notion of the citizen soldier is incompatible with the all-volunteer force (AVF). In strong opposition to this belief, Morris Janowitz has argued that the citizen soldier and the AVF ought to and can be consistent with each other.[1] The concept of the citizen soldier, as articulated by Janowitz, is congruent with the all-volunteer framework in so far as we accept the utility of short-term service to perform national goals, the need for a representative segment of youth to perform such service, and the desirability for those who serve the nation to reflect core and widely shared civic values. Janowitz proposes, moreover, that to the degree these conditions can be met in national service options extending beyond those exclusively found in the military, the concept of the citizen soldier is enlarged and enhanced.

This essay takes the direction pointed to by Janowitz. The AVF experience is examined from the vantage of those elements most germane to the concept of the citizen soldier. In turn, a set of concrete proposals is offered that aims to reinvigorate the citizen soldier ideal in the all-volunteer context.

## Social Trends in the AVF

Since the end of the draft in 1973, the military services have been hard
pressed to meet recruitment goals. Enlistment has fallen particularly
short among those who will serve in the ground combat arms and aboard
warships. More than one in three service members do not complete their
initial enlistments. With a growing number of skilled technicians leaving
the military, retention of qualified people in the career force has become
an acute problem. Army Reserve components are well below the peacetime manning objectives set by Congress. Little wonder that the reintroduction of draft registration in the summer of 1980 was seen by
many as the precursor of a return to full-fledged conscription.

Yet for over eight years Defense Department reports announced the
AVF was working well and, indeed, was attracting a quality of youth as
good if not better than that of the draft era. The problems of the AVF are
not the results of the end of conscription, nor of the declining youth
cohort of the 1980s, nor of the efforts of service recruiters. The crucial
flaw has been a redefinition of military service in overly econometric
concepts and models. The redefining process was given powerful expression by the 1970 President's Commission on the All-Volunteer
Force—the Gates Commission.[2] It is a theme that recurs in officially
sponsored assessments of the AVF.[3] The American military profession is
being defined, not according to an institutional format, but as another
occupation in the marketplace. This redefinition has led to an ignoring
or glossing over of the difficulties the AVF has confronted since its
inception. The main fault stems from the assumption that the armed
forces are just another part of the labor market. It is this faulty theoretical
underpinning, not the end of conscription, that has brought the American military to its present plight.

Sustained by their resilient authority among the policymakers in the
Pentagon under both Republican and Democratic administrations, the
econometricians have overcome the collapse of their arguments with
remarkable ease. They present themselves as hardheaded realists. Although they do not say so in so many words, it is hard not to read in the
econometricians' analyses the premise that the desire for middle class
youth participation in the rank and file is an irrelevant sentiment with
no bearing on AVF manpower issues. The perplexing aspect of their
arguments is that they are not subject to refutation. Declines in the
representativeness of the forces (when such declines are admitted) are
dismissed if end-strength figures are met. If initial strength targets are not
achieved, then new ones are set forth with downward adjustments. If

even these lowered goals are not met, then it is argued that marketplace mechanisms were never tried. Instead of rethinking their propositions or admitting that their earlier data were distorted, they admonish us to try .more of the same, to recruit at the margin to fill empty spaces.

Within the Defense Department there has been a failure to take the advice of those military leaders who were aware of the realities but unable to transmit a sense of them past the self-deceptions and conceptual predispositions with which the proponents of the AVF had equipped themselves. Because the official evidence on the workings of the AVF was suspect, military manpower hearings on Capitol Hill became increasingly strained, if not antagonistic, when Congress questioned Pentagon spokesmen. A 1980 report of the House Armed Services Committee includes this telling statement: "Rather than attempting to reorient the recruiting process to attract people from broader segments of the civilian population and instead of exploring new alternatives to energize a faltering recruiting program, Defense officials appear to be expending their efforts to justify the continuation of past policies."[4]

The most important, but least commented upon, effect of the shift to the AVF has been the sharp decline in the peacetime military force level, from over 2.6 million on active duty in the early 1960s to slightly over two million in 1981. To maintain an active-duty force even at this reduced level, with attendant understrength units, the military must recruit around 350,000 enlisted persons annually. Over 80 percent of enlisted military entrants are non-prior service (NPS) males, the group with which most of the ensuing discussion will deal. Problems of enlisted recruitment and retention plague all four services, but, generally speaking, recruitment problems are most severe in the Army and Marine Corps, and those of retention in the Navy and Air Force.

## MENTAL GROUP AND EDUCATIONAL LEVELS

A stock argument among defenders of the AVF was that the mental quality of recruits, as measured by aptitude tests, had improved since the draft era. There was always a certain amount of misdirection in this argument. No one could deny that the proportion of recruits in the top mental categories of I and II had declined, from 42 percent in 1964 to 27 percent in 1979. But this was countered by the purported drop in those scoring in mental category IV, the lowest from which the military is allowed to recruit. In early 1980 it was revealed that the aptitude tests may have been "misnormed" and that the proportion of category IV recruits has, in fact, expanded greatly.[5] Evidence on this issue may never be conclusive, but the revised test results could only further reinforce concerns about the quality of enlisted recruits.

We turn from the ambiguities of the mental aptitudes of AVF recruits to the more clear-cut data on educational attainment. There are major differences between the services. Over the course of the all-volunteer era, the number of NPS males with a high school diploma has averaged about 86 percent for the Air Force, 69 percent for the Navy, 60 percent for the Marine Corps, and 55 percent for the Army. The overall trend across all four services has been toward a lower number of recruits with high school diplomas. Moreover, some studies show that high school graduates who do enter the military, especially those entering the Army, tend to come from the lower levels of their graduating class. But even if we look only at the high school completion rates, it is indisputable that the educational levels of male enlistees in the all-volunteer Army are far lower than either the equivalent civilian population—82 percent of all 19-year-old males possessed a diploma in 1978—or the Army entrants of 1964, the last peacetime year before the war in Vietnam.

The data also reveal an even sharper decline in the proportion of Army entrants with some college between pre- and post-Vietnam periods. Whereas 17.2 percent of the draftees and 13.9 percent of the enlistees in 1964 had some college training, the corresponding figure in the all-volunteer Army has been around 4 percent. It is startling to learn that in 1980 among first-term soldiers in the entire U.S. Army there were only 276 college graduates (out of 339,678 members), and only 25 college graduates in all the combat arms (out of 100,860 men).

## RACIAL CONTENT

The various services differ in their racial composition. The pattern has been for the Army to have the highest proportion of blacks, followed in order by the Marine Corps, Air Force, and Navy. In 1979 blacks accounted for 28.9 percent of the Army, 19.8 percent of the Marine Corps, 13.8 percent of the Air Force, and 9.7 percent of the Navy. These percentages include both officer and enlisted personnel. The issue of racial content has been most prominent in the Army, the largest of the services. Blacks in the Army made up 11.8 percent of enlisted personnel in 1964, 17.5 percent in 1972, the last year of the draft, and 32.2 percent in 1979. Among Army senior sergeants, blacks were considerably better represented in 1979 than at any earlier time. This reflects the fact that the black reenlistment rate in the 1970s was 1.6 times greater than that of whites. Blacks continue to be underrepresented in the officer corps, with the partial exception of company grade officers in the Army.

It is a well-recognized fact that the educational levels of blacks in America have trailed behind those of whites. Contrary to national patterns, however, the intersection of race and education is quite different among entrants in the all-volunteer Army. Since the end of the draft, the proportion of NPS black males with high school diploma has been 65 percent compared with 54 percent for whites. In point of fact, today's Army enlisted ranks are the only major arena in American society where black educational levels surpass those of whites, and by a significant degree. What may be happening in the all-volunteer Army, I suggest, is something like the following. Whereas the black soldier is fairly representative of the black community in terms of education and social background, white entrants are coming from the least educated sectors of the white community. In other words, the all-volunteer army is attracting not only a disproportionate number of minorities but also an unrepresentative segment of white youth, who, if anything, are even more uncharacteristic of the broader social mix than are our minority soldiers.

## WOMEN

No change in the makeup of the AVF has received as much media attention as the growing number of women service members. An argument could be made that the margin of success in AVF recruitment has been in the sharp rise of female entrants, virtually all of whom until late 1979 were high school graduates. Before the Vietnam War, the utilization of women as military personnel was essentially token. In 1964, only 1.1 percent of uniformed personnel were female. In 1974, the figure had risen to 3.5 percent, and by 1979 it reached 7.5 percent. Projections for 1984 show women comprising about 12 percent of the enlisted force. The role of females has expanded rapidly in the first phase of the AVF. That many male soldiers believe women shirk full responsibilities so that the men end up with added work-loads and late night shifts may speak more to informal policy and personal preference than to innate capabilities. But in the years to follow the increase in female utilization will in all likelihood be much slower than anticipated. One important factor in this regard is the emotion-ladened decision as to whether women will be recruited for combat roles, even though there has already been an undeniable movement of females into near combat roles where they would surely suffer casualties in the event of hostilities.

There have also been difficulties in incorporating enlisted women into non-traditional assignments even outside the combat arms. These include rates of attrition much higher than those for comparably educated males, the incidence of pregnancies, and the reluctance on the part of many women to accept permanent assignments outside clerical and health settings. This is not to argue that the ceiling on female personnel has been reached, but that further expansion into non-traditional tasks will be very gradual. The 1979 policy change to accept female high school dropouts will only further complicate the utilization of women soldiers.

### MARITAL STATUS

Although it is usually not commented upon by students of all-volunteer trends, there has been a significant change in the marital composition of the junior enlisted ranks. Since the end of the draft, the proportion of marrieds at grade E4, the modal junior enlisted pay grade, has apprxoimately doubled to around 45 percent. The high incidence of junior enlisted marrieds is all the more noteworthy in that it runs directly counter to national patterns, where the clear trend is toward later marriage. The new phenomena of intra-service marriages and fraternization between officers and enlisted personnel of the opposite sex have hardly been acknowledged, much less appraised for their effects on organizational readiness.

## Serving in the Ranks

One of the main presumptions of the Gates Commission was that, with longer-term enlistments, there would be less personnel turnover than in a military system heavily dependent upon draftees and draft-motivated volunteers. This has turned out not to be the case. Since 1973, over 600,000 young people have been prematurely discharged from the military for reasons of indiscipline, personality disorders, job inaptitude, and the like. The striking finding is that high school graduates are twice as likely as high school dropouts to complete their enlistments. Even more revealing is that this finding is virtually unchanged when mental aptitude is held constant. High school graduates from the lower aptitude levels are actually much more likely to finish their tours than high school dropouts in the higher aptitude levels. Other measures of soldierly performance, such as enlisted productivity and low disciplinary actions show precisely the same correlates as found for attrition rates. In the aggregate, high school graduates significantly outperform high school dropouts. Possession of a high school diploma, it seems, reflects the acquisition of social traits (work habits, punctuality, *Sitzfleisch*) which make for a more successful military experience. The facts also show unambiguously that higher educated soldiers do better across the board—in low as well as in high skill jobs.[6]

The military has always recruited large numbers of youths, white and black and brown, who had no real alternative job prospects. It will always continue to do so. But present trends toward labeling the Army as a recourse for America's underclasses are self-defeating for the youth involved precisely because they directly counter the premise that military participation is one of broadly based national service. Whatever success the military had as a remedial organization for deprived youth was largely due to the armed forces being legitimated on other than overt welfare grounds, for example, national defense, citizenship obligation, patriotism, even manly honor. In other words, those very conditions peculiar to the armed forces which serve to resocialize poverty youth toward productive ends depend directly upon the military not being defined as a welfare agency or an employer of last resort. It will be increasingly difficult for the Army to avoid characterization as a recourse for dead-end youth, unless enlisted membership reflects more of a cross-section of American youth.

The rising minority content in the Army actually masks a more pervasive shift in the social class bases of the lower enlisted ranks. To what degree the changing racial composition of the Army reflects white reluctance to join an increasingly black organization is unknown, though it is surely a factor. Yet, I am unpersuaded that any significant number of middle class whites—or middle class persons of any race, for that matter—would be more likely to join the Army, under present recruitment incentives, even if the Army was overwhelmingly white. That the disproportionately white Navy and the racially balanced Air Force also face recruitment problems indicates that there is more than racial content at work in attracting a cross-section of youth to serve in the AVF. It is a social reality that the combat arms especially will never draw proportionately from middle and upper class youth. But to foster policies that accentuate the tracking of lower-class youth into such assignments is perverse. To rationalize the outcome as the workings of the marketplace is duplicitous. This is not to argue that the makeup of the enlisted ranks should be perfectly calibrated to the social composition of the larger society, but it is to ask what kind of society excuses its privileged from serving in the ranks of its military.

By no means does being middle class necessarily make one braver or more able. There are many outstanding members of the AVF who have modest educational attainments. But our concern must also be with the chemistry of unit cohesion which requires an optimum blend of talents and backgrounds. Research evidence serves to confirm the observations of commanders and NCOs who remember the draft period that college educated members enrich the skill level and commitment of military units, in peace as well as in war.[7] The distinctive quality of the enlisted experience starting with World War II was the mixing of the social classes and, starting with the Korean War, the integration of the races. This gave poor youth an opportunity to test themselves, often successfully, against more privileged youth. Such enforced leveling of persons from different backgrounds had no parallel in any other existing institution in American society. This state of affairs began to diminish during the Vietnam War when the college educated avoided service; it has all but disappeared in the all-volunteer army.

A major outcome of the AVF has been a dramatic compression of pay scales within the enlisted force. In the 1960s, the basic pay of a sergeant major was better than seven times that of an entering recruit. Since the end of the draft, that same sergeant major makes only three and a half times the pay of the recruit. The paradox is that this "front loading" of compensation toward the junior ranks, along with changes to improve lower enlisted life, cannot be appreciated by those new to the service because they have not experienced the old ways. Instead, junior enlisted members see little monetary or lifestyle improvement over the course of a military career, a situation which reduces the likelihood of their choosing to remain in the service. Once upon a time sergeants measured their incomes and perquisites against those of the soldiers they led, and felt rewarded; now they see a relative decline of status within the service, compare their earnings against civilians, and feel deprived.

## Making the AVF Work

The difficulties of the AVF have led to renewed talk of restoring conscription. A return to the draft would pose anew the question of who serves when most do not serve. Under present manpower requirements, less than one in five males would be drafted or otherwise serve in the military. If women were to be drafted, the proportion of youth serving would, of course, be only one in ten. To have a workable conscription also requires a national consensus as to its necessity, especially within the relevant youth population. It is unlikely that such a consensus can be created. A draft could lead to turbulence on college campuses, making ROTC units again an object of attack. If compulsion is used, moreover, many will attempt to avoid induction, which will bring on its own problems. Even under a seemingly "fair" lottery system, decisions would have to be made which will corrode the induction system. These would include determination of conscientious objection and ersatz physical disabilities. That the rate of non-compliance under the reintroduced draft registration will probably remain a mystery does not inspire confidence in the probability of an equitable system of conscription. In any event, only a small and, by definition, unlucky minority would ever be called to serve. A bungled draft would leave us in even worse straits than the undesirable status quo. In a peacetime situation, we must make the AVF work rather than find ourselves embroiled in a debilitating draft controversy.

Granting that conscription is not in the offing, what about management steps that could be taken to improve manpower utilization within the all-volunteer framework? Here we run into the difficulty that almost all proposals in this vein do not address the core issue: getting young qualified men into the combat arms and related tasks. Neither lowering physical or mental standards for men, nor increasing the number of women, nor greater reliance on civilian personnel suits the imperatives of the combat arms.[8] Large raises in military pay for lower enlisted personnel, a central Gates Commission recommendation, were the principal means used to induce persons to join the AVF. However, this has turned out to be a double-edged sword. Youth surveys show that pay motivates less qualified youth (for example, high school dropouts, those with poor grades) to join the armed services, while having a much lesser effect on college bound youth.[9] Any policy based on increases in lower enlisted pay will only aggravate the present AVF trend to recruit at the margins.

Underlying many of the difficulties of the AVF is a source of enlisted discontent that had no real counterpart in the peacetime draft era. This is post-entry disillusionment resulting from unrealistic expectations as to what the military would offer. The peacetime draftee never held high expectations as to what he would encounter and therefore was not unpleasantly surprised; indeed, he might often—at least in hindsight—find the Army favorable on its own terms. In all-volunteer recruitment, however, a consistent theme has been the self-serving aspects of military life, that is, what the service can do for the recruit in the way of training in skills transferable to civilian jobs. Post-entry disillusionment speaks directly to the excessive attrition rate. The irreconcilable dilemma is that many military assignments—by no means exclusively in the combat arms—are not transferable to civilian jobs.[10]

The central issue remains: is there a way to meet military manpower needs without direct compulsion or excessive reliance on cash inducements for recruits? To put it differently, is there a way to obtain the analogue of the peacetime draftee—the citizen soldier, if you will—in the all-volunteer era? I believe there is. First, link federal aid for higher education to a program of voluntary national service, including military reserve duty or civilian work. Second, introduce a GI Bill for the AVF. Third, construct a two-track military personnel and compensation system which differentiates between a short-term volunteer and one who makes a long-term commitment. The total costs of these proposals could easily be contained within present federal outlays and, probably, be even lower.

## EDUCATIONAL BENEFITS IN CONFLICT WITH THE AVF

The major barriers to more effective recruitment have been the elimination of the GI Bill in 1976 and the concurrent expansion of federal assistance to college students. Congress has created a system of educational benefits which offers more to those who do not serve their country than to those who do. Under the Veterans Educational Assistance Program (VEAP), which replaced the GI Bill, the government matches, within prescribed limits, voluntary contributions made by service members.[11] It is estimated that governmental expenditures for VEAP will be under $100,000,000 annually. But, for 1980 alone, federal aid to college students will reach more than $4.4 billion. This sum is projected to increase to over $7 billion for the year 1985.

The funds allocated to civilian students in major assistance programs in 1980 were (in billions): Basic Educational Opportunity Grants, $2.275; Supplemental Educational Opportunity Grants, $0.370; College Work-Study Program, $0.550; National Direct Student Loan, $0.286; and Guaranteed Student Loan, $0.960. With passage in 1978 of the Middle Income Student Assistance Act (MISA), eligibility for Basic

Educational Opportunity Grants can extend to families earning over $25,000 annually. Also, under MISA there is no need requirement for the Guaranteed Student Loan Program. The Work-Study Program is becoming a major source of graduate student support. A college student who can establish self-supporting status, moreover, is eligible for most federal assistance programs. Such governmental policies can hardly be thought of as part of a poverty program. In effect, we have created a GI Bill without the GI.

It is surprising that no public figure has thought to tie such student aid to any service obligation on the part of the youths who benefit. A program of voluntary national service should be introduced on a step-by-step basis over the next five years.[12] In the interim, those who enlist in military reserve units or perform one year of civilian service would have priority for federal aid to college students; in time, participation in such national service would become a prerequisite for eligibility for federal college assistance. Only persons medically exempt from national service would not be held to this standard.

PROVISIONS OF AN AVF GI BILL

Concurrent with linking federal educational assistance beyond high school to national service, there must be an introduction of post-service educational benefits for members of the AVF along the lines and scale of the GI Bill following World War II. In this way maximum federal educational benefits will be allotted to those who serve on active duty. A person who enlists in the armed forces and completes his or her two-year obligated period of active duty would be entitled to college or vocational school assistance as follows: (1) the costs of tuition and fees up to $3,000 per academic year in a private institution, or up to $1,000 per academic year in a public institution, for a maximum of four years; (2) a subsistence stipend of $300 per month while enrolled in school for a maximum of 36 months; and (3) such entitlement would depend upon an appropriate reserve obligation, say four years, following active duty.

On the bases of analyses conducted by the Congressional Budget Office, the maximum direct costs of such a program would be under 1.5 billion dollars a year. There would also be substantial countervailing reductions in the net costs of an AVF GI Bill. These include: a lower attrition rate, smaller recruitment outlays, an end to combat arms bonuses, and, most likely, fewer lower-ranking service members with families. With these savings, the real costs of a GI Bill would be well under one billion dollars annually, a figure less than a quarter of present federal expenditures for college assistance programs.

## CITIZEN SOLDIER AND CAREER SOLDIER: COMPLEMENTARY ROLES

The definition of military service in the all-volunteer context needs overhauling as much as the machinery of military recruitment. The armed services can set up a two-track personnel system recognizing a distinction between a "citizen soldier" and a "career soldier." ("Soldiers" as used here also refers to sailors, marines, and airmen.)

The career soldier would initially enlist for a minimum of four years. He or she would receive entitlements and compensation as in the prevailing system, but there would be significant pay raises at the time of the first reenlistment and throughout the senior NCO grades. Most such persons would be trained in technical skills, though others would make up the future cadre in a variety of military specialities. In certain skill areas with extreme shortages, an extra reenlistment bonus might be required. In addition, a reenlistment bonus might be offered in lieu of GI Bill benefits. Or, a career soldier's benefits might be transferred to an interest bearing account from which sums could be disbursed to dependents. Alternatively, a career soldier's GI Bill might be used to take a "sabbatical" involving an engineering or science curriculum for future technical work in the military. The career force must also be given adequate housing allowances and reimbursement for government ordered change of stations. Steps such as these would go a long way toward the retention of the experienced and trained personnel required for a complex and technical military force.

The citizen soldier would enlist for two years of active duty (the term of the old draftee) and be assigned to the combat arms, low-skill shipboard duty, aircraft security guards, clerical work, and other labor intensive positions. Excepting clerical work, these are the kind of assignments in today's AVF where recruitment shortfalls, attrition, and desertion are most likely to occur.[13] Active-duty pay for the citizen soldier would be lower—say by one-third—than that received by the career soldier of the same rank. Other than the GI Bill, the citizen soldier would receive no entitlements, not excluding off-base housing and food allowances. This would reduce the frequency of marriage at the junior enlisted levels and restore unit cohesion in the barracks. Because there would be no presumption of acquiring civilian skills in the military, the terms of such service would be honest and unambiguous, thus alleviating a major source of post-entry discontent in the AVF.

A college or graduate education or vocational training in exchange for two years of active duty would be the means to attract highly qualified soldiers who can learn quickly, serve effectively for a full tour, and then be replaced by similarly qualified recruits. Enlistment studies show that a combination of short enlistments and educational benefits attract a wider cross-section of youth than does higher entrance pay.[14] The AVF, if it is to survive, must attract those middle class and upwardly mobile American youth who would find a temporary diversion from the world of school or work tolerable and perhaps even welcome.

One feature of the two-track system presented here is that, because of the higher active-duty compensation in the career track, some of the two-year joiners will opt for the longer commitment to the service. This will further reinforce retention in the career force. But the overwhelming number of citizen soldiers will undoubtedly leave active duty after two years and, if they take advantage of the GI Bill, go on to the reserves. This is to be preferred—without much greater reliance on prior-service personnel, there seems to be no way to salvage Army reserve components in the all-volunteer context.[15] The dominant economic model of the AVF relies on the mistaken notion that long initial enlistments are always to be preferred over short enlistments. Thirty-six percent of all enlisted entrants in 1964 signed on for four or more years compared with 72 percent in 1979. Yet with the high attrition rate, the personnel turnover is almost as great now as it was in the peacetime draft era, not to mention the differences in organizational costs between a service member who is prematurely discharged and one who successfully completes an obligated tour.

The overriding strategy is to make governmental subsidies of higher education consistent with the ideal that citizen obligation ought become a part of growing up in America. Such a realization would also clarify the military's role by emphasizing the larger calling of national service.

## Notes

1. Morris Janowitz, "The Citizen Soldier and National Service," *Air University Review*, 31, 1 (1979), pp. 2–16.
2. *The Report of the President's Commission on the All-Volunteer Force* (Washington, D.C.: Government Printing Office, 1970).
3. Notable in this regard are Richard V. L. Cooper, *Military Manpower and the All-Volunteer Force* (Santa Monica, Calif.: Rand Corporation, 1977); and U.S. Department of Defense, *America's Volunteers* (Dec. 31, 1978, processed).

4. U.S. Congress. House. Armed Services Committee. *Department of Defense Authorization Act of 1981.* 96th Cong., 2d sess. H. Rept. No. 96-916 to accompany H.R. 6974. Washington: April 30, 1980, p. 21.

5. Office of the Assistant Secretary of Defense (Manpower, Reserve Affairs, and Logistics), *Aptitude Testing of Recruits* (July, 1980, processed).

6. Cooper, *Military Manpower*, p. 139.

7. Studies for the army during the Korean War show that educational background is positively correlated with combat effectiveness. Roger L. Egbert and others, "An Analysis of Combat Fighters and Non-Fighters," *HumRRO Technical Report 44* (Washington, D.C.: Human Resources Research Organization, September, 1957, processed).

8. See, for example, Martin Binkin and Shirley J. Bach, *Women and the Military* (Washington, D.C.: Brookings Institution, 1977); Martin Binkin with Herschel Kanter and Rolf H. Clark, *Shaping the Defense Civilian Work Force* (Washington, D.C.: Brookings Institution, 1978); and Martin Binkin and Irene Kyriakopoulos, *Youth Or Experience? Manning the Modern Military* (Washington, D.C.: Brookings Institution, 1979).

9. See the periodic reports found in *Youth Attitude Tracking Study* (Washington, D.C.: Market Facts, Inc., annually since 1975, processed).

10. For survey and demographic data on this point, see John D. Blair and Robert L. Phillips, "The Military as a 'Normal' Organization: Youth in Military and Civilian Work Settings," paper presented at the conference of the Inter-University Seminar on Armed Forces and Society, Chicago, Illinois, Oct. 23–25, 1980. See also Choongso Kim, Gilbert Nestel, Robert L. Phillips and Michael E. Borus, *The All-Volunteer Force: An Analysis of Youth Participation, Attrition, and Reenlistment* (Columbus, Ohio: Center for Human Resource Research, Ohio State University, May, 1980, processed).

11. Data on the VEAP program are reported in Mark J. Eitelberg, "The Attitudes, Experiences, and Expectations of VEAP Participants," paper presented to the Seminar on Military Educational Assistance, Congressional Budget Office, Oct. 9, 1980.

12. A good summary of civilian national service options and needs is found in Potomac Institute, *National Youth Service: What's At Stake* (Washington, D.C.: Potomac Institute, 1980).

13. In the armed forces of the Federal Republic of Germany during the late 1970s, the following proportions of serving members were committed to a military obligation of two years or less: Army 59.2 percent, Navy 30.2 percent, and Air Force 35.6 percent. *White Paper 1979* (Bonn: Federal Minister of Defence, 1979), p. 221.

14. The earliest data on the differential effects of higher pay versus educational benefits on military enlistments is found in Jerome Johnston and Jerald G. Bachman, *Youth in Transition: Young Men and Military Service* (Ann Arbor,

Mich.: Institute for Social Research, University of Michigan, 1972), pp. 179–90. See also Jerald G. Bachman, John D. Blair, and David R. Segal, *The All-Volunteer Force* (Ann Arbor, Mich.: University of Michigan Press, 1977), pp. 142–48.

15. On the relative attractiveness of short term versus higher pay incentives, the experience of the military of the Federal Republic of Germany is informative. Although two-year volunteers receive over twice the pay of 15-month draftees, only 8.6 percent of draftees in 1978 elected to shift over to the longer term but higher paid volunteer track.

8

# Two Conceptions of
# Military Professionalism

SAM C. SARKESIAN

Changes in the international security environment and the complexity
of national security policy inevitably raise issues concerning the military
institution and military professionalism. It is no surprise therefore that
the most important assessments of military professionalism have occurred
over the past two decades. These were decades in which the United
States moved from a situation of virtual monopoly of nuclear weaponry
to an era of increasing nuclear proliferation; from relatively clear national security interests to a period in which national security issues have
become obscure; from a relatively clear military posture and capabilities
to one in which serious questions have arisen regarding military effectiveness; and a period of military manpower riches to one of poverty.

A number of those engaged in the study of military professionalism
have published important works focusing on such concepts as convergence-divergence, managerial skills, to a call for political professionals. All of these studies notwithstanding, the two most influential
works remain Samuel Huntington's *The Soldier and the State* and Morris

Janowitz's *The Professional Soldier*. Most students are familiar with both of these works and little needs to be said regarding their substantive issues.

The purpose of this essay is to examine the major philosophical premises of the works of Huntington and Janowitz to ascertain their relevance and conceptual coherency over the past two decades. The intent is not another comparison of the substantive differences and similarities, but rather a macro view that focuses on the "world view" regarding professionalism. Examining scholarly theses from a "universalistic" perspective is a useful intellectual undertaking since it focuses attention on the underlying philosophical premises and provides reference points for critical inquiry based on a disciplinary landscape. In this respect, the Huntington and Janowitz theses are examined in light of the changing nature of international security, the domestic political environment, and the military posture of the United States.

At the outset, it should be noted that there are now a number of variations on the Huntington-Janowitz theses. There are also very useful assessments of both of these works. Much of the literature uses one or the other, or both, as a basis for examining military professionalism. As such, the contributions to the study of military professionalism by both Huntington and Janowitz are of singular importance. In the case of Janowitz these contributions have expanded over the years and have taken root in the organization of the Inter-University Seminar on Armed Forces and Society (IUS).

Huntington's political science perspective is concerned with civil–military relations and control of the military. Underlying his study is a political scientist's concern with state control over coercive instruments, legitimacy, and the proper functioning of the political system.[1] Janowitz's sociological perspective is primarily concerned with the political-social system within the military, the socio-economic characteristics of those who are professionals, and the impact these have on the character of professionalism.[2]

Using such an analytical framework, Janowitz examines attitudes and values to draw conclusions regarding the military professional—the now well-known "absolutist-pragmatic" categories. Beginning with different perspectives both scholars focus on the state of the profession, projecting their concepts into the future as the basis for professionalism. Where Huntington concludes that the best professional is an apolitical one, well entrenched in the specifics of military skills, Janowitz argues that the professional must also develop political-social insights to deal with political-military issues and the ambiguous nature of the security environment.

The label of military professional has, by and large, been reserved to the officers corps. This is not to denigrate the professional enlisted man, i.e., the professional warrant officer or non-commissioned officer. However, as Huntington notes and most scholars recognize, the nature of civil–military relations and the character of the political dimension of military professionalism, as well as the esprit and morale of the military is in no small measure the result of the character of the professional officer, his education and socialization, and the relationship of the state to the officer corps. Equally important, the concept of officership makes the officer an agent of the executive department of the government, providing him with a legitimacy to control and supervise an important institution within the political system.

In examining both the Huntington and Janowitz theses in relation to the international security environment, the domestic environment, and military posture, therefore, we must note the direct relationship between professionalism and the officers corps. Similarly there is a need to examine these works from their own perspective, i.e., political science and sociology. Some of the criticism regarding these works neglect to focus on the purpose and disciplinary orientation of the authors, thus provoking in some instances misinterpretations and invalid critique.

## Professionalism and the International Security Environment

It is self-evident to most scholars that the nature of the international environment has changed significantly since the late 1950s. Yet this was not immediately reflected in the literature. Following the Korean War, a number of scholars began to examine the concept of limited war. The idea that politics established constraints on military operations and indeed, limited strategy and battlefield tactics was difficult to reconcile to the professional perspective. More astute historians recognized the political leverage gained by the Soviet Union in combining political advantage with military operations in World War II. Whereas the American concern remained primarily military, the Soviet and British concerns were political as well as military, i.e. the shape of the post-War world, the relationships of present military operations to the emerging control of Europe. The demand for unconditional surrender was a manifestation of the military view that "there is no substitute for victory." One either won or lost. War appeared to be a clear zero-sums game, particularly from the American viewpoint.

In Korea, the concept of limited war, in which the nature of targets and the extent of military operations were limited by policy makers, was difficult to accept by most military men. The controversy over General Douglas MacArthur was a reflection not only of concern about civilian-control of the military, but more specifically of the attitude of the president that military operations had to be confined to specific political guidelines. It had been axiomatic that politicians were in command until the moment that war occurred. On the battlefield and in the conduct of the war, military men predominated. Many military men and scholars alike viewed this kind of delineated responsibility as historically legitimate—particularly with respect to the United States. The concept of limited war, with all of its political-military implications, was difficult to reconcile with this view. Following the Korean War, some scholars and military men attempted to reconstruct a military perspective incorporating a limited war dimension. However, most returned to the idea of the political war delineation.

It was to be expected that one major perspective for the study of military professionalism in the immediate post-Korean war era perceived military efficiency in terms of apolitical military men whose primary focus was on developing military skills for the proper and successful conduct of war. Underlying this was the return to the idea that politicians negotiated and military men fought wars. Equally important, such a posture for the military professional was relatively easy to translate into education and training, and into a clear state of civil-military relations. The military served society, and in this service, the military was intellectually wedded to military skills and military matters conceived in a narrow professional sense.

In addition, military professionalism according to this perspective viewed the world in pessimistic terms. In light of the late 1950s and early 1960s this appeared to be a logical conclusion, founded on historical evidence. The turmoil of colonial struggles combined with the dramatic events in China seemed to predict decades of constant confrontation and struggles in the international arena. This was reinforced by the realization that other nations, among them the Soviet Union, possessed nuclear weapons and that nuclear war was indeed a possibility. Accordingly, military men could best perform their professional duties by preparing for war and becoming expert in military skills, while the politicians struggled to respond to the fluid and unpredictable international order. Huntington's thesis about the apolitical military and a strict interpretation of professionalism appeared to be the most appropriate and relevant perspective at this time.

Without a detailed recounting of the changes that took place in the early 1960s, it is necessary to note that dramatic events in the international environment stimulated shifts in U.S. political-military perspectives. The collapse of the colonial empires, the increasing capability of the Soviet Union in nuclear weaponry, and the rise of Communist China provided an impetus for rethinking political-military matters. Particularly important was the victory of the Chinese Communist Party over the Nationalists using unconventional strategy and tactics. This gave increasing relevance (or so it appeared) to revolutionary strategy against colonial or authoritarian systems and eroded the relevance of traditional professional views of the battlefield.

The concern of many military men regarding contingencies in various parts of the world with possible unconventional tactics sparked a renewed interest in the reassessment of military professionalism. Huntington's construct of military professionalism appeared to some not to be enough in light of these changing international security issues. The employment of force for less than battlefield victory and for political and symbolic purposes became increasingly important in terms of America's national interest. This thesis was best expressed by Janowitz's idea of a "constabulary" force. A force not in the traditional sense of a constabulary, (a para-military police force), but one in which professionalism included consideration of political-social dimensions and employment of force in non-battle configuration. Most important, Janowitz's thesis insisted that professional socialization include such a dimension.

The Janowitz approach did not abandon the traditional perspective on military professionalism, but used this as the basis for developing a more flexible political-social professional perspective. Equally important Janowitz recognized that the socio-economic character of the military profession had changed and was changing. For example, the concept of professionalism as a lifetime career, was revised. The military now might be only one of several careers. Society had developed linkages with military profession which provided a number of alternative sources for socialization. Moreover, the self isolation of the military was eroding, partly a reflection of societal changes and partly a reflection of the changing demands of the international security environment.

Thus during the early years of the 1960s both the Huntington and Janowitz theses appeared relevant, or appeared to provide a useful framework for understanding professionalism, but for different reasons. One stressed the need for an apolitical military totally immersed in military training and skills in a traditional sense, and the other argued the need to go beyond this if the military was to remain effective.

The Vietnam experience brought dramatic challenges to the concept of professionalism. In terms of the international environment, the Vietnam war appeared to show that professional socialization and professional competence in the traditional sense were not adequate to meet the demands of counter-revolutionary conflicts. Moreover, the U.S. experience in Vietnam seemed to indicate that the existing views on military intervention had become outdated. There have been volumes written on the U.S. experience in Vietnam—more are in the works. Yet, much still needs to be done to develop some objectivity in the U.S. experience in Vietnam. The only point to be made here is that the profession went through a very traumatic soul-searching regarding its own capacity to deal with Vietnam type situations. The demands of counter-revolutionary war went beyond traditional perspectives, kill ratios, real estate; and battlefield victories appeared to be almost irrelevant to the outcome of the war. More important were political symbols, ideological orientation, and the psycho-political environment. Most of these were factors that had little relevance in conventional military terms.

The Huntington thesis seemed to be less relevant in such an environment, while Janowitz's perspectives appeared particularly valid as political-social issues dominated the international conflicts of the 1960s. Equally important, Janowitz's scholarship stimulated an increasing number of scholars to focus on military professionalism, the nature of military education and socialization. This is not to denigrate Huntington's work. Indeed, even during the worst years of the U.S. involvement, there remained a group of military men as well as civilians who argued that the outcome in Vietnam would have been different if policymakers recognized that the battlefield belongs to the military—if professionals had been allowed to operate according to their own professional expertise, the Viet Cong would have been handily defeated early in the war.

Interestingly enough, both Huntington's assessment that professionals had a Hobbesian view of the world and Janowitz's view of the absolutist-pragmatic delineation appeared valid in examining professionalism during the Vietnam era. Not only did many professionals feel that communism and the wars of national liberation were the major challenges, but that such struggles would continue in the foreseeable future. In response to this challenge there were professionals who felt that a strict application of military skills and the use of weapons technology (absolutists) was the best response. Another group of professionals (pragmatists) perceived the need for a more flexible and adaptable employment of force to respond to the political-social as well as military challenges.

The post-Vietnam era has brought with it another shift in professional orientation. It ought to be noted here that these shifts and those referred to earlier did not develop overnight nor were they necessarily perceptible at the outset. By and large such shifts were incremental and in some instances imperceptible. Chastened by the Vietnam experience and threatened by what they perceived as a Soviet build up of conventional and nuclear power, military professionalism reverted to a European orientation (i.e., the "no more Vietnam" syndrome). The battle in the central plains of Europe became the crucial contest within which professional training and education took place. Indeed, it can be reasonably argued that a reaction against political-social dimensions of professionalism occurred with many professionals arguing that the concern with such matters detracted from the main purpose of the profession which was to develop military skills to fight the enemy: in this case military skills and proficiency to fight the Soviets in Europe. This was and is reflected in senior service schools, in the training of units, and in the military budget.

The Huntington thesis again reasserted itself, to be sure in revised form. The professionally proficient military officer was one who gave little heed to politics. He concentrated almost exclusively on the development of military skills. The revised perspective did acknowledge the need to appreciate the political-social environment in the target area, but this was only a background to the development of a military profession, narrowly construed, and emmeshed in technical military matters. Yet, the Janowitz view persisted. There remained a continuing need for a political-social dimension of professionalism, particularly in light of the probable conflicts that would characterize the post-Vietnam era. Equally important, most of the Western world was moving, and indeed had moved, to a different form of military recruiting: from selective service to volunteer service. This had an effect on the character of professionalism and the relationships between the officer corps and the enlisted structure. Moreover, this had an important influence on the capabilities of the military institution.

## Professionalism and the Domestic Political Environment

Both the Huntington and Janowitz theses are well suited to a democratic political system in one dimension and unsuited in another—but for differing reasons. Huntington stresses the apolitical nature of the military and persuasively argues that military men have no business whatsoever in politics. It is particularly concerned with the character of civil-military control. This control is exercised not only through constitutional arrangements, but also through the democratic value system as it interacts with the system in the military. Military socialization processes stress civilian control and the subordination of the military. The subordination of political-social matters in the profession is thought to reinforce the subordination of the military to civilian leadership.

Janowitz's thesis also focuses on the subordination of the military to civilian decisionmakers, not only as a result of the democratic political system, but also because of the professional value system. However, the argument for a political-social component to professionalism and the need for the military to seriously concern itself with such matters provides evidence to some critics that the military officer in Janowitz's perspective is more than a "military" professional—he is one that becomes involved in politics which may open the way for undue influence in the political system. However, the burden of Janowitz's thesis is that the political-social dimension is one that should be directed outward, toward the employment of force in external contingencies.

In terms of the unsuitability of parts of both theses to democratic systems, it can be argued that Huntington's professionalism and Janowitz's constabulary concept both contain the potential for erosion of civilian control. Huntington's stress on the apolitical professional has the potential for developing a military professionalism that is insensitive to democratic values and processes just as it can be insensitive to politics as a whole. To expect a military system to be insensitive to its own political-social system is not realistic, particularly in light of civilian socialization processes and alternatives. Similarly in Janowitz, the study of the professionalism involvement in political-social matters cannot be limited by regulations to the application of force. The inculcation of political ideas and political analysis opens the door to a political assessment of domestic society and the implicit involvement in a variety of informal political alliances. In both cases, the military profession can operate contrary to the values and ideals of the democratic system. Finally, Huntington's argument that professionals have a Hobbesian view of the world bodes ill for the military professional who views his own democratic society in such terms.

Much has been written about the civil rights domestic turmoil of the 1960s compounded by the reaction to the U.S. involvement in Vietnam. One result of such political conflict was reflected in the denigration of the military profession's status. This negative view lingers on to a certain degree in the volunteer era. But more important, the volunteer concept provides another useful measure for examining the influence of Huntington and Janowitz. The Huntington thesis provides support for the volunteer concept since the manpower base would allow the military to isolate itself from the constant input of civilian political-social attitudes and subdue the political concerns and activity of military men. The volunteer military in such circumstances, could be trained as a truly professional force, isolated from the eroding (and some would say corroding) influences of the political-social system. The problems of military effectiveness that first appeared during the Korean War and again emerged in dramatic form in the later parts of the Vietnam War could have been avoided by such a professional posture—according to the logical extension of this argument. In applying the Janowitz thesis to the Korean War, it could have been argued that a better political-social understanding of the nature of the war and the role of the United States and the U.N. could have rectified much of "why we are fighting?" rhetoric as well as cementing and reinforcing the legitimacy and credibility of the military's role on Korea.

The greatest divergence of the two approaches is in their applicability to the military profession during the Vietnam era. As suggested earlier, both views were used by groups of officers, not only to defend the role of the profession in Vietnam but to establish guidelines for the military in the post Vietnam era. In terms of the domestic political environment, the Huntington thesis gained strength as the U.S. involvement in the war became more questionable. Using his thesis, professionals could argue that the battlefield belongs to the military. What needs to be done to gain victory should be left in the hands of the professional. The nature of the weaponry and the strategy and tactics for success in *any* battlefield conflict must be in the hands of the professional—so the argument goes. The failure of the military—if it can be called a failure, was not in the military professional, but in the political constraints and civilian interference in the proper conduct of the war. One need but review some of the most recent memoirs of the war published by high ranking officers to understand the frustration and indeed bitterness with which civilian interference has been viewed. This kind of attitude was not limited to high-ranking officers. Many other professionals also felt that major institutions in the political system did little to assist in the proper conduct of the war. In sum, the Huntington thesis that military men should remain apolitical and focus on their own purpose—success in battle both directly and indirectly—was seen as the answer to failures in counter revolutionary conflict.

Using Janowitz's thesis, military professionals could argue that it was the lack of a real appreciation of the political-social nature of the Vietnam war that was ultimately the basis for the American military failure.

The traditional and conventional perspective could not cope with the highly political and social nature of the revolution in Vietnam. This led to an irrelevant strategy and equally irrelevant tactics. Both civilian and military leaders can also be faulted in such a perspective for not allowing the political-social aspect of the profession to be seriously weighed in the conduct of the war. Equally important, the political-social dimension could have better prepared the military to respond to the domestic turmoil and social issues that spilled over into the military in the middle and late 1960s. The drug scene, racism, dissidence, and insubordination, to a degree unknown previously, caught many military professionals by surprise. Yet it is argued that political awareness and appreciation of the political-social changes taking place in society could have alerted military professionals to the problems of maintaining discipline, morale, and a fighting spirit in the military system.

In the post-Vietnam era, there remain adherents to the Huntington thesis as well as those to the Janowitz thesis. In its extreme form, the Huntington thesis is interpreted to mean isolation from society so that the military can enjoy the freedom to engage in the necessary training to succeed in battle. If it is taken to its extreme the Janowitz thesis is interpreted to mean that the military professional must also be a social scientist concerned about solving the military's problems—problems which have been injected into the military by society, i.e., illiteracy, race, drug abuse, dissidence, and job dissatisfaction. In reviewing the literature, one can identify a variety of themes articulated by scholars on these matters—themes that owe their inception to the scholarship of Huntington and particularly to that of Janowitz.

## Professionalism and Military Posture

The philosophical distinctions between the Huntington and Janowitz conception of professionalism are most clearly seen in their impact on military posture. The definition of military posture can include a variety of considerations, from force structure to defense budgetary considerations. As it is used here, military posture refers primarily to the professional view as to the most probable use of the military institution, the substance of education and training of the professional, and his "world view."

The Hobbesian view of the world underlies the professional intellectual dimension, according to Huntington. Whether military men actually identify themselves as Hobbesian is not important. Rather, it is the fact that military men perceive the world in which states must operate as fundamentally hostile and one in which military conflicts are frequent. For any state to survive, it must therefore have a military force capable of protecting its political system.

The "conservative" orientation complements the Hobbesian view. Professionals are characterized as men who see the world populated by selfish men, who can only be controlled by strong leaders. Even then, the irrationalities of world politics make disorders imminent. Living in this type of world, military men accept "law and order" as a primary objective of any political system and as something to be sought as inherently "good." With this kind of perspective, it is difficult for military men to completely reconcile themselves to the dynamics, changes, and inherent instabilities that usually characterize a liberal democratic system.

Finally, military men see virtue in existing institutions—a virtue that requires loyalty and commitment. Thus, it is difficult for most military men to accept criticism of American political institutions. This was evident during the Vietnam era. For example, military men felt that the mass media were major culprits in presenting a distorted view of the Vietnam War and of the military institution. This professional view remains by and large true today.

The professional world, however, is fundamentally rooted in a philosophical premise that accepts the apolitical nature of the military institution. According to Huntington, this is necessary if the profession is to perform its military role without the erosion from political influences. Involvement in politics shifts the energy of the profession from its main task to the corrupting nature of politics. The more professional the military, the more it is isolated from politics. Military education and training, according to this argument, must therefore focus on the special skills necessary to win battles and wars. The study of political-social phenomenon may be an intellectual luxury and irrelevant to the main tasks of the profession.

Huntington argues that this kind of professional posture is best suited for a liberal democracy that prides itself on civilian control of the military. The variety of democratic controls, institutions, the value system involved, and the inculcation of military men with a commitment to the acquisition of military skills provides not only "objective" but "subjective" controls—those that derive from value systems and ethical considerations.

A major thread of current professionalism is characterized by this

Huntington perspective. As discussed earlier, not only can this be used as an explanation of the Vietnam debacle but it also provides a reference point for the future professional training and socialization.

Less a philosophy than a professional orientation, Janowitz's constabulary concept not only views professionalism in certain political terms but also sees the military institution as a political instrument as well as one in the traditional sense. The military should not be used as a partisan political tool, nor is it to be construed as *primarily* a "political" instrument, but military men must understand, according to this view, that battlefield victory is only one aspect of professionalism. Limited war with all its political-social characteristics must be part of the military professional baggage.

The constabulary perspective does not eliminate the traditional view that military professionalism is primarily based on military skills and competent performance. Rather, it adds a political-social dimension that is characteristic of Vietnam-type wars. This is manifested in the role of the military in such relatively non-traditional contingencies as arms control, conflict limitation, and international peacekeeping.

According to Janowitz, the world view of military men is not monolithic but is basically reflected in two perspectives, the "absolutists" and the "pragmaticists." Where the former views the world in "good" and "evil" terms, the latter accepts shades of gray, in which there are times when "good" and "evil" may not be discernible. For the absolutists, the employment of force to respond to world events parallels Huntington's apolitical professional. In its purest form, this means the application of all the means at the disposal of the military to achieve "victory." For the pragmaticists, however, the employment of force is a more complicated matter, with a number of political considerations. In a number of instances, military men must constrain their use of force, and may become involved in essentially non-military contingencies—according to the pragmatists.

The professional socialization process, including the components of military education, reflects the more complex dimension of the constabulary force. Military men need to do more than learn purely military skills. Military schools, particularly the senior schools, must study a number of political subjects, such as arms control, conflict limitation, problems of political and social change, as well as economics of national security. In the final analysis, the professionalism of Janowitz requires a military competence, but also a political-social sensitivity. This must however be qualified by severely circumscribed political involvement and activity by individual professionals.

## Summary and Conclusions

The examination of the Huntington and Janowitz views of politary professionalism must be tempered by the recognition of their disciplinary perspectives. Huntington's political science focus directs him to the operation of the political system and the military's proper role in that system. Janowitz is primarily concerned with the political-social character of the profession and how this affects the military institution. Both scholars draw conclusions from their disciplinary roots relating to the needs of the military profession and the political system. Thus, it can be argued that the nature of professionalism advanced by both scholars compliments each in many respects. This is not to deny the basic disagreement between Huntington's apolitical military and the Janowitz constabulary force concept. Nevertheless, to articulate these disagreements without recognizing their complementary nature is to misinterpret the scholarship and contributions of both men.

Examining the philosophical premises of the scholar's works does not necessarily reveal the details nor the extent of the substantive analyses. But if one seeks to identify the intellectual thrust and philosophical dimensions which establish the context within which the scholars address the subject, then a macro view is valid—one unencumbered by the incremental details (not that these are unimportant). Interestingly enough, the philosophical basis of the Huntington and Janowitz works is reflected in the present debate in the U.S. Army regarding the utility of *Field Manual 100-5* and all that it suggests regarding the battle in the Central Plains. This debate is generally an operational manifestation of the Huntington-Janowitz perspectives.

Any attempt to draw conclusions regarding the contributions and long-range impact of the scholarship of Huntington and Janowitz will surely fall short. The fact that these two works remain central to the study of armed forces and society is an important clue to the excellence and timelessness of the scholarship. In the case of Janowitz, not only has the scholarship been a significant contribution but the academic career has followed a similar path. Janowitz's disciplinary contributions to the literature and his influence upon the military institution and individual professionals are in no small measure responsible in making the study of armed forces and society a legitimate scholarly concern—one that crosses disciplinary boundaries. While one may not always agree with Janowitz regarding his interpretations and assessments of armed forces and society, one must surely acknowledge his intellectual stature and his impact on the military profession.

## Notes

1. Huntington has much to say throughout his book regarding the political impact on the profession and the military mind. The selections quoted here illustrate his views.

   A political officers corps, rent with faction, subordinated to ulterior ends, lacking prestige but sensitive to the appeals of popularity, would endanger the security of the state. A strong, integrated, highly professional officer corps, on the other hand, immune to politics and respected for its military character, would be a steadying balance wheel in the conduct of policy. . . . In a liberal society the power of the military is the greatest threat to their professionalism. Yet as long as American security is threatened, that power is not likely to diminish significantly.

   Only an environment which is sympathetically conservative will permit American military leaders to combine the political power which society thrusts upon them with the military professionalism without which society cannot endure. . . . (p. 464)

   The military ethic emphasizes the permanence, irrationality, weakness, and evil in human nature. It stresses supremacy of society over the individual, and the importance of order, hierarchy, and division of function. (p. 79)

2. Janowitz refers to the absolutist-pragmatic approach, and the constabulary force concept at a variety of points throughout the book. The selections quoted here provide clear views of his definition and concept of these categories.

   Each theory has its own philosophy of long-range political goals, a conception of politico-military strategy, an image of enemy intentions, and an estimate of the uncommitted nations. The absolute doctrine . . . emphasizes the permanency of warfare and continues to be concerned with victory . . . the pragmatic doctrine emphasizes the revolutionary character of atomic energy, and the discontinuity of the military past with the future. . . . The "absolutists" assume the end as given—total victory; the means must be adjusted in order to achieve it. The "pragmatists" are concerned not only with adapting military means to achieve desired political ends, but insist that the end must be conditioned by what military technology is capable of achieving . . . the distinction between "absolute" and "pragmatic" codes is roughly equivalent to that which obtains between conservative and liberal doctrine. . . . The meaning of these terms—absolute-pragmatic, or conservative-liberal—is clarified by reference to the issue of the inevitability of war, and the political objectives of military action. (pp. 264–265)

   The military establishment becomes a constabulary force when it is continuously prepared to act, committed to the minimum use of force, and seeking viable international relations rather than victory because it has incorporated a protective military posture. The constabulary outlook is grounded in, and extends, pragmatic doctrine. (p. 418)

   Most fundamentally, the professional soldier is conservative. . . . (p. 33)

# 9

# The All-Volunteer Force in a Multidisciplinary Perspective

DAVID R. SEGAL

## Social Science and Social Policy

The world of science is a world of autonomous disciplines, each of which makes assumptions about the nature of reality that allow it to establish priorities regarding what variables must be studied and what variables can be left, at least temporarily, unstudied. The complexity of reality seems to demand such assumptions, for it is only by agreeing to exclude large areas from current consideration, and by assuming that among those remaining some are more important than others, that scientists working in a particular discipline can focus on a slice of reality that is sufficiently manageable. Thus, scientific disciplines are abstractions from reality that differ not only in their levels but also in their planes of abstraction, that is, in the angles at which they intersect with reality. Given that these angles differ, the disciplines may intersect with each other in the abstract world of ideas. Although the social sciences study the same broad phenomena—men and women and the ways in which they structure their lives and relationships—they emphasize different elements of these relationships. Psychology focuses on the individual's adaptation to reality. Economics emphasizes the importance of market processes. Anthropology studies the ways in which cultures persist and change. Political science analyzes the many ways that people establish and relate to bodies that govern them. Sociology studies the institutionalized patterns of interaction which constitute our social lives.

While the world of science is divided into disciplines, the world that scientists study is not. To get a full picture of the richness and complexity of social life, it is necessary to reweave the several threads of social organization that the social science disciplines single out and isolate to expedite their analyses. This is particularly true in the realm of social policy, where the totality of social science research efforts is only one input—and usually a very minor one—to the policy process. Thus, the impact of any single discipline is likely to be insignificant, the claims of discipline-based social scientists to "policy-relevance" notwithstanding.

The all-volunteer armed force looms large as one of the most far-reaching and exciting social experiments in twentieth-century America. Both the planning for and the evaluation of the all-volunteer force have drawn heavily upon social science analysis. Rather than an integrated effort at social understanding, however, the social science community has produced three relatively large but disparate research literatures, coming from three different quarters, addressing three different sets of questions, and suggesting potential solutions to three different audiences. A fourth discipline has made a somewhat smaller contribution in terms of the magnitude of the literature produced, although not in terms of policy significance, since none of the three major contributors seem to have made an impact that is likely to be regarded as significant in the long run. By emphasizing competition between disciplines rather than integration of disciplinary perspectives, the contribution of the social sciences to the understanding of the strengths and weaknesses of the all-volunteer force is likely to be fragmented. This contribution of the social sciences to the understanding of so important a social innovation as an all-volunteer military force in a major world power during an era of nuclear military technology, however, does shed light on the individual roles of several social science disciplines in the policy process, and on the nature of that process itself.

Economics, for at least the past two decades, has been the single most influential social science discipline at the highest levels of the executive branch of the federal government. The President of the United States, lacking councils of influential social, psychological, cultural, and political advisors, does have a Council of Economic Advisors, reflecting the primacy of economic determinism in our national ideology.

Psychologists have been second to economists among the social sciences in recognizing the legitimacy of plying their trade outside the bounds of academe. They have followed the economists into government and industry, and, while they have not penetrated as deeply into the corridors of power and influence as have the economists, they abound in mid-level research positions in executive branch agencies that are responsible for the implementation, rather than the development, of policies having to do with the utilization of human resources.

Sociology has been among the more critical of the social science disciplines, not so much because it opposes much national policy (although to some extent it does), as because it has tended to operate outside the formal policy process, with the most influential sociologists using the lectern and the pen, rather than the government forum, to influence the policy process. While such input has increasingly been attended to by policymakers, and sociologists have increasingly been invited to participate in government forums, there are few sociologists in mid-level positions, and virtually none in senior-level positions, in the executive branch of the federal government.

The role of political science in the formulation of domestic policy, is highly limited. To be sure, many of our elected officials studies political science in college, and the American Political Science Association takes great pride in the number of its members who have, historically, assumed positions of power in local, state, and federal governments. These individuals, however, have become practitioners of politics rather than of science, emphasizing the substance rather than the analysis. To the extent that the scientific study of politics has played a role in the policy process, it has tended to be confined to international affairs. While this realm includes national security matters, the issue of national security did not figure largely in the analysis of the transition from a conscription force to an all-volunteer force, save in the recognition that foreign military threats were the reason for the maintenance of a large standing force, regardless of the means of personnel accession. In the domestic arena, political science also indicates to policymakers how acceptable various policy alternatives are. However, such scientifically based indicators are not the only, or even the major, information used by officials.

## The Background of the All-Volunteer Force

America's military traditions were inherited from the British: a distrust of the kind of standing peacetime force that James II had used to suppress the freedom of the English people and a predisposition to associate the role of soldier with that of citizen. In the colonies, all free, white, able-bodied men were members of the "common militia" and liable to be drafted into active service. With American independence, the militia tradition was kept alive. The Militia Act of 1792, while it did not establish a standing force, did enunciate the principle that all white, able-bodied males were part of the military mobilization base.

When the concept of state militias liable for federal service under specific conditions was shown to be inadequate in the War of 1812 and the Mexican War, both the North and the South established military drafts in the Civil War. The draft was not used in the Spanish-American War, but in 1917, a new draft law was passed, and three million American men were conscripted for service in World War I. After the war, the draft was allowed to lapse, and for two decades the American military depended on voluntary recruitment. However, with the advent of another war in Europe, America established its first "peacetime" draft in September 1940. The draft helped supply personnel to the American armed forces for more than thirty of the next thirty-two years. More than ten million men were inducted into the World War II forces, and a series of extensions prolonged the draft until March 1947.

Army strength dropped considerably without conscription, and as relations between the East and the West became more tense, particularly after the February 1948 communist coup in Czechoslovakia, President Truman and the Congress again turned to conscription to meet America's military personnel needs. A new Selective Service Act was passed in June 1948, after fifteen months of a volunteer force. Few people were inducted under the Act, and the Congress was considering letting it expire when, in late June 1950, the North Korean Army crossed the 38th parallel. The Selective Service Act was extended, and continued as a peacetime draft after the Korean police action. During the post-war period, however, manpower needs decreased. The Selective Service System had to find criteria for *not* drafting young men. Deferments on the basis of age, education, occupation, and parenthood made the draft appear increasingly inequitable. In 1963, as the post-World War II baby boom began to come of military age eligibility, the Selective Service began to defer all married men.

The deferment system was coming under increased criticism, both from the public and from the Congress. But for the Vietnam War, conscription might have been phased out in the United States a decade earlier than it was. Just as America's involvement in the Vietnam War required the extension of the draft, the unpopularity of the war, the peace movement, demonstrations on campuses and in Washington, and

increasing hostility to the draft itself as draft calls increased all contributed materially to the demise of conscription in 1973. During the 1968
presidential campaign, Richard Nixon promised to end the draft once
the Vietnam War was over. Within three months of his inauguration,
Nixon had appointed the President's Commission on an All-Volunteer
Armed Force, which was charged with the development of "a comprehensive plan for eliminating conscription."

## Social Research on the All-Volunteer Force

The deliberations of the President's Commission were not conducted in
an information vacuum. Indeed, it is unlikely that any policy deliberation in the United States has been as informed (or overinformed) by
social science research. In response to opposition to the Vietnam War,
criticisms of the draft, and concerns about high draft calls, all of which
were highly visible on college campuses, as well as a Department of
Defense study of the draft in 1964, economists had started studying and
publishing papers on the draft and its all-volunteer alternative in the
mid-1960s. The existence of this growing body of literature, in turn,
helped fan the flames of governmental debate on the all-volunteer force.

The economic research focused on labor market factors, and attempted to estimate the cost of military service borne by those who were
drafted (the "conscription tax"), and the cost to the nation of recruiting
an all-volunteer force at competitive wages. The issue of a conscription
tax was highlighted by the President's Commission on an All-Volunteer
Force.[1] The distinction made by the Commission, which focused on
costs which show up in the budget as opposed to those absorbed by the
men who serve, did not originate with the Commission. It had been
metnioned repeatedly at a 1966 University of Chicago conference on the
draft, particularly in the presentations of economists Milton Friedman
and Walter Oi.[2] The research literature that evolved was contradictory;
some analyses showed that veterans experience a loss in lifetime earnings; others showed no differences between veterans and non-veterans
when factors such as age were taken into account, and the most recent
analyses showed income gains as a function of military service.[3]

Research on the costs of an all-volunteer force focused on the pay
elasticity of military enlistees: the increase in enlistments that could be
expected as a function of pay increases. As in the case of research on the
conscription tax, results were contradictory and inconclusive, although
they did suggest that at competitive pay levels, it would be possible to

recruit sufficient personnel to fill the ranks of an all-volunteer armed force.[4] Extending the issue of pay elasticity to the evaluation, rather than the planning, of an all-volunteer force, the manpower shortfalls in recent years have been attributed, at least in part, to the fact that the basic assumption of the all volunteer force, that military pay can become with comparable civilian pay, has not been met.[5] In the face of continued economic costs of military service borne by those who serve, that is, lower pay in the military than in the civilian sector, the market model predicts an inability to achieve manning goals.

The contribution of psychology to the solution of military manpower and personnel issues was drastically altered by the advent of the all-volunteer force. Starting with the World War I period, psychologists had contributed materially to the development and validation of selection and classification tests that would assist the defense establishment in determining who was qualified to serve and to which jobs they might best be assigned. In 1917, when war was declared, Robert M. Yerkes, then president of the American Psychological Association, encouraged his colleagues to contribute to the defense effort by devising methods for examining recruits. The results of his call were reflected in the Army Alpha and Beta tests, for the classification of literates and illiterates, respectively. The Army General Classification Test (AGCT) was developed for use in World War II. The most widely used test, the Armed Forces Qualification Test (AFQT) was developed in 1950. It was the first psychological screening test with a mandatory cutting score set by an Act of Congress, and the first to be used by all the services to determine mental fitness. Military psychology became deeply involved in training research in the 1950s, but selection and classification testing remained a major area of exploration, leading to the development of the Armed Services Vocational Aptitude Battery (ASVAB), which in the mid-1960s replaced all previous selection tests used at Armed Forces Examining and Entrance Stations (AFEES), and the mis-norming of which led to a drastic increase in the proportion of enlisted personnel in the lowest acceptable mental category in the late 1970s.

The error in norming was widely cited in Congress as evidence of the decline in personnel quality in the all-volunteer force, as compared with the conscription based force. Psychological screening did indeed become a problem for the services after the end of the draft, but the problem was not simply one of norming errors. It was the failure of the proponents of the military's selection and classification tests to recognize the processes of screening that had taken place in a draft environment. The effective use of selection tests to meet personnel needs with high quality individuals assumes a favorable selection ratio. The services must be able to afford the luxury of rejecting a considerable proportion of those who present themselves, as volunteers or as conscripts, for service. In the absence of a favorable selection ratio, the best of selection and classification tests could not play the role in the military personnel system of the all-volunteer force that the Alpha, Beta, AGCT, and AFQT had played during conscripton.

The psychologists employed by the defense establishment recognized this shift, and turned their attention to two other areas of research that were perceived to be crucial to the success of the all-volunteer force: studies of the motivations of young Americans regarding military service, and studies of ways to improve the quality of life in the armed forces to make them more attractive as employers.

As America prepared to move into an all-volunteer force era, the Defense Department was concerned with the impact of the anti-Vietnam War, anti-draft, and perhaps anti-military attitudes that it felt pervaded American society. Three series of attitude studies were designed to monitor youth's motivation to join the military: one concerned with inter-cohort changes in the military age-eligible population over time,[6] one concerned with the attitudes of people who actually enlisted, and one concerned with intra-cohort changes in attitudes of American youth over time. The major findings derived from these surveys were that (1) the proportion of young Americans who expected to serve in the military varied very little from year to year, roughly between 12 and 15 percent of each male cohort; (2) the Army was seen as the least attractive service; (3) the recruitment incentives most important to the highest quality recruits were opportunities for training and education, rather than pay, as the econometric models suggested. The major drawback of the survey approach was that there was a poor fit between attitude and behavior. Many of the civilian respondents who indicated that they expected to join the armed forces did not do so. Nonetheless, the surveys did provide information to recruiting commands and policymakers regarding the images of the services.

Research to improve the quality of life in the services began with the Army's Project Volar, started at four experimental posts in 1971, which aimed at improving living conditions and removing some of the sources of dissatisfaction from Army life. The actions taken included hiring civilians for K.P. duties, establishing short-order food service in dining facilities, allowing beer in the barracks, and the abolition of reveille. Project Volar was evaluated against a criterion of reenlistment intentions among personnel at the experimental posts. However, the research conducted was unable to demonstrate that the Volar innovations had any effect on either reenlistment intentions or actual reenlistment behavior.[7]

The lack of demonstrable impact of perceived quality of life on personnel retention notwithstanding, all of the military services have continued to invest resources in, and conduct analyses of, programs to improve the quality of service life. To a great extent, this has involved borrowing organizational development strategies developed in the civilian sector to improve job satisfaction, and adapting them (or merely adopting them) in military environments.

The success of these strategies in improving organizational effectiveness, organizational climate, job satisfaction, and personnel retention has been no greater than the success of Project Volar. All three services have noted a decline in job satisfaction since the early 1970s and the advent of organizational development.[8] This is not to say that organizational development is responsible for this decline. Indeed, the decline in job satisfaction might have been more extreme in without such techniques. At a minimum, however, organizational development cannot be credited with improving job satisfaction.

More local attempts to evaluate the effects of organizational development against other criteria have been similarly unsuccessful. J. P. Fry and R. E. Cliborn evaluated a series of workshops designed to improve the leadership skills of officers. They found no evidence that the training had any impact on the behavior of officers or on organizational effectiveness. Holmes and his colleagues conducted a study of Army leadership using survey feedback as the organizational development technique. Against a criterion of unit effectiveness measures, no significant differences were found between units trained to use survey data and units that were not.[9] Johns conducted an evaluation of a laboratory training exercise and a follow-up team-building exercise oriented toward changing the leadership styles of battalion-level leaders. He found no significant differences in the ratings of the behavior of battalion commanders between experimental and control units.[10] In short, psychological research does not seem to have contributed materially to the understanding or solution of personnel accession and retention problems in the all-volunteer force. What it has done has been to urge policymakers to emphasize the ways in which the military is similar to a civilian employer, and to deemphasize the characteristics that make the military unique, in order to make military service more attractive. While the psychologists have not confined themselves to the fiscal rationality assumptions contained in econometric analyses of the all-volunteer force, they have, like the economists, tended to ignore that which is organizationally unique about the military.

The political science research that was brought to bear on the decision to end the draft was for the most part concerned with public opinion on policy alternatives. In retrospect, however, the government appears to have led, rather than followed, public opinion. From the mid- to late-1960s, public opinion polls showed majorities of the population favoring the draft, although the size of the majorities diminished from more than three quarters to somewhat more than half between 1966 and 1969. During this same period opposition to the draft increased from 15 percent to more than a third. Facing a choice between a conscription based force and a volunteer force, the public preferred the draft by a ratio of about 2:1. The draft was continued through the Johnson administration.

In March 1969, the month in which President Nixon appointed his Commission on an All-Volunteer Armed Force, a small majority of the public still preferred the draft and favored the selection system then in existence over the lottery that the President was soon to suggest. Nonetheless, the lottery system was established in December 1969, and that month almost three-quarters of the public decided that they approved of the new system. With the President calling for an end to conscription, by January 1970 a small majority of the public indicated support for an all-volunteer force, as opposed to the lottery system. In short, the public opinion research seems not to have provided input to the policy process so much as it demonstrated the ability of the administration to garner support for its favored policies, at least in the short run.

Sociological analysis of the all-volunteer force in the late 1960s and early 1970s reflected a change in the field of military sociology. Military sociology in the 1950s, as exemplified by *The American Soldier,* had focused on the individual soldier primarily from a social psychological perspective. In the early 1960s it focused on the military as an occupation and a profession (Janowitz's *Professional Soldier*). By the dawning of the era of the all-volunteer force, the field of military sociology was beginning to grapple more extensively with macrosociological relationships between armed forces, their host societies, and the world system.

At the 1966 University of Chicago conference on the draft, Janowitz argued in favor of replacing the selective service with a system of national service that made service in the armed forces one of the alternatives available to American youth. Correctly anticipating the events that were to unfold, he suggested that "an Armed Forces based on "competitive" salaries is not a real possibility. . . . The military would always be disadvantaged relative to the private sector. . . ."[11] However, his arguments in favor of national service were not primarily based on market principles. Rather, he saw such a service as an opportunity to build a new social institution that would direct social change constructively. He saw the new system as ensuring that the burden of national defense would no longer be borne disproportionately on the shoulders of young black males who did not qualify for educational deferments, but shared more widely. It would help to equalize educational and social welfare opportunities. Perhaps most important, although more implicit, was the idea that national service was to establish linkages between the armed forces and civilian society, and between the behavior of the individual citizen and national purpose.

As the all-volunteer force moved from concept to policy, Janowitz continued to voice concerns about the potential social isolation of the armed forces from civilian society, and continued to argue for institution-building, this time within the structure of the armed forces. In particular, he stressed a "constabulary" notion of military mission, and a definition of military professionalism based "more on contractual and public service conceptions and less on sheer traditional authority."[12] The themes of social isolation, both ideological and structural, the constabulary concept, and the redefinition of military professionalism continued to be major foci of the sociological analysis of the all-volunteer force through the decade of the 1970s.[13]

When the move to an all-volunteer force became a reality in the early 1970s, two critical themes surfaced in the sociological literature. The first was that the armed forces were becoming increasingly unrepresentative of American society, and that, in particular, the increasing concentration of black males in the ground combat forces might exacerbate racial tensions, raise questions about the internal reliability of the force, put the black community, which has received less than its share of the largess of American society, in the position of bearing more than its share of combat casualties and fatalities in protecting that society, and most important in structural terms, produce a military structure from which the educated, white, middle class is alienated, leading to questions of the legitimacy of the military institution.[14] Discussions of the racial and more general socioeconomic composition of the all-volunteer force, and the implications of this composition, have continued to pervade the literature.[15]

The second theme focused on a major transformation of military organization, rooted in ending conscription and imposing an econometric model of military manpower. In a presentation on enlisted personnel, at the 1973 meeting of the American Sociological Association, Moskos noted, almost in passing, "an organizational shift from a predominantly institutional format (i.e., legitimized by normative values) to one more resembling that of an occupation (i.e., akin to civilian market-place standards)." The hypothesized transformation of military organization from a unique institution to a civilian-like workplace, and of military service from a calling to simply a job, has generated much controversy and debate in both the policy and scholarly communities.[16] In the former, there has been considerable discussion in both the Army and the Air Force about whether it is possible to recapture the pre- all-volunteer force days, when personnel "served" rather than "worked," and when their service was seen as a duty rather than a job. In the latter, there has been debate on whether Moskos correctly identified the major trend in military organization and whether the model of the military as an institution is incompatible with that of the military as a workplace.[17]

The juxtaposition of the institution and workplace models itself reflects the historic lack of contact among scholarly disciplines concerned with the analysis of military organization. The workplace orientation is found primarily in studies of the military rooted in industrial psychology and labor economics and assumes a similarity between military and industrial organization. The institution orientation, on the other hand, is embedded in the traditions of military history and military sociology. Here the focus has been on those aspects of the military that differentiate it from civilian organizations: engagement in combat operations in wartime, willingness among peacetime soldiers to go to war should the need arise, and attitudes regarding obedience to authority, the role of force in international relations, and the appropriate role of the military in domestic politics. This perspective assumes that the soldier is different from the civilian employee.

Research conducted from these two perspectives through the period of the Cold War kept them distinct. It has only been during the past few years that attempts have been made to integrate them. What research has been done has shown them to be not incompatible: military personnel in the all-volunteer era seem to have both institutional and workplace orientations.[18] However distinct military sociology, military psychology, and labor economics are from each other, they all seem necessary in explaining the reality with which they are trying to come to grips: the orientation of the volunteer soldier.

## The Transformation of the Military in the 1980s

The United States has embarked on a major national debate that will define the nature of the armed forces in the years to come. The issues raised by the debate lend themselves well to social science analysis. The degree to which such analysis effectively informs the debate, however, is likely to be constrained by how well social scientists can transcend disciplinary boundaries and biases and integrate their several perspectives.

The central focus of the national debate concerns whether we will continue to have an all-volunteer armed force, or whether we will resort, at least in part, to some less voluntary form of military service. These forms range from an outright military draft through a system of choices among alternative forms of national service (where one of the alternatives may be entering a military draft pool to be used should not enough people elect the armed forces alternative), including a "minimally coercive" national service system, in which service is not compulsory, but where receipt of certain citizen benefits might become contingent upon voluntarily fulfilling citizen responsibilities. Continuation of the all-volunteer force, of course, continues to be an option in the debate.

Four major interdependent themes have been raised in this debate, and they are worthy of specification since they help identify the areas in which the social sciences might make their major contributions to policy deliberation. At the same time, the very interdependence of the themes highlights the importance of integrating the collective contribution of the social sciences.

One of the earliest issues raised in the debate was cost. The expense of maintaining America's armed forces increased markedly with the demise of conscription, and the greatest increases have been in personnel-related costs. Some critics of the all-volunteer force have pointed out that it is the cost of recruiting an all-volunteer force, and paying that force at a level that makes military service economically attractive, that has made the expense of an all-volunteer force prohibitive. Actually, the personnel costs would seem less excessive if we subtracted those costs that are after-effects of the mobilization of the Vietnam War rather than of the conversion to an all-volunteer force. We also need to weigh recruiting costs against the expense of establishing and maintaining a selective service system or national service system as well as maintaining as much of a recruiting system as we had during previous periods of military conscription. We never depended wholly on drafted personnel; the issue is not one of high recruiting costs versus no recruiting costs.

With regard to savings in compensation, it is important to note that the President's Commission on an All-Volunteer Force separated the issue of compensation level from that of conscription. The argument made was that a differential in compensation that favored the civilian labor force did not represent a saving, but rather a reallocation of cost, so that it was borne by those who served rather than by the taxpayers. The commission felt this "conscription tax" was inequitable and recommended that even if we maintained military conscription, military compensation should be brought into line with the civilian labor market. As noted above, we managed to do just the opposite: we have abolished conscription and allowed military compensation to fall below civilian pay level.

The analysis of economic costs must also take into account the cost of veterans' benefits, particularly those related to education and training. One of the major justifications for the original G.I. Bill educational benefits was the assumption that those who served under the draft would be economically disadvantaged relative to their peers who did not serve, and that assistance in achieving higher education or job training might resynchronize them with their age cohorts. These G.I. Bill benefits were among the casualties of conscription's demise. Although the Defense Department is currently experimenting with additional educational incentives, there has not been a thorough accounting of the costs and benefits of military educational benefits. Clearly, there is much economic analysis left to be done on military manpower issues. Unfortunately, should these analyses be undertaken, they will have to be interpreted in light of the fact that recent economic analyses of military manpower issues have been, for the most part, incorrect.

The second theme in the debate is that of military effectiveness. There is a widely held view in the policy community that the all-volunteer force is not very effective. This lack of effectiveness is, in turn, attributed to the quality of personnel attracted to serve under the all-volunteer system. It is clear that since the advent of the all-volunteer force, there has been a decline in the representation of college educated people in the enlisted ranks, and particularly in the ground combat elements. It is equally true that major problems in organizational effectiveness, rooted in the scale of military organization and in the structure and process of decision-making and resource allocation, were noted before the demise of conscription. These same problems persist today.[19] Were we, through conscription, national service, or some other means, able to solve the problems of personnel quantity and quality, we would still, in all likelihood, not have an effective military. In this sense, the manpower issues raised by the debate serve as smokescreens for deeply rooted structural problems that need to be addressed by organizational sociologists, organizational psychologists, and experts in management.

The third theme that has been raised in the debate focuses on the demography of the American population and the related issue of utilizing women in the armed forces. The post-World War II baby boom ended in the 1960s, and the cohorts produced during this birth dearth will come of military-age eligibility during the 1980s. Were the armed services to maintain their current size, given the decrease in the number of age eligible young men, they would have to attract a larger proportion of these men to serve, change the age distribution of the force by using older men to broaden the recruitment pool, or expand the utilization of women in service.[20] Given the general trend in American society toward reduction of gender-based inequalities in activities and compensation, the most compelling arguments have addressed this last possibility. Indeed, there has been a broad expansion in the number of women in the United States armed forces and in the number of jobs to which they can be assigned. However, they are still drastically underrepresented in terms of the American population and are excluded from combat specialities.

When President Carter announced early in 1980 that he would seek authority to register both women and men for selective service, he ran into opposition from, among other groups, conservatives who opposed the utilization of women in the armed forces generally and who argued for the reintroduction of a military draft as a means of reducing military dependency on womanpower. The traditionalists won, and registration was limited to males. This restriction has been challenged in court on the basis that gender-based exclusions are a denial of equal protection, but, in 1981, in *Rostker v. Goldberg,* the Supreme Court ruled that Congress has the right to exclude women from registration. There is a clear need for research on how gender integration affects military effectiveness, research that will go beyond historical analyses of the Soviet and German experiences in World War II and of the involvement of American, Russian, and Israeli women in unconventional warfare. There is also a continuing need for legal scholars and anthropologists to study the changes in the law and the social changes that reflect and articulate the values and gender role definitions of American society in this transitional period.

The fourth theme that has been raised is the meaning of citizenship in American society. The economic incentives used as inducements to serve in the all-volunteer force, a military organization that increasingly resembles an industrial organization, and a societal context that becomes progressively more rationalized and alienating, all contribute to heighten individualism, increasing disengagement, and a weakening of social control, as Janowitz has shown. The available evidence suggests that, as a nation, we have lost sight of the fact that citizenship involves responsibilities as well as rights. Service to the state, whether in a military or civilian capacity, has traditionally been one of those responsibilities.

The advent of the all-volunteer armed force contributed to the re-definition, and the moral reduction of that responsibility. Much of the contemporary discussion of registration, of reintroduction of a draft, of compulsory or voluntary national service, and of tying some of the bene-fits of citizenship, such as financial assistance for higher education, to fulfilment of citizenship responsibilities, are all implicitly concerned with the issue of responsibility to the state. Sociologists have begun to address this issue explicitly,[22] but increased attention from political scientists, and indeed from philosophers, is warranted as well.

We need integrated scholarly consideration, by a variety of disci-plines, both positivistic and humanistic, to inform the national debate on the nature of military service in the United States in the last two decades of the twentieth century, indeed, on the very nature of the relationship between the military and society. This is a challenge which has been, in the past, beyond the abilities of most discipline-based scholars.

Implicit in the challenge to scholars is a challenge to policymakers as well: a challenge to be patient. The greatest costs of wise counsel are measured, not in dollars, but in time. And new forms of military organi-zation are experimental social innovations which must also be given time to prove themselves or to fail. There is no organizational quick-fix, and the benefits of even a vastly improved system will not be apparent in much less than a decade, for a whole new generation of citizens must be socialized to accept a participatory definition of integration with the state.

## Notes

1. *The Report of the President's Commission on an All-Volunteer Force* (Wash-ington, D.C.: U.S. Government Printing Office, 1970), p. 9.
2. Sol Tax, ed., *The Draft: A Handbook of Facts and Alternatives* (Chicago: University of Chicago Press, 1967). See, in this volume, Milton Friedman, "Why Not a Volunteer Army," pp. 200–208; and Walter Y. Oi, "The Costs and Implications of an All-Volunteer Army," pp. 221–51.
3. Wayne J. Villemez and John D. Kasarda, "Veteran Status and So-cioeconomic Attainment," *Armed Forces and Society* 2 (Spring 1976): pp. 407–420; O. B. Kassing, "Military Experience as a Determinant of Vet-erans Earnings," in *Report of the President's Commission on an All-Volunteer Armed Force*, pp. III-8-1–III-8-22.

4. Alan E. Fechter, "Impact of Pay and Draft Policies on Army Enlisted Behavior," *Report of the President's Commission on an All-Volunteer Armed Forces.*

5. Melvin R. Laird, *People, Not Hardware* (Washington, D.C.: American Enterprise Institute, 1980).

6. Allan A. Fisher, Jr., et al., *Attitudes of Youth Toward Military Service* (Alexandria: Human Resources Research Organization, 1972).

7. Robert Vineberg and Elaine N. Taylor, *Summary and Review of Studies of the VOLAR Experiment* (Alexandria, Va.: Human Resources Research Organization, 1972).

8. David R. Segal and Joseph J. Lengermann, "Professional and Institutional Considerations," *Combat Effectiveness: Cohesion, Stress, and the Volunteer Army*, ed., Sam C. Sarkesian (Beverly Hills, Ca.: Sage Publications, 1980), pp. 154–84; David R. Segal, Ann Lynch, and John D. Blair, "The Changing American Soldier," *American Journal of Sociology* 85 (July 1979): pp. 95–108.

9. J. P. Fry and R. E. Cliborn, *Development, Implementation, and Evaluation of Leadership/Management Training within Army Battalions* (Alexandria: Human Resources Research Organization, 1975); Douglas S. Holmes, et al., *Survey Feedback in Combat Units in the U.S. Army in Europe* (Alexandria, Va.: U.S. Army Research Institute for the Behavioral and Social Sciences, 1978).

10. John H. Johns, "Organizational Change in the U.S. Army as a Function of Applied Social Science Knowledge" (Ph.D. diss., Washington, D.C.: The American University, 1979).

11. Morris Janowitz, "The Logic of National Service," in *The Draft*, ed., Sol Tax, pp. 73–90.

12. Morris Janowitz, "Volunteer Armed Forces and Military Purpose," *Foreign Affairs* 3 (April 1972): pp. 443–72; Janowitz, "Toward an All-Volunteer Military," *The Public Interest* 27 (Spring 1972): pp. 104–17.

13. On social isolation, see Jerald G. Bachman, John D. Blair, and David R. Segal, *The All-Volunteer Force* (Ann Arbor: University of Michigan Press, 1977); David R. Segal, Mary Senter, and Mady W. Segal, "The Civil-Military Interface in a Metropolitan Community," *Armed Forces and Society* 4 (May 1978): pp. 423–48. On the constabulary force, see Charles C. Moskos, Jr., *The American Enlisted Man* (New York: Russell Sage, 1970). On military professionalism, see Sam C. Sarkesian, *The Professional Army Officer in a Changing Society* (Chicago: Nelson-Hall, 1975).

14. Morris Janowitz and Charles C. Moskos, Jr., "Racial Composition of the All-Volunteer Force," *Armed Forces and Society* 1 (Fall 1974): pp. 109–23; Janowitz, "The All-Volunteer Force as a Sociopolitical Problem," *Social Problems* 22 (February 1975), pp. 432–49.

15. Alvin J. Schexnider and John S. Butler, "Race and the All-Volunteer System," *Armed Forces and Society* 2 (Spring 1976): pp. 421–32; Charles C.

Moskos, Jr., "The Enlisted Ranks in the All-Volunteer Army," in The *All-Volunteer Force and American Society*, ed., by John B. Keeley (Charlottesville: University of Virginia Press, 1978), pp. 39–79; Morris Janowitz and Charles C. Moskos, Jr., "Five Years of the All-Volunteer Force," *Armed Forces and Society* 5 (Winter 1979): pp. 171–218.

16. Charles C. Moskos, Jr., "Studies on the American Soldier: Continuities in Social Research" (Paper presented at the Annual Meeting of the American Sociological Association, 1973); Moskos, "From Institution to Occupation," *Armed Forces and Society* 4 (Fall 1977): pp. 41–50.

17. David R. Segal, John D. Blair, Joseph J. Lengermann, and Richard Thompson, "Institutional and Occupational Values in the U.S. Military," in *Changing Military Manpower Realities*, ed., by James Brown, Michael J. Collins, and Franklin D. Margiotta (Boulder, Co.: Westview Press, 1980).

18. Charles A. Cotton, *Military Attitudes and Values of the Army in Canada* (Toronto, Ontario: Canadian Forces Personnel Applied Research Unit, 1979).

19. Segal and Lengermann, "Professional and Institutional Considerations."

20. Martin Binkin and Irene Kyriakopoulos, *Youth or Experience* (Washington, D.C.: Brookings Institution Press, 1979); Mady Weschler Segal, "Women in the Military," *Youth and Society* 10 (December 1979): pp. 101–26.

21. Morris Janowitz, *The Last Half-Century: Societal Change and Politics in America* (Chicago: University of Chicago Press, 1979).

22. Morris Janowitz, "The Citizen Soldier and National Service," in *Evolving Strategic Realities: Implications for U.S. Policy Makers*, ed., by Franklin D. Margiotta (Washington, D.C.: National Defense University Press, 1980), pp. 127–44.

# The Ordeal of Tradition
# in the German Militaries

WILFRIED VON BREDOW

## Difficulties of Comparison

A comparison of institutions and their functioning in the two contemporary German societies does not seem, at first glance, to be problematic. Comparative studies of this kind are in vogue both in sociology and in political science. The confrontation of some aspects of the political culture of countries belonging to the Eastern or Western camp has become one of the usual tasks of academic frontier-guards.

This task and its usually not very stimulating results will not be criticized in this chapter. There are, however, some problematic features of the comparative approach that should be mentioned.

If one understands the East-West clash as a deep structural conflict in current affairs which takes effect not only on the level of international relations but also on nearly all levels of national political cultures,[1] one should be careful with East–West comparisons because of the danger of (mostly unconscious) distortions of the social reality by means of ideological blinkers. A survey of studies in Eastern Europe about Western countries and of Western studies about Eastern Europe does not generate optimism.

The two different German political units are, on the one hand, relatively easy objects for East–West comparisons. But, on the other, they produce, because of their dramatic confrontation, a considerable amount of sociological analysis about one another, which, for the most part, is less analysis and more a combination of hopes, wishes, and bad futurology. It is not at all easy to get the information you want because it is frequently wrapped in lots of rubbish. This may sound arrogant, but it is nevertheless true. You will find no sociological study of the Bundeswehr by an East German author that is seriously discussed in West Germany (FRG). Nor will you find a sociological study of the Nationale Volksarmee (NVA) by a West German author that is seriously discussed in East Germany (GDR).[2]

So how to begin a comparison?

Sociological research is an effort to overcome one's own prejudices. And even if Max Weber's *Wertfreiheit* is an ideal that we shall perhaps never attain (as Mr. K. never entered the palace in Kafka's novel), it is always possible to rise above the level of political propaganda and mutual invectives.

A special problem of inter-German comparisons is the different "weight" of the two states. The FRG is at least about three times bigger if you compare the population, territory, or gross national product. And the status of both states within their respective alliances is different, too. It is not sufficient to use the notion of a "penetrated system" because it only stresses the common features of their situation, but does not cover the fact that the degree of integration of the GDR into the Warsaw Pact is much higher. There are more differences of this kind.

A methodological remark: this chapter is based on the unquestioned self-understanding and self-image of the political and military elites in both political units. There will be no discussion of the limits of these images and of their relevance in the everyday-life of the armed forces. Presumably, I would have difficulties in carrying out empirical research on the NVA.

## The Ideological Triangle

The FRG and the GDR are young states, just over thirty years old. The FRG understands itself as the successor of the German Reich. The GDR has always rejected all political, judicial, and moral responsibility for the actions of the German Reich. Both states have to cope with problems of legitimacy; once again the FRG seems about three times better off. The past is a heavy burden: the regime of the Third Reich with its internal and external crimes, World War II and its end in total surrender, the division into four zones after the cutting off of some parts of the territory. From the perspective of 1945, the idea of an anti-fascist reconstruction of Germany seemed not unrealistic. But it soon lost its political grip. The East–West conflict entered the cold war phase. It was this climate that determined the development of the four occupied zones into two German states, incorporating two hostile principles for the organization of a society. The reconciliation was a "natural" option at first. But by 1955 that option had faded away. The build-up of "real" armed forces and their integration into NATO and the Warsaw Pact meant a big jump toward the existence of two German states which were no longer provisional.

In 1945, 1949, and once again in 1955, the question of personal continuity became particularly urgent. Were Germans who had been involved in the political, economic, cultural, and military life of the Third Reich to be allowed to participate in the reconstruction of a "new" Germany? Should one decide with moral rigidity? Or should one be flexible because of the need for skilled persons? Evidently, these questions led to a moral and technical dilemma; the situation of 1945 and the following years demanded all sorts of compromises. In general, the political leaders of East Germany were more rigid.

The strong and principal rejection of the aims, methods, and ideology of national socialism became, however, part of the fundamental base of both German states' legitimacy. It is still nearly as important as it was over thirty years ago. But this rejection was and still is quite differently motivated. There is no common "anti-fascism" on both sides of the frontier. On the contrary: anti-fascism became a propagandistic Marxist slogan intended to function as decoy for the bourgeois-national minority in the FRG. (It didn't, by the way.)

The condemnation of national socialism amalgamated in both German states with the rejection of the opposite regime. Western studies in totalitarianism compared common features of fascist and communist regimes, and this descended to the political sphere as the formula red = brown. Eastern studies in modern imperialism underlined the common features of fascist and capitalist regimes. This led to the belief that in the FRG neo-fascist political forces and ideologies were of real or even dominant importance, sort of strange ideological triangles.

## The New Armed Forces

The implications of the ideological triangles would, of course, not be acceptable in the state being criticized. In the GDR, studies in total-

itarianism are regarded as devilish bourgeois propaganda. And the undeniable continuity of leading persons in several sections of society from
(in some cases) the Kaiserreich to the FRG[3] is mostly regarded in the
West as the consequence of a decent process of re-education and re-
orientation.

The general problem of how to reject national socialist values and
behavior came up once again during the discussion about rearmament.
The Reichswehr, although certainly not Nazi-minded, had played a sin-
ister role in 1933 and 1934. The Wehrmacht had not only followed
Hitler's armament policy but had even accelerated it.[4] It had led Hitler's
war. If now new armed forces are to be founded, asked a West German
historian, will there not be the real danger of a revitalization of all the
negative traditions in the relationship between the political and the
military power?[5]

The political leaders in both German states were strictly determined
to prevent the possibility of a strong military influence on the political
system. So the process of building up the new armed forces took place
with an unusually high display of civil control. As the years went by, this
display developed more and more into routine (perhaps also because the
concept of civil control became inadequate). But there is no doubt that
both the Bundeswehr and the NVA are the loyal instruments of their
political leaders. As both societies demonstrate different ways of functioning, so do their institutional and ideological frameworks of civil
control differ.

Not only must civil control extinguish national socialist and, in a
broader sense, Wilhelminian-militaristic traditions, but it has another
(and increasingly important) task: to prevent the establishment of apolitical, professional, and technological traditions incorporated by the
Nur-Soldat ("just-a-soldier-don't-care-for-the-rest"). This type of soldier
was cultivated by Seeckt during the Weimar Republic. The soldier and
especially the officer of the Bundeswehr is expected to be a "citizen in
uniform" and therefore a firm and convinced democrat. The soldier and
especially the officer of the NVA is expected to develop a firm "socialist
conviction."

We can see that the configuration of the ideological triangle is reflected on the level of the armed forces. "The soldier of the Bundeswehr—and this distinguishes him from his predecessor in the
Wehrmacht and from the comrades of his year's class serving in the
NVA—is to define himself as a 'soldier for peace'. . . . He does not obey
because he has to, but because he is conscientious; he does not serve
because he has to, but because he feels responsibility."[6] In a new publica-

tion from the GDR one can read: "The soldiers of a socialist army do not only possess considerable military and military-technical knowledge. This and good shooting-results may also be a characteristic of well-trained soldiers of an imperialist army. Socialist armed forces, however, have a greater fighting capacity because they have a higher fighting morale than any imperialist army."[7] The compulsory service is regarded in both states as a politically necessary type of army!

The permanent purpose of the political and military leaders of both armed forces in order to assure a possibly total subjective (ideological) *and* objective (institutional) political control of the soldiers is two-fold. Probable conflicts between civil and military parts of the elites are to be prevented. In addition, the integration of the soldier augments his efficiency. If a soldier, so goes the philosophy, understands and accepts the overall purpose and sense of his work, he can better resist the pitfalls of everyday routine.

## Resolute Cultivation of Traditions

The public debate on military traditions in the FRG started vehemently at the beginning of the 1950s.[8] Wolf Graf von Baudissin, the most impressive and consistently reform-oriented member of the founding fathers of the Bundeswehr, recalls the fact that the Dienststelle Blank (the predecessor of the Ministry of Defense) was confronted with that subject without being prepared to take a position.[9] At that time, former members of the Wehrmacht intensified the discussion because they expected a general rehabilitation *before* the start of rearmament. Their plea was that "the" German soldier had been "misused" by the political leadership, but that this "misuse" had nothing to do with their old military traditions, values, and behavior. Baudissin and some other future officers of the Bundeswehr did not agree with that opinion, and they were strongly supported by leading political representatives of the two big parties CDU/CSU and SPD. The small liberal party advocated the "traditionalistic" position.[10] But this position was overruled, not only because of interior reasons but also because of considerations concerning the international situation of West Germany. The revival of too many symbols from the German Reich would have increased the already existing political mistrust in Eastern and Western Europe.

The Bundeswehr thus tried to get rid of a considerable number of the German military traditions. In 1957, the not very popular *Handbuch Innere Führung* was published by the Ministry of Defense. It was intended

to help the new armed forces to find their way through the obscure jungle
of rightist, leftist, and all other sorts of political ideologies. As to the
problem of military traditions, the manual remarked:

> The new laws of our FRG have re-installed the basis of our German tradi-
> tion. The Third Reich had interrupted the continuity of our history and
> removed the ramparts of western tradition. It is now our task as soldiers of
> the Bundeswehr to fill our heritage with new life. This needs two precondi-
> tions, (1) that we choose deliberately an already established tradition which
> is characterized for instance by the name of General Ludwig Beck . . .
> (2) that we develop patience and confidence and wait for the growing up of
> new symbols, new forms and new manifestations of tradition.[11]

Patience and confidence were rare at times. This was mainly the
consequence of the dilemma concerning the Wehrmacht. Which type of
Wehrmacht soldier should be praised as a model? The officer who fought
bravely, because he was a nationalist or perhaps even for some time a
national socialist? Or the officer who fought bravely and did not care for
politics? Or the one who joined the resistance? Or all together, providing
they accepted now the norms and values of the democratic society? (And
it was, of course, not only a problem at the officer level.)

For many soldiers of the Bundeswehr this kind of question seemed to
be rather dull. They preferred a more or less apolitical, professional
tradition. Therefore the Ministry of Defense intervened a second time.
In 1965, after a long period of preparation, the "Decree on Tradition"
came into being.[12]

The decree consists of three chapters. The first chapter deals (it is,
after all, a German document) with "principles." It defines tradition as
the *valid* heritage of the past. The cultivation of tradition is seen as part
of the soldier's education. The focus of all cultivation of tradition in the
Bundeswehr has to be the overall military mission. Thorough knowledge
of the historical development of human institutions, deep moral convictions as well as individual and social virtues such as fearlessness, courage,
and bravery will form the fundaments of a military tradition worthy of
the name. The Bundeswehr should be self-confident enough to generate
new traditions of its own.

The second chapter summarizes "Valid traditions of German military
history." There one finds, among other information, remarkable words
about the military opposition to Hitler: "If the head of the state (Dienst-
herr) breaks the oath, resistance out of a sense of responsibility is legitimate. Resistance cannot and should not, however, become a principle in
and of itself."

The last chapter provides some more detailed instructions. The limits of acknowledged tradition are clearly drawn. There is no official connection between units of the Bundeswehr and units of former armed forces in Germany. The soldiers are encouraged to stay in contact with veterans. No veteran should be excluded from those contacts, but any official meeting with veterans should at the same time underline the substantial differences between the armed forces of the past and the present. The decree finishes with a programmatic wish: "Every arrangement for the cultivation of military traditions is to serve as an instrument of education and to strengthen the commitment of the soldier of the Bundeswehr to his present mission."

The decree is still binding. Its impact, however, has not been paramount. For a longer period, problems of military tradition seemed to have lost relevance. This development changed direction in the middle of the 1970s. Some single, and as such, not so important, cases of deviant behavior in the field of military traditions aroused public attention. But it is, apart from these incidents, mostly a general need within the civil society of the FRG to deal with the past roots of the present political, social, and cultural life that has initiated a growing military need for tradition. The 200th birthday of Clausewitz in 1980 was, for instance, a welcome and well-employed occasion for looking back mildly. One can easily suppose that military tradition—its contents and forms—will be a subject of growing importance in the coming years.

In the GDR, the NVA was confronted from the beginning with a resolute political directive "from above" to cultivate some positive traditions. The great awareness of this need is partly due to the desire to fix the limits of Western influence. One can always find in East German publications on military tradition a strong condemnation of the "negative" traditions of the Bundeswehr. Another part of the East German method of cultivating military traditions is intended to prove that the NVA is the first democratic, socialist army in Germany and that it is therefore the continuation and peak of all German revolutionary and progressive military traditions.

As in the Bundeswehr, the cultivation of military traditions in the NVA is regarded as part of the political education of the soldiers. In a 1973 study, Dale Herspring has observed a particularly successful instance of this political education:

Although there was concern with building the foundation of a modern military, politicisation of the NVA officer corps nevertheless took precedence. Despite the importance of the technical skills of former members of the Wehrmacht, the party quickly decided to dismiss any of them judged less than completely reliable politically. It would be better to sacrifice skill and start from the beginning to build a dependable force, rather than take the chance that the gun might one day control the party rather than the other way around. At no time did the level of political control decrease throughout the course of this study.[13]

Nor has it decreased up to the present.

In 1966, the Minister of National Defense, Hoffmann, published an article in the theoretical organ of the SED, *Einheit*, that gives a well-documented survey of the different endeavors to cultivate revolutionary and progressive military traditions in the NVA. Hoffmann defines cultivation of military traditions as a means for the better fullfilment of the NVA's historical mission. "We understand by cultivation of traditions all measures which inform the members of the NVA about their exemplars and precursors in Germany's past, which develop their feeling for honour and which help them to fulfill their fighting mission more conscientiously."[14] This definition is representative of numerous publications in the GDR, because it is authoritative. Tradition, to sum up, has to sustain the ideological beliefs of the soldier.

No wonder that the NVA has its own decree on tradition. The aging process of these directives seems to be unusually quick: the first (April 1969) "Order for the Cultivation of Revolutionary and Progressive Military Traditions and for the Occupation with Tradition in the NVA" (*Traditionspflegeordnung*) was replaced in January 1978 by the "Order of the Minister for National Defense for the Cultivation of Military Traditions in the NVA and in the Border-Troops of the GDR" (*Traditionspflegeordnung*).[15] The new version is a signal for some new accents. (Unfortunately, I was not able to read either of the quoted documents, but one can reconstruct their main contents.)

## Tradition and History

"There may be men in the German military history who were excellent and very brave and highly decorated soldiers. But when they deny our constitutional state, on which we, soldiers of the Bundeswehr, have taken an oath or when they even insult it, they and their names are not worthy to belong to our tradition."[16] The former Generalinspekteur, Wust, underlined with these words (directed toward Colonel Rudel, a former pilot of the Wehrmacht and a political right-winger) the Bundeswehr's difficult task of separating valid, that is, "good" from "bad" traditions. This task should not, in the words of Walter Scheel, then

President of the FRG, imply a directive "to put aside all dark and prob-lematic times of our history."[17] The decisive criterion for separating different elements of history should be their possible convergence with a democratic-republican constitution. This is not so difficult in theory. However, at times when only a handful of people are really interested in history at all, it *is* difficult to fulfill in practice. Even now, the growing interest in the past has not yet found enough "good" traditional material. One has to recognize a sort of a spiritual vacuum.

This is not the case in the GDR. The Marxist ideology offers a stable image of what history is about and where it leads to. The leaders of the NVA always had a consistent description of the past in mind. "Not every occupation with history is cultivation of tradition. Cultivation of tradi-tion means a deliberate selection and a resolute underlining of certain actions, objective contexts, and developments and their use for socialist education of the mind."[18] Yet, if we examine what has been selected and used, we have to cancel the word "consistent." For the list of useful historical traditions is a rather short one. It is reduced mainly to the following events: the farmers' war at the beginning of the 16th century; the national liberation war against Napoleon at the beginning of the 19th century; the revolution of 1848; the revolution or half revolution of 1918–1919; the fights against the *Freikorps* and rightist movements (Kapp-Putsch) during the Weimar Republic; the anti-fascist fight of the international brigades in Spain 1936–39; and the anti-fascist fight during World War II.

German military history does not, it seems, offer many "revolution-ary and progressive military traditions." This is one of the reasons why the traditions of the international labor movement and of other coun-tries—especially of the Soviet Union and its Red Army—appear on the list of "good" and cultivatible traditions. From the 1950s to the present time a steady stream of publications with short descriptions of these traditions have ensured their popularity among the soldiers of the NVA.[19]

## New Traditions

On both sides of the frontier the leaders of the armed forces were eager to develop new traditions. This is understandable in light of Germany's difficult history. In the FRG the initiatives for new traditions have come mainly from the moderate left. As there are only a few moderate-left soldiers (the best-known is Graf von Baudissin), it is left to groups of civilians to act. Thus a workshop of the SPD published in 1977 a number of "Principles concerning the cultivation of traditions in the Bundeswehr." The last of these principles reads: "Tradition for the Bundeswehr begins *mainly* with the construction of a democracy after World War II."[20] As one can imagine, a great number of the officer corps of the Bundeswehr do not favor this principle greatly. Neither do the other two parties in the Bundestag and the moderate-right wing of the SPD. They all have different arguments for their opposition. A good point is scored by the speaker of the FDP-faction for military affairs in the Bundestag, Möllemann: "If we restrict tradition in the Bundeswehr to the time of its existence, we cut off many experiences and actions of former generations. These experiences, when liberal, republican or democratic, do have a certain meaning for today."[21]

The discussion is still going on. Evidently, there is not a real dichotomy between old and new traditions. Both are possibly useful. The question is where and how to put the correct emphasis.

The NVA seems to be a little ahead in this discussion. We may suspect that the new version of the *Traditionspflegeordnung* of 1978 brought exactly that emphasis: to carry on with historical traditions, but to double the endeavors to initiate new traditions. Thus the decree orders that newly founded "tradition circles" within the units be occupied with the histories of their units. A number of publications have already appeared (mostly for internal use only). As one reviewer puts it: "More and more units recognize the educational benefit for and the mobilizing influence of the troop-historiography on the solution of military tasks."[22] The study of current history has had, it seems, a direct practical effect, unlike the preoccupation with the past or with heroic victories that distinguish other armed forces. The problem of personal identification is smaller. Everyone can see that there is some progress and, furthermore, the integration of the soldier into *his* unit is accelerated. There is also some skepticism. This can be deduced from a passage in an article by one of the experts in the NVA for all questions of military tradition: "Some people argue that our new military traditions lack heroic elements, because they did not . . . originate in fighting and war."[23] But this sort of argument is strictly rejected.

## Conclusions

Most attempts to cultivate traditions in either of the German armed forces are not very efficient. As a rule, all efforts with direct and personal reference are more successful. Therefore, the practice of troop historiography seems to be a good idea. The traditional military folklore, naming ceremonies for ships, and barracks for model-soldiers or model-civilians (mostly politicians, by the way), and other rituals are of higher importance for the civil public and perhaps for retired and retiring generals than for the rank and file.

There is one remarkable exception, but only in the FRG because of its political system. As soon as there is a public debate about a certain military tradition, an emotional escalation starts, and its political relevance increases rapidly. The cultivation of a well-chosen set of military traditions is after all an elegant means of demonstrating the armed forces' conformity with the political and social norms and values of the civil society. That is why responsible leaders of armed forces cannot neglect this aspect of education, leadership, and organizational "foreign" policy.

Both German states and their armed forces have to bear a heavy load of "bad" traditions which they try to rid themselves of. Both try to select what are in their eyes "good" traditions from the past. That is relatively easy within the framework of historical materialism and not quite so easy in an ideologically pluralist society like the FRG.

In the official view of the NVA, the Bundeswehr incorporates all the "bad" traditions of German militarism and imperialism. The empirical basis of this argument is very thin indeed. Since the middle of the 1970s, the NVA has been encouraging the founding of new traditions which are meant to strengthen the rather weak position of historical traditions.

The Bundeswehr is really suffering from the ordeal of tradition, but in a specific way. Ideological pluralism determines the cultivation of military traditions, and that often means a low profile for any tradition. The efforts of the political and military leaders of the Bundeswehr to create elements of a democratic military tradition are noteworthy. So are the difficulties of its implementation. There is often an ideological compromise. In the future, the relationship with military traditions of both the past and the present will improve.

## Notes

1. Although this assumption is contested by most of my colleagues, my remarks about the difficulties of East–West comparisons are still apt. The sometimes vigorous debate about a possible convergence of the systems in the East and the West is a hint of those difficulties.

2. And I am afraid there are only a handful of studies that would warrant serious discussion.

3. See, for example, Wolfgang Zapf, *Wandlungen der deutschen Elite. Ein Zirkulationsmodell deutscher Führungsgruppen 1919–1961* (Munich: Piper, 1961); Detlef Bald, *The German Officer Corps: Caste or Class?*, in *Armed Forces and Society* 5(1979), pp. 642 ff.

4. Wilhelm Deist, "Die Aufrüstung der Wehrmacht," in *Deist/Messerschmidt/Volkmann/Wette, Ursachen und Voraussetzungen der deutschen Kriegspolitik* (Stuttgart: Deutsche Verlags-Anstalt, 1979), pp. 418 ff.

5. Hans Herzfeld, "Die Bundeswehr und das Problem der Tradition," in G. Picht, ed., *Studien zur politischen und gesellschaftlichen Situation der Bundeswehr*, vol. 1 (Witten/Berlin: Eckart, 1965), p. 37.

6. Peter von Schubert, "Introduction," Wolf Graf von Baudissin, *Soldat für den Frieden. Entwürfe für eine zeitgemässe Bundeswehr* (Munich: Piper, 1969), pp. 7 f.

7. Edgar Doehler, Rudolf Falkenberg, *Militärische Traditionen der DDR und der NVA* (Berlin: Militärverlag der DDR, 1979), p. 130.

8. See, for example, Wilfried von Bredow, "El problema de la 'tradición rota' en las Fuerzas Armados de la República Federal de Alemania," in *Revista de Estudios Politicos* (Madrid), 12(1979), pp. 163 ff.

9. Wolf Graf von Baudissin, "Gedanken zur Tradition," unpublished paper, July 1978.

10. *Handbuch Innere Führung. Hilfen zur Klärung der Begriffe* (Bonn, 1957), pp. 73 f.

11. Dietrich Wagner, *FDP und Wiederbewaffnung. Die wehrpolitische Orientierung der Liberalen in der Bundesrepublik Deutschland 1949–1955* (Boppard: H. Boldt 1978), pp. 155 ff.

12. "Bundeswehr und Tradition" (Fü B I 4 Az. 35-08-07)," in *Information für die Truppe* (Beilage), 9 (1965).

13. Dale Roy Herspring, *East German Civil-Military Relations: The Impact of Technology 1949–72* (New York: Praeger, 1973), p. 186.

14. Heinz Hoffmann, "Traditionen und Traditionspflege der Nationalen Volksarmee," in *Sozialistische Landesverteidigung. Ausreden und Aufsätze 1963–1970* (Berlin: Deutscher Militärverlag, 1971), p. 463.

15. The decree of 1969 is mentioned in Horst Syrbe, "Zur Pflege der revolutionären Traditionen in der Nationalen Volksarmee," in H. Meier, W. Schmidt, eds., *Geschichtsbewusstsein und sozialistische Gesellschaft* (Berlin: Pub 1970), p. 157. The decree of 1978 is quoted by Siegfried Heinze, "Zur Erforschung und Propagierung der Geschichte von Truppenteilen der NVA und der Grenztruppen der DDR," in *Militärgeschichte*, 18 (1979), p. 539.

16. Harald Wust, "Bundeswehr und Tradition" (Address at the Mührungsakademie of the Bundeswehr, June 30, 1978), mimeo., p. 27.

17. Walter Scheel, "Über die sittlichen Grundlagen von Verteidigungsbereitschaft und demokratischem Bewusstsein," in *Bulletin der Bundesregierung*, April 7, 1978: 280.

18. Karl Greese, "Alfred Voerster, Zur Herausbildung sozialistischer Traditionen der Nationalen Volksarmee," in *Militärgeschichte*, 16 (1977), p. 263.

19. The newest publication in this vein is Doehler and Falkenberg's *Militärische Traditionen*.

20. *Frankfurter Rundschau*, August 31, 1977.

21. Jürgen W. Möllemann, "F.D.P. und Innere Führung," in G. Verheugen, ed., *Das Wichtigste ist der Frieden* (Baden-Baden: Nomos 1980).

22. Heinze, "Zur Erforschung," p. 543.

23. Paul Heider, "Militärische Traditionen der DDR und ihrer Streitkräfte. Probleme ihrer Kontinuität und ihres Entstehens," in *Militärgeschichte*, 18(1979), p. 443.

# The Israeli Woman in Combat

NANCY L. GOLDMAN
WITH
KARL L. WIEGAND

In the general cross-cultural and historical study of women in combat[1] in the twentieth century, Israel occupies a unique position. It is often cited as a country in which women have served in combat and, by implication, can be looked upon as a model, or at least as a source of information, to assist today's policymakers who are dealing with the question of utilizing women in combat. A more recent viewpoint, however, almost laments

This research was supported by contract agreement DAH19-78-C-0011 from the United States Army Research Institute for the Behavioral and Social Sciences. The views expressed in this article are those of the authors and do not necessarily represent those of the sponsor.

We wish to express our appreciation to Brig. General Ben-Porat, and Col. M. Eini, Assistants Defense and Armed Forces Attachés Embassy of Israel; Tamar Eldar-Avidar, Attache for Women's Affairs, Embassy of Israel; Capt. Nurit Rosen, Public Relations Officer, Israel Defense Forces; Mrs. Devora Nechushtan, Washinton, D.C.; and to other Israeli officials with whom we have spoken.

that Israeli women have "regressed" because they no longer serve in combat, serving instead in an auxiliary role. We contend that the reverse of both viewpoints is true, i.e., that the combat use of women in Israel's twentieth-century history provides little information directly applicable to the questions posed by today's policy makers and that women in the Israeli Defense Forces have not "regressed," but have gradually expanded their role in the recent past.

The extent to which women have functioned in the defense organizations of Israel since the early 1900s has varied with a number of factors: manpower needs, the dominance of tradition in sex role definition, the status of the military organization (irregular or regular), and the method of raising manpower (volunteer or conscription). The Zionist ideal of sexual equality did not have major impact upon the definition of women's roles in the military organizations although these ideals did have an indirect and long-term influence. After statehood the opinions of the political electorate had to be considered when defining the roles of women in the military.

This paper will examine the roles of women in the defense organizations of Israel in terms of the factors cited above. It will highlight the social conditions which gave rise to the use of women in combat, and it will trace the conditions which led to the more common case of their being excluded from combat roles. We will view women's participation chronologically, in four periods: the prestatehood period, the War of Independence, the early statehood period (the first twenty years), and the contemporary period. Official statistical data concerning the utilization of women in the defense organizations during these periods are unavailable. The Israel Defense Forces' (IDF) official policy does not permit disclosure of this information.[2] The data given are, therefore, approximate and obtained largely from the published literature.

There also are no published official histories focusing specifically on women in the Israeli military. Our analysis, therefore, draws largely upon information offered in published histories of the Israeli army and the War of Independence, in biographical material, in recently published and unpublished reports and studies on women in the IDF and in Israeli society, in available official documents, and in informal interviews which we have conducted in the United States with a small sample of men and women who have been associated either with the prestatehood, underground paramilitary groups, or with the IDF within the past ten years. Every effort has been made to weigh the information obtained from these sources for potential bias and accuracy.

## Women in Jewish Defense Units Prior to the War of Independence

While Orthodox Judaism placed women in traditional female work roles, which stressed their nurturing attributes and taught that a woman's place was in the home, the Zionists who settled in Palestine had an ideology that admitted of an expanded, more equal role for women in the agrarian social structure which they established. "In Europe we planned and dreamed about our future in Zion; there there would be no distinction between men and women."[3] Zionism was a partly secular-sectarian movement which stressed sexual equality, especially with regard to work roles. Many women believed that they had the right to labor exactly as men did and that in so doing they would be emancipated; however, neither in production, agriculture, nor defense did they make great strides in achieving this emancipation. The expansion of woman's role followed an arduous and uneven path.

The stereotype of Israeli women, equal with men, has its roots in this Zionist social ideology, but, although some of the women settlers in Palestine did work in "men's production jobs" as laborers and in agriculture, many did not. "The girls who had the opportunity to work in the fields were . . . few and far between, and even within the pioneering, revolutionary labor movement in the Land of Israel women were relegated to their traditional tasks—housekeeping and particularly kitchen work."[4] Traditional sex role definition was still in evidence even among those settlers who were most committed to the ideology of Zionism.

During the early years of the kibbutzim (circa 1914) women filled traditional service jobs while men were involved in production jobs. The male pioneers resisted equality in work opportunities, believing women to be less "productive." A shortage of work also contributed to a lack of opportunity for women to work in the fields. In the first kibbutz, Degnia, women were not even considered full-fledged members. They served as cooks and laundresses for the kibbutz while the men were paid by the Palestine office for their work in production.

During these early years, prior to World War I, the male population was much larger than the female population. This fact helped to perpetuate a traditional division of labor. Unless men were to share in the kitchen and laundry work, all of the women were needed to do these jobs. For a time the growth of the female population was great enough to produce an overflow who could work in the fields. Furthermore, as the kibbutz movement developed, men were sometimes assigned to service jobs on a temporary basis.

Although there were women who wanted to implement the egalitarian ideals of Zionism, and wanted to work in agricultural or production jobs, the percentage of women engaged in agriculture or production actually decreased with time. For example, Garber-Talmon's 1956 study of eight kibbutzim in the Ichud Federation shows that in this group the percentage of women so employed decreased from 50 percent in the early 1920s to 15.2 percent in 1948, and 10.4 percent in 1954. Concurrent with this decrease was an increase in the percentage of women engaged in service jobs. The demand for services increased, in large part because of an increase in the number of children. Child care was considered a woman's task.[5] In short, the division of labor on the kibbutz for the most part followed traditional male–female lines—a trend that became more pronounced as the years passed.

When it came to the matter of armed defense, the traditional values and ideology of Jewish society clearly prevailed. The first of the defense organizations formed by the Jews in 1909, the Hashomer (literally meaning the Guard) was a small organization of paid, full-time, armed guards hired by the Hashomer Association (or "Shomer") to serve as watchmen and to protect the Jewish settlements from Arabs.[6] Although *Sepher Hashomer* (*The Book of Hashomer*) contains the names of twenty-four women among the total of 105 members,[7] these women were members of the Hashomer Association, not guards in the Hashomer. These women members helped to plan the defense system and hire the male guards. Also, many women may have been listed as members because they were related to male members. Mania Schochet, for example, was a "spokesman" for the Hashomer and was the wife of one of the founders of the Hashomer Association.

Despite the fervor of the early Zionist movement, sex role differentiation was prevalent in the pre-World War I period. Both external and internal pressures fostered this differentiation. According to one authority, the Arabs would have considered the Jews unmanly if they allowed their women to defend the community.[8] At the same time, according to Maimon, those women who did take a turn at guarding their settlement in the absence of a professional were considered "freakish" by the other women.[9]

The tug-of-war between woman's role according to traditional Jewish values and that role as envisioned in Zionist ideology was not only to be found on the kibbutz. It continued as Jewish women faced the decision of what role to play during World War I. Many members of the women's movement were reluctant to serve in the military. When the Jewish Legion was formed in 1918 to fight with the British, there was no automatic consensus among the members of the Working Women's Council that the women of Palestine should volunteer for service with the Legion or, if they did volunteer, should seek the same work roles as men. This was in spite of the fact that the Working Women's Council was composed of women who were seeking equal work roles with men in the Jewish civilian sector. Some members thought that women should stay at home to replace men in any type of job, menial or not, which was vacated as the men volunteered. Some of those who thought women should volunteer for the Legion along with the men "went so far as to assert that they should seek the same type of military service as men. Others thought they should assist the Legion by working as cooks, nurses and laundresses."[10] In a speech at the Women Workers' Conference in July 1918, Rachel Katznelson, a leader of the women's movement, discussed this controversy "and emphasized the historic significance of Jewish women fighting shoulder-to-shoulder with their husbands and brothers—*an unprecedented development in Jewish history.*"[11] Katznelson clearly implied that women had thus far not participated shoulder to shoulder with men in defense. In the end, it was the British who determined the role to be played by women in the Jewish Legion. While 200 women from Palestine volunteered, only those trained in nursing were accepted. This limited role, as well as the roles which the British gave to their own women's auxiliaries during this war, seems to have influenced the defense roles permitted to Israeli women after the war.

In the 1920s, following the establishment of the mandate government in Israel, the Arabs conducted bitter attacks against the growing Jewish community. In response to these attacks a people's defense organization, the Hagana (meaning defense) was organized clandestinely to replace the Hashomer guards. The Hagana was forced to be clandestine because the British forbade the Jews to bear arms, though they did not provide adequate defense for the Israeli settlements. Unlike the paid, full-time professional guards of the Hashomer, the Hagana was composed entirely of part-time volunteers. They received just enough training to guard the community during Arab attacks. During the early period of its existence, the Hagana was loosely organized and was designed for localized self-defense of the many isolated Jewish settlements against the Arab attacks of 1920, 1921, and 1929.

With the Arab terrorist attacks in 1929, which were much more severe than earlier attacks, the Hagana began to plan for defense on a "national" scale. It began to form a centralized organization. During the crisis period of 1936–1939, the Arab threat reached an unprecedented level. The Arabs' aims were to destroy as many Jewish settlements as possible, to prevent the development of new settlements, and to prevent Jews from establishing an independent state. It was during this period that the Hagana began to prepare for offensive military actions and to recognize the need for a permanently established military force instead of the semi-autonomous local home guard groups. The Hagana became a centrally controlled militia consisting of all able citizens willing to volunteer.

At this critical time the British military failed to provide appropriate defense for the Jews. The British mandatory administration proved to be an additional obstacle to Jewish ambitions for an independent homeland. Although the Nazi party had come to power in Germany in 1933 and many Jews wished to emigrate, the British issued a White Paper which restricted immigration and effectively revoked the Balfour Declaration (which had allowed for the establishment of a homeland for all Jews who wished to emigrate). Thus, the Jews in Palestine who were seeking an independent state identified the British mandatory administration, along with the Palestinian Arabs, as its enemy. All of these pressures were important in the Hagana's decision to expand and develop from a group of local home guard units into a people's militia—a military force. These factors likewise had their influence on the utilization of women in defense activities.

Yigal Allon, one of the Hagana's first professional soldiers, writes of the situation during this period: "Under the pressure of militant Arab nationalism the *Hagana* grew in size and strength; its membership included almost every Jew and Jewess working in an appropriate unit."[12]

Maimon, who was also actively involved in the work of the community at this time, indicates that the composition of the Hagana by 1936 included most "citizens" of the Jewish community including women, who participated in the "passive" methods of territorial defense.

> The entire Yishuv, on all levels, stood guard over each settlement; villages were expanded and production increased. In those difficult years, and directly following, new border settlements—'wall and tower' as they were called—were set up all over the country. . . . The numbers joining the *Hagana* grew steadily. The Yishuv was forced to arm itself, in the face of opposition from the Mandatory Government. . . . Many women belonged to the Hagana, and they too stood guard on the roads along with the men.[13]

This increased utilization of women should not be considered an expansion of their defense role. Since the 1920s, it had been necessary for women in Israel to be able to protect themselves and their children. Most of the women of the kibbutzim, because of the remote locations in which these settlements were built, received some training with shotguns and revolvers from the Hagana. This did not make them military personnel or combat soldiers. They are more accurately described as "armed pioneers"—citizens guarding their homes. Many were not even registered members of the Hagana. Furthermore, even though the women were trained for armed self-defense, it was usually the men who performed the defense duties.[14]

Of course, some women were more active than others. In 1937, on one kibbutz, women were given roles in all aspects of protective defense, that is, all non-offensive roles. In this same year, in another kibbutz, the first training course for women commanders was organized. Its title, *coursa*, which means "armchair," indicates both the passive character of the course, compared to the training given to men, and the attitude of the male commanders toward the appropriate role for women.[15] Some women were commanders of mixed groups, although usually as instructors. In one case, a woman was appointed post commander of her kibbutz in preparation for Arab invasions. Her job was to instruct immigrants, teenage youths, and some of the women in rifle practice. This was but token training, however, because each person was allowed to fire only five shots.[16] Membership in the Hagana after 1936 was, therefore, no longer unusual for women. Indeed, it was invited and expected once the defense organization was forced by serious threats from the Arabs and the British to reorganize and expand.[17]

As the Hagana's military policy became more aggressive and preparations began for the Jewish resistance against the mandatory government at the end of World War II, a sharper delineation could be seen between the protective defense roles of women and the offensive assault roles of men. The Hagana in 1940 added a field corps, called HISH, a permanent, mobile force consisting of part-time volunteers whose function was to carry out offensive operations. A garrison army, HIM, meaning guard corps, was established as a static home guard force consisting of "older men" (over twenty-five) and women. The women served principally as nurses and signalers. Most volunteers served in the HIM, the central function of which was to man defensive positions at the borders of each settlement. Girls and boys fourteen to seventeen years old were expected to train in paramilitary youth groups for service with the HIM if needed. The training they received was similar to that given to women—signals, self-defense, and first aid.

It is a piece of historical irony that as the Hagana developed militant, mobile forces and became less self-restrained, women were used in greater numbers, but the role they played was the same one of static defense which they had been performing as "citizens" without military status. Of course, this appears ironic only if it is assumed that women were eagerly seeking to serve in offensive operations. This was not unanimously the case, as can be seen in their attitude toward active military service in World War II.

Despite the fact that during World War II women were needed for military service, women themselves, even those in the working women's movement, were initially reluctant to volunteer. The dominant attitude was the traditional one that suitable roles for women during wartime were "guarding and all areas of noncombatant defense work at home." This attitude was explicitly spelled out by the Working Women's Council. A memo which was circulated during the war to its members stated: "Women must take an active part in guarding the settlements and in all areas of noncombatant defense work."[18] In 1942 a proclamation of this council further highlighted the sexual distinction between defense roles: "Let us as women soldiers, assume appropriate tasks."[19]

During the war, increasing numbers of women joined the Hagana for service at home and the British Auxiliaries for service abroad. In September 1943, there were 4,511 enlisted women and 245 women officers from the Jewish community of Palestine serving as volunteers with the Auxiliary Territorial Service (ATS), the British women's auxiliary.[20] They served mainly as drivers, nursing orderlies, switchboard operators, and store women. Most were sent to Egypt and Italy where they helped with the survivors from the Nazi extermination camps at the end of the war. Some also served with the Women's Auxiliary Air Force. This military experience was to be extremely influential in the definition of women's roles in the Israeli Defense Force to be formed after the state of Israel was established. Many of the women who stayed in Palestine became actively engaged in its defense, replacing the men who were serving with the British forces. Like the civilian women in Great Britain, women in the Hagana were trained in traditional (civilian) wartime roles for women: civil defense, first aid, and firefighting.

During this period the Palmach (literally translated, this abbreviation means commando battalions) was formed as the striking arm of the Hagana. In this organization the role of women was, for a while, somewhat different. The Palmach, formed in 1941, was a standing, mobile force of full-time volunteers, women as well as men. Compared to the HISH and the HIM, which were really paramilitary organizations, the Palmach, although part of an irregular army, was a professional military organization with professionally trained, full-time soldiers. It was formed as a standing reserve for mobilization in the event of Arab or German invasion. Initially it cooperated with the British to defend the Jewish community against German invasion. The members of the Palmach were, for the most part, Jews born in Palestine, known as sabras. At least 30 percent of these sabras had grown up on the kibbutzim. Compared to the Hagana, which was open to all who volunteered, the Palmach was an elite group of selected members. Although technically under the authority of the Hagana, the Palmach was an autonomous organization which was, in effect, a private army with its own regulations. Although elitist in its selection procedures, the Palmach ideology espoused the egalitarian principles of the Zionist movement.

The establishment of the Palmach, consisting of nine companies of commando troops, marked the beginning of the explicit use of women in Israeli combat units; however, the numbers of women (and men) were small. In 1944 there were 300 women and 1,000 men, plus 400 reservists, mostly men. In the fall of 1947, there were 2,100 active members and 1,000 in the active reserves. A recent news article reported that of the total Palmach membership of 6,000 in the 1948 war, 1,000, or approximately 16 percent, were women.[21] Although the number of women was small, the approximate proportion of the group represented by women was relatively high compared to that of the regular armies of Great Britain and the United States during World War II.[22]

If women in the Palmach enjoyed equal status with men during the early days, this equality was not long-lived. Within two years after its formation, sexual polarization had taken place. Even those women who had initially had training identical to the men's were, for the most part, assigned to the units as secretaries, nurses, and signalers.[23] Some served as guards along the roads and coast and some were commanders of mixed units—but usually not of units engaged in fighting. The traditional Israeli concept of the women's roles was generally in evidence. In 1943 the Hagana established rules that clearly relegated women to static defense positions. When a woman's unit was engaged in combat, the women were located at headquarters level. The policy established at this time reflected the Hagana officials' attitude toward coeducational training as well. It was stated that training in mixed units resulted in women competing with men—competition believed to be detrimental to their performance.[24]

The Palmach, in many respects somewhat autonomous from its Hagana parent unit, shared similar attitudes about women. Yigal Allon describes women's main contribution to the Palmach as "humanizing":

> The presence of women in combat units blurred and decreased the harshness of military life; it lent substance to the *Palmach* concept of an armed force free of militarism; and it precluded the brutalization of young men thrown

into an all-male society for months on end. The mobilization of daughters, sisters, sweethearts, and often wives turned the *Palmach* into a true people's army. . . .

Allon also writes in his history:

> The girls stormed at any proposed discrimination, arguing that it ran counter to the spirit of the new society being built in Palestine to restrict women to domestic chores, particularly since they had proven their competence as marksmen and sappers. In the end, the wiser counsel prevailed. The girls were still trained for combat, but placed in units of their own, so that they would not compete physically with men. Whenever possible, they were trained for defensive warfare only."[25]

These statements, coupled with the rules established by the Hagana, make it reasonable to infer that, although egalitarian with regard to roles in principle, in practice the Palmach relegated most women to auxiliary roles, as did the Hagana's HISH and HIM.

In spite of the general practice, there were several heroines among the Palmach volunteers who, during World War II, were involved in secret missions for the Allies. Two women, Hanna Senesh and Haviva Reich, were among twelve Palmach parachutists who were dropped into Yugoslavia. Both were captured and executed. Another heroine was Bracha Fold, who was killed in 1946 while defending Tel Aviv. Several other members of the Palmach became well known for their combat activities during the War of Independence.

At the end of the mandate period, the Hagana was still a volunteer and amateur militia. Even though it had expanded to include a mobile field force and commando units, it still had no full-time soldiers except those in the Palmach. The HISH field force was composed of part-time soldiers, and the HIM garrison force, which consisted of the majority of the members of the Hagana, had minimal, if any, training. Of 30,745 registered members of HIM in 1944, only 4,372 or 14 percent of the home guard were considered "trained."[26]

While a few women of the Palmach were reported to have been involved in sabotage activities against British installations, most women during this period (1945–1947) were used to aid illegal immigration, to guard the beaches and roads, to nurse, and to operate communications equipment.[27] Other women conducted terrorist activities against the British. These were women associated with Irgun and the Stern Gang, nonsocialist organizations which had split from the Hagana to pursue more aggressive tactics in the struggle against the British. There are no data available indicating the numbers of women in these guerrilla bands, or exactly what their roles were prior to the start of the War of Independence in 1947. Neither group was large. It has been estimated that by the end of 1947, at the groups' peak, the Irgun had 2,000 and the Stern Gang had 400 members. They concentrated on terrorism, street fighting, and sabotage. According to one estimate, women accounted for 50 percent of the membership;[28] however, there is no evidence as to the source or accuracy of this figure.

Even though it appears that the majority of women who participated in military activity during this period were given auxiliary roles, the few who did engage in direct combat activities helped to sustain the image of the Israeli liberated woman during the prestatehood period.[29] The civil sector also had its liberated women, as some women engaged in nontraditional work roles, ordinarily defined as male ones.

Thus in the period prior to the War of Independence, women generally played a limited, auxiliary role in the Jewish response to military threats, either in the local semi-autonomous units or in the Hagana or the Palmach. On the frontier and outlying settlements women were on occasion involved in armed self-defense and a few were used for secret missions during World War I and World War II; however, in the main, the Zionist egalitarian principle of sexual equality was not extended to the realm of defense.

## The Mobilization of Women During the War of Independence

In November of 1947 the United Nations voted to terminate, as of May 1, 1948, the British mandate government and establish a Jewish state in Palestine. The Palestinian Arabs protested with full-scale hostilities. By the time the mandate government would be fully dismantled, the Jews knew that they would likely face five additional regular Arab armies in neighboring nations, which would surpass them in numbers of men and quality of equipment. The Jews had only the Hagana and the other small irregular guerrilla organizations at the onset of these hostilities. In the first stage of the War of Independence (before conscription had mustered enough men and women into the standing army to mount an offensive), fighting was just as it had been during past guerrilla wars with the Arabs—ambush, sniping, terrorism, and street fighting.[30] The Hagana's goal was survival for the Jewish state, and with the shock of the Arab attack the official Hagana policy restricting women to noncombat roles was not enforced. Whether a registered member of the Hagana or not, every able-bodied Jew participated in the defense of the state (excepting the ultra-Orthodox Jews who were pacifists).

Upon the outset of hostilities the Hagana hastened its transformation to a regular, full-time army. Registration began immediately and all men seventeen to twenty-five years of age were called up for duty. The number of full-time soldiers increased as men left their work to fight for their country.[31]

Most women served in the HIM in traditional female military roles, nursing and signals, which many had learned in England. The men and women of the HIM guarded the defensive positions at the perimeter of each settlement. Many women in the HISH had served in the British forces during World War II and continued to serve in similar auxiliary capacities. Women of the Palmach, HISH, Stern Gang, and Irgun were used in armed defense in the first phase of the war, during the "Battle for the Roads." This "battle" took place when the Arabs tried to starve out the Jews by preventing their convoys from transporting supplies on the Jerusalem Road. Women then served as armed escorts for the convoys because, unlike men, they could hide weapons under their clothes where members of the British army and police were not allowed to search. The girls accompanied the convoys disguised as passengers. This role was similar to those of smuggling and guard duty, which they had previously played. Some women members of these groups were also involved in guerrilla warfare. Throughout the war, however, most women were in support roles as signalers, runners, and nurses. These vital roles subjected them to the dangers of combat but were not, in fact, direct combat roles. Women in the kibbutzim served as guards and defended their settlements against attack, usually as "auxiliaries" to the men. Most of these women were cooks, nurses, and signalers. "Women took their turn with the men, but it was understood that in the case of real trouble the women would remain in the shelter."[32]

The Palmach took the shock of the initial Arab attack in November 1947. Although women had been trained along with men for such a national emergency, their actual mobilization with the Palmach units was more a result of the dire emergency than of an intentional plan. As noted above, in 1943 military policy had decreed that women were to be restricted from going into battle with their units. They were to be used in "static defense" roles.

In spite of the policy, there is evidence that some women did, in fact, fight along with the men. Yigal Allon, commander of the Palmach during the period, described the activities of some of these women. He wrote that on April 3, 1948, a company platoon consisting of ten men in various jobs and fifty women seized a commanding position on the Safad-Ein Zeitim road to ensure the safe crossing of a convoy. A few other heroines were involved in combat missions. One was Netiva Ben-Yehuda, the "Yellow Ghost," as the Arabs called her because of her hair. She was a demolitions expert and commander of a Palmach unit. She reportedly signaled the attack on Safed by detonating an explosive charge. She also set an explosive charge against a wall of an Arab police station while under heavy fire.[33]

Another heroine was Judith Jaharan, "The Black Devil," known also as "the girl in the green skirt." A member of the Irgun, she was said to have served as an infantryman and medic. On one occasion she fired from a rooftop at passing Arabs and killed many of them. Lorch also writes of a girl who, leading a Palmach section, had been instructed to "assault a building and lob in a hand grenade, and break inside."[34] Yet such women fighters were the exception. Even in the Palmach during the first part of the War of Independence most women served in combat support roles. There is no indication in any of the sources of the numbers of women who actually engaged in either assault or even defensive combat. All sources agree that the great majority of registered women were in the HIM (garrison army) and that the Palmach, Irgun, and Stern Gang were all small groups.

In the meantime, registration and conscription of Jewish men and women were transforming the Hagana from the irregular guerrilla group into a regular standing army. The registered membership in the Palmach at the beginning of the war, November 1947, was approximately 2,000 members (300 women); in the HISH, 6,000–10,000 members (some women); in the HIM and the youth battalions, approximately 32,000. Altogether there were about 50,000 men and 10,000 women serving. By October 1948, the peak strength reportedly reached 120,000, of whom 12,000 were women.[35]

With this growth in the number of men and drop in the percentage of women (from 16 percent to 9 percent), the Hagana reached a condition which permitted it to embark on offensive operations against the Arabs and enforce its policy concerning women in combat. The women were removed from direct fighting roles and remained with their units as clerks, nurses, runners, and signalers. Many who had been trained in the Palmach were used as teachers of new troops. Some women in the kibbutzim continued their guard duty in cases in which there were insufficient numbers of men. All these roles, while auxiliary, exposed women to grave dangers because the whole country was a battleground. As Shoshana Raziel, a former Irgun officer, stated in an interview, "There was terrible danger in everything that we did. You didn't have to be in combat to fight. You can do as much with a telephone. It is no big deal to put that gun in a violin case and stroll down the street past British officers as though you're just coming from your music lesson."[36]

The restriction of women to noncombat jobs, or jobs of "static defense," was in accord with official Hagana policy set in 1943, but it was also the result of several other concerns. Women were thought to be a distraction, in the sense of a worry (not sexual) to the men.[37] Of particular concern was the fact that the Arabs were especially humiliated by having a woman kill any of their men and were known to be particularly brutal in their retaliation. In fact, Netiva Ben-Yehuda had to be moved to a different location because the Arabs were seeking revenge for her attacks. Another woman fighter who had been captured by the Arabs had been brutally raped, killed, and mutilated.[38]

The women felt great pressure to prove themselves to the men, but there was reportedly some concern about their performance in battle. In one instance a girl had been accused of delaying a raid against an Arab community because she did not, as instructed, throw a hand grenade into a building and break in. She had heard a baby crying. There are two interpretations of this event given in the published literature. One indicates that the woman had been explicitly instructed to hit only gang leaders and agitators and, therefore, was following instructions. The other is that, being a woman, she was too soft to hurt a baby. She was therefore inadequate to the job.[39] Whichever interpretation is correct, her behavior influenced men's attitudes toward all women in combat.

Another concern emerged as the Hagana was transformed to a regular standing army. As a regular force it was in the public eye. Its members were no longer anonymous. Its manpower conscription and utilization policies were to be publicly legislated by the new state. In order to make the conscription of women consonant with the values of a nation with a politically powerful conservative minority, it was important to define women's military roles as clearly noncombatant and similar to those which women held in the civil sector. Similarly, in England during World War II, when women were conscripted, their status was clearly defined as noncombatant even though many argued that those women serving on the antiaircraft sites were in fact "gunners."[40]

In summary, some women performed combat tasks in an emergency period; however, during the Hagana's transformation into a regular army, women were removed from such tasks. When those participating in the army were no longer anonymous, when the army came out into the open, when warfare became conventional instead of irregular, when military service was no longer voluntary, when there were enough men to fulfill the combat missions, women were removed from combat roles and were assigned to support, and later educational, duties. The dominant attitude

toward women's utilization in paramilitary and regular military organizations throughout this entire period was traditionalist. Egalitarian principles did not make substantial inroads into this traditionally male realm of
endeavor. In the following sections, we will show that political pressures
were added to the traditional social pressures that influenced the roles of
women in the new Israel Defense Forces.

## Women's Roles in the Israel Defense Forces: The First Two Decades

The state of Israel was established on May 14, 1948, a state of emergency
was declared on May 20, and the Israel Defense Forces (IDF) were
organized on May 28, 1948, when Israel Defense Order No. 4 was issued
by Israel's provisional government providing the legal framework for the
military forces of the state. In September 1949 national conscription for
women as well as men was established; however, women were not to
serve in integrated units with equal responsibilities in the new IDF. The
women's organization was based on the British Women's Auxiliaries in
which many women had served during World War II. The new women's
organization was called CHEN, which means "charm." An official pamphlet indicates that this was the image which the IDF desired its women's
service unit to portray in the contemporary period.[41] Women in the
CHEN were trained in self-defense by officers of the Hagana and the
Palmach. Eventually the CHEN was to serve only as a training unit. In
the 1970s women were integrated into IDF units after their training.
    With statehood, the Israeli government and the armed forces pur-
posefully decided to eliminate women from combat units and, in effect,
to implement the policy with regard to the utilization of women set forth
by the Hagana in 1943 and informally implemented the month prior to
independence, as discussed above. In summary, their combat-related
roles became those officially defined as ones of "indirect reinforcement of
the IDF's combat forces." Women were limited to a variety of administrative, professional, and service duties to release male soldiers for
fighting missions. They were also to be trained for emergency self-defense. Women were removed from combat units. They were taken out of
the tank corps, the artillery, and the infantry units in which some had
served in the earlier stages of the War of Independence. The Defense
Service Law, adopted in 1949, made women between the ages of eighteen and thirty-four liable for conscription for service with the CHEN in
peacetime as well as wartime. Conscripts were also required to serve in
the reserves after their active duty tour.
    The restriction of women's roles to those of indirect combat support

clearly separated women's roles from combat functions. This was a political decision meant to satisfy both those religious parties which opposed any military service for women and the general public, which held conservative attitudes towards suitable roles for women. It was, however, also a decision that was consonant with the attitudes and strategy of the military leadership. The Israeli defense establishment believed that with its forward strategy it could defend the nation without using women in combat roles. There was no immediate manpower requirement for women in such positions. It was decided to use women in a narrow range of specialized tasks which would free men for combat duty.

During the first years of the state of Israel major demographic changes took place which were to influence the roles for women in the IDF. A large influx of immigrants entered Israel. Between 1948 and 1951 a total of 665,500 immigrants entered the country. This figure exceeded the total population of the country (649,000) at the time of independence. In May 1948 the population consisted of persons largely of European or American heritage. The percentage of immigrants from these areas was 89.6 percent between 1919 and 1948. Only 10 percent of the immigrants during this period came from Asia and North Africa; by January 1, 1952, that percentage had reached 27 percent of the total Jewish population of Israel (1,404,400). In the 1952–1966 period, the number of immigrants from Asia and Africa exceeded those of other areas, and accounted for approximately 43 percent of all the immigrants to Israel since 1919.[42]

Both the size and cultural background of these immigrant groups affected the utilization of women in the IDF after independence. The position of women in Asian and African societies was more visibly inferior to that of men. Thus, the Afro-Asian immigrants would reinforce the traditional concepts toward women's military roles. Furthermore, most of these newcomers required education and help in becoming integrated into Israeli society. Filling this need became important to the nation-building function of the IDF. "Service in CHEN gives the women spiritual and moral assets which find their expression in good citizenship, the awareness of a mission, and a feeling of identification with the State of Israel."[43]

Not only were new immigrant conscripts educated during their service in the IDF, but an important role for some women in the IDF became that of teaching recent civilian immigrants to Israel. One of the three major functions of CHEN is: "Combining security duties with educational activities—by spreading educational and cultural values, particularly among new immigrants and in outlying settlements."[44]

Thus with the establishment of the state, traditional rather than egalitarian values prevailed with regard to women's military roles. There were many differences between male and female military services. In order to preserve national unity many concessions were made. In 1953 the government passed a compromise national service law which exempted married women, mothers, pregnant women, and women who observed Christian or Muslim religious practices. In addition, those claiming religious objections to military service could obtain exemption by proving their religious convictions to a board of rabbis or accepting an alternative, nonmilitary form of national service. In addition to reiterating these exemptions, the Defense Service Act of 1959 declared a shorter period of military service for women than for men, different training periods, and different roles. In spite of these exemptions for and concessions to women, the ultra-Orthodox parties (Agudat Israel and Poeley Agudat Israel) continued to voice their objection to women in military service.

Along with the general societal resistance to a non-traditional military role for women, another important factor in the determination of women's noncombatant status was the morale of the male soldier. The Jewish male is raised to be extremely protective of women, and the prospect of a woman being wounded or taken prisoner by the Arabs is believed by the military leadership to be a grave threat to efficient male performance in battle. In fact, when rumor spread during the October War that a female soldier had been captured and raped, it was necessary for the mass media to reassure the public and military personnel that this was not the case.[45] Colonel Dalia Raz, Commander of the Israeli Women's Corps, stated that Israeli society would not tolerate the idea of women being taken prisoners of war, especially after the tragic experiences which had occurred in previous years.[46]

One function of women in the military is to provide a humanizing influence. The family is a very important institution in Israeli life, and, in some ways, women's function in the Israeli military is analogous to their function in the family. This was evident in the Palmach during the War of Independence. After women were removed from combat duties, one woman stayed with each unit to nurse, cook, and sew.[47] Because the family is of primary importance in Israel, women are expected to marry and have children. A commander of the CHEN has said, "We never disregard the fact that the girls here are going to be married and become mothers. We don't want to impair their femininity in any way."[48] Furthermore, Landrum observes that women in the IDF enjoy being protected and do not want to compete with men.[49]

Thus, a complex set of factors underlies the differences between the conscription and service of men and women. According to Dickerson, the IDF only conscripts the number of women it needs to meet its manpower requirements. When possible, only women with high school degrees are conscripted; however, if more are needed, those with less education are drafted. As a result of the different basis upon which women are drafted, only approximately 50 percent to 60 percent of the females see military service compared to 95 percent of eighteen-year-old males. Length of service is also different for men and women. From 1949 until 1963 men aged eighteen to twenty-six were conscripted for only thirty months. Unmarried women aged eighteen to twenty-six were conscripted for only twenty-four months. In December 1963, because of an increase in the numbers of men and women in the age goups conscripted, the period of service for both men and women was reduced by four months. In November 1966 men were again required to serve for thirty months; however, women's service was not increased at that time.[50] Since 1974 women have served for two years. Women's reserve obligations also differ. While men are in the reserves until the age of forty-nine, only unmarried women are required to be in the reserves and only until they marry and/or become mothers. Women receive less training than men. The men receive several months while women are given only three and one-half weeks. Those who volunteer to do their service in the Nahal (Fighting Pioneer Youth Corps who live on and develop defensive agricultural settlements) receive eight weeks of training.

According to Landrum, the training given by the CHEN to female conscripts is "basically a transition from freer civilian life to that of the more disciplined military way. The women have no field exercises nor any night training. They do take a short hike, but more for physical fitness than for meeting any requirements. Their use of weapons is at a bare minimum, and the emphasis is put on familiarity rather than use."[51]

The Israeli attitude toward the utilization of women as combatants is dramatized by the fact that women in the IDF, although given some training with weapons, are not expected to use them. The training they receive is limited and is a form of morale building to make them look and feel like soldiers. Landrum concludes that women's arms training serves to familiarize women soldiers with the weapons in the event that those living in isolated areas need to defend themselves or their families. This is an extension of the type of training that women had received in the Hagana. Even though the women of the Nahal carry small arms as a part of their uniform, they are sent to the bunkers in the event of an attack. Tiger, visiting a Nahal unit, commented:

It is pointless for women to try to shoot their weapons; they were too heavy for them and of relatively poor quality, being old Czech rifles, regarded as weapons of last resort. The Commander agreed that the women's activities with weapons were purely symbolic; they were good for their morale and offered them a sense of participation in Nahal's most serious function, the military.[52]

Women are given practice with weapons only once a month. The day Tiger visited, he reported a derisive attitude on the part of men, as well as some women, toward the women's weapons practice taking place at the time. The IDF has been unwilling to give more training to women because most women will marry and have children, thereby becoming ineligible for the reserves. In wartime, they cannot be called up. Thus, the IDF does not believe it will get sufficient return on the money invested in training.

The first decades of the use of women in the IDF were thus a period of no advancement in their egalitarian utilization. Their use in strictly noncombat endeavors was firmly entrenched in response to the conservative attitudes of the men and women in Israeli society—a society whose demographic characteristics had changed dramatically in the two decades following the attainment of statehood and whose attitudes were respected by politically astute, elected officials. As the next section will show, even though elected officials had to be sensitive to the electorate when considering roles for women in the military, manpower needs could force a measure of expansion in women's roles which had not yet been attained in the IDF.

## The Expansion of Women's Roles in the Israeli Defense Forces, 1967–1979

In spite of the official policy to place women only in noncombatant jobs, women had never been totally removed from direct combat support roles. During the Sinai War of 1956 and the Six Day War of 1967, some women served as pilots in reconnaissance squadrons and at least one woman dropped paratroops over the Mitla Pass in Sinai.[53] During these wars, some women served in communications and as nurses, roles which brought a few onto the front line. Brigadier General S. L. A. Marshall's field notes in 1956 record that a woman signaler whose radio had been knocked out went in person while under fire to instruct the tanks to charge.[54] In the October war of 1973 at least three women were killed and many others injured.[55] One radio operator was killed by Syrian attack and two were killed by enemy fire in Sinai. Women in Israel, while assigned to noncombatant roles, do sometimes come under fire during hostilities because of their proximity to the front line, a line that has been increasingly difficult to distinguish in Israel's wars. These women were at the front as exceptions. They were not, according to official policy, supposed to be there.

The official definition of women's roles as ones of "indirect reinforcement of the IDF's combat forces" became increasingly ambiguous in the 1970s as the military leadership opened some nontraditional jobs to women. After the 1967 war, when Israel's borders were expanded to include a large hostile population and the manpower pool was not large enough to meet the need for men to fulfill additional military duties, the Israeli military leadership chose to extend the range of assignments open to women. This expansion of roles constituted a major change in assignment policy from the nation-building roles to which most women had previously been restricted. Women were once again in military roles after some two decades of largely administrative and teaching functions. Following the 1973 war, when, to meet manpower shortages, recruitment was increased to include even handicapped men heretofore exempted, women were utilized in a wider variety of jobs.

In 1977, in order to free additional men for combat assignments and to some extent in response to pressure from civilian women's groups, eighteen new nontraditional specialties were opened to women. Among these were weapons technician, fighter aircraft mechanic, communications repairman, radar and telecommunications operator (aboard missile boats), artillery reconnaissance, and combat arms instructor in the infantry, artillery, and armor schools. As reported by the press, women were allowed to serve for the first time as officers on warships. Most, however, were reportedly assigned to naval bases.[56] Women have also been admitted to the Intelligence Corps as intelligence officers. Women in these jobs could come under fire in the event of war. These jobs are clearly ones of direct combat support. But since women are removed from the front line during war, the IDF is able to continue to define women's service as "indirect reinforcement of the IDF's combat forces."

In 1977 women were also allowed to train as pilots, but the program was discontinued after a short time. Since the IDF trains only fighter pilots and women were not allowed to be combatants, their expensive training could be used only to fly cargo planes.[57] Until 1956 women were used as noncombatant pilots for troop transport, but this practice was stopped because their training was considered too expensive for the

length of service which they gave. Today women selecting the nontraditional jobs are required to serve at least an additional year in order to
make their training cost effective; in 1979 the IDF considered filling 15
percent of these jobs with women.[58] In the Israeli Air Force, 45 percent
of the military jobs have recently been opened to women. Female attrition in these jobs has, however, been higher than expected. 16 percent
of the jobs are reserved for men only and 6 percent for women only.[59]
There are no official data released indicating the numbers of women
actually in these jobs.

Currently, women in Israel are permitted to serve in Category I
combat units (units which actively engage the enemy in combat) but in
noncombatant roles only, e.g., administrative or technical specialties.
Women are not involuntarily assigned to these units. They must volunteer. If the unit engages in combat, the women are to be evacuated. This
policy causes difficulties for the IDF because they must find replacements
for these women. Furthermore, women with children do not serve in the
reserves, and most women marry and become mothers. Thus it is incon-
sistent to put women in combat support roles—to meet manpower shortages—when they cannot be mobilized with their units into the front line
during wartime, the period in which they are most needed and for which
they are trained. Despite the persistence of this indirect combat support
ideology, women's roles since 1967 have become increasingly military in
character and increasingly important to the functioning of the IDF.
There has been no alternative for the Israeli military other than to
expand women's roles to meet manpower shortages. Therefore, despite
the contradictions implied, they have chosen this policy.

Now two opposing forces affecting women's military service are at
work. On one side the mobilization manpower requirements are impell-
ing the Israeli military leadership to extend the range of assignments
open to women. The high level of mobilization after the 1973 war has
increased the manpower requirements of the IDF, but the manpower
pool from which to conscript has declined. On the other side, Menachim
Begin's party, the Likud, required the votes in the Knesset of the religious political parties which are opposed to military service for women.
The result is a contradiction of national proportions. Although there are
valid military requirements for more women to fill a broader range of
assignments, the ruling coalition passed a new religious exemption law in
July 1978, making it even easier for women to be exempt from military
service. All that a woman needs to do to avoid military service is to attest
before a judge that her religion precludes such service and sign affidavits
stating that she observes Jewish dietary laws and does not travel on the

Sabbath. The procedures and regulations operate so that women are underutilized for any type of military assignment. The religious exemption has become so easy that military service for women could become, in effect, voluntary despite the operation of the universal conscription law. However, according to an Israeli official, since the passage of the exemption law in 1978, the loss of women conscripts for religious reasons has been limited because the conscription law has been strictly enforced. Also, such measures as permitting pregnant women to remain on active duty and lowering the entrance standards have been taken to try to prevent additional loss of women available to the military.[60]

On the other hand, the Committee on the Status of Women, an official fact-finding commission, has suggested that the interest of more women would be sparked if there were a greater variety of jobs available to them. The commission recommended that women be involved in every military function short of active combat. However, only 210 of the 700 military jobs in the IDF have been opened to women. Of the women conscripted, 50 percent to 60 percent are still in secretarial and clerical jobs. The fact is that most women's attitudes reflect the culturally conservative elements of the country. The conservative attitude of Israeli society toward women's roles can be seen from a recent survey. In 1976 Bar-Yosef reported her large-scale survey of seventeen-year-old girls. She found that the largest proportion (68.8 percent) ranked motherhood first as very important. The second highest proportion (68.4 percent) chose wife as a very important role. Only 3.2 percent chose public activity as very important, and 13.9 percent chose voluntary action as very important.[61]

Insofar as women actually performing in combat roles is concerned, it has been noted that the small group of women seeking combat roles for females is not supported by the majority of women. Clearly the small but vocal group pushing expanded combat roles for women receives little support from women soldiers themselves.[62]

Women will serve only in jobs which would not involve them directly in fighting if hostilities begin. By regulation, those who are in combat units will be evacuated in the event of war. No pressing military need for women to serve in combat roles in the IDF is acknowledged in the 1980s. Nor is there a great demand on the part of women to do so. An unusual interplay of social forces has rendered a noncombatant status for women vital to making conscription acceptable to the public and allowing religious exemptions vital to making the expansion of women's roles in the IDF possible.

As nontraditional jobs open up to them in the 1970s, women are moving into direct combat support roles which *could* put them in the battlefield during war. The official definition of women's roles as "indirect combat reinforcement" no longer accurately defines many of these jobs, though it helps to perpetuate a stereotype accepted by traditionalist elements in Israeli society in general.

In short, the decade of the 1970s saw a curious balancing act take place in Israeli defense manpower policy. National security needs were balanced against sociopolitical pressures to achieve a compromise. Women now are assigned to support tasks which, by regulation, they will have to evacuate in case of war. What will actually happen is problematic. On balance, the new policy is the most significant substantive egalitarian advance for women in the IDF since its inception.

## Summary and Conclusion

The utilization of women in the paramilitary and military organizations in the Jewish community from its prestatehood period to the present time reflects varying degrees of divergence from the country's traditional social values which are influenced by their conservative religious foundations. This divergence, sparked both by the secular, egalitarian ideology of Zionism and by manpower requirements, has at times extended so far as to permit some female members of a clandestine paramilitary self-defense militia to be armed and trained for emergency self-defense. However, it was not expected that women in these assault units would be mobilized.

It was circumstance alone that caused women to be in combat. They fought in the War of Independence because of an emergency situation in which survival was the overshadowing objective. These women can best be characterized in nonmilitary terms as "fighting pioneers" with semimilitary status in semimilitary organizations—the Hagana, the Irgun, and the Stern Gang. Furthermore, they were a minority of the female members of these groups. Even at the critical time of the War of Independence, most women were given the support jobs that women have traditionally filled—communications, nursing, and domestic duties. Although often serving under fire, most women were not in direct (offensive) combat operations. What is more, after the immediate military emergency was over in spring 1948, women were removed from the combat units. At the time of statehood, when the military organization became professionalized and formalized as the Israel Defense Forces, women's roles were clearly defined as noncombatant ones and reverted to those dictated by the dominant social traditions of the country. Thus, while many individual women performed valiantly in combat, Israeli women have not played an historically unique role that reflects sexual equality in the course of defending their settlements and their country during the prestatehood period, the War of Independence, or the poststatehood period.[63] They have consistently been valued in the irregular military units and in the IDF for releasing men for active combat operations and for their feminine, nurturing qualities, their ability to bring a touch of family atmosphere and of charm to the starkness of military life.

The utilization of women in the IDF represents the outcome of policy decisions linked both to domestic Israeli politics and the requirements of national security. There is a complex and delicate sociopolitical balance among the demands of the religious political parties which oppose military service for women, the majority of Israeli society which holds traditional, conservative values with regard to sex role definition, and the unusual military manpower requirements of the IDF. This balance has been strikingly stable since the formation of the IDF in 1948, but in the contemporary period it has become unstable, leading to strain and political fragmentation.

There is conflict between the policies of excluding women from combat and releasing married women and mothers from the reserves and the new practice of opening some technical, nontraditional military jobs in direct combat support fields to women. These jobs require extra training time and are vital during war. Extra men must be trained to replace these women, and there is a shortage of men. In addition, with the nature of modern warfare, persons in the second or third lines can find themselves in combat during war. These strains notwithstanding, we would contend that this programmed expansion of women's roles in the IDF over the last ten years to include direct combat support roles constitutes more substantive, egalitarian achievement than was demonstrated by those women who participated on a one time basis in combat under the duress of external threat.

This study confirms observations that advanced industrial democratic nations are gradually expanding the role of women in the military.[64] It is true that the uniqueness of Israeli history coupled with the lack of any systematic survey data or performance analysis of mixed-sex units during combat periods makes it impossible to predict from the Israeli experience in the War of Independence how U.S. women would perform in mixed-sex combat units.

In a more general vein, the investigation of women in combat in Israel suggests a working hypothesis which can be used in looking at other nations. It appears that if a military organization in a country with a multi-party system of government must conscript women, or utilize a large number of women volunteers in its armed forces to meet manpower requirements, it will define women's military status as "noncombatant," despite the actual nature of the roles.[65]

## Notes

1. In this paper, combat is defined as the direct use of lethal weapons in opposition to an enemy force. The term "offensive action" is sometimes used to indicate active or direct combat to differentiate it from "defensive action." "Combat support" is defined as activities to aid those engaged in combat that could involve the agent in the line of fire. "Indirect combat support" activities do not involve the agent in the line of fire.

2. Official correspondence from the IDF Spokesman, December 7, 1978, and March 13, 1979.

3. Sara Malchin, "The Woman Worker in Kinneret," *Hapoel Hatzair*, nos. 11–12 (1913) (Malchin was a leader of the women's movement in the Jewish community of Palestine), quoted by Ada Maimon, *Women Build a Land* (New York: Herzl Press, 1962), p. 23. The following four paragraphs are also based on Maimon's book which presents an excellent discussion of the women's movement in this community from 1904 to 1954. Although a chief promoter of the working women's movement there, she presents a view, based on academic research as well as personal experience, of their problems and accomplishments. Chapter XV, "Fighting Women," provides an overview of women's military roles in Israel since 1929 which was especially useful to my research. Maimon immigrated to Palestine in 1912 at the age of 21 (see *Who's Who in Israel*).

4. Maimon, *Women Build a Land*, p. 24.

5. Cited in Lionel Tiger and Joseph Shepher, *Women in the Kibbutz* (New York: Harcourt Brace Jovanovich, 1975), pp. 84–86. See this volume for a full discussion of women's roles in the kibbutz based on the authors' extensive research. See especially Chapter 8, "The Military Service of Women in the Kibbutz," which includes a brief overview of the historical background of women's military roles.

6. Described by Yisrael Shochat, founder of that association, in a memorandum dated December 1912 entitled, "A Proposal for the Defense of the Jewish Community in the Land of Israel," which is included in *Toldot Ha-Haganah* (Ma'arachot, 1954), I, i, pp. 235–36, reproduced in Yigal Allon, *The Making of Israel's Army* (London: Vallentine, Mitchell, 1970), p. 113.

7. *Sepher Hashomer* (Tel Aviv: Dvir Co., 1936), pp. 475–76.

8. Cited in Tiger and Shepher, *Women in the Kibbutz*, p. 184.

9. Maimon, *Women Build a Land*, p. 24. It should be noted that women throughout the prestatehood period "guarded" their settlements. During the mandate period of illegal immigration, they guarded the beaches. During the "Battle of the Roads," at the initiation of the War of Independence, they guarded the convoys. "Guarding" did not mean that women were military personnel. They were, in effect, civilians engaged in home guard duty—civil defense. They primarily performed watch or patrol duties and were often armed.

10. Maimon, *Women Build a Land*, p. 57.

11. Maimon, *Women Build a Land*, p. 60. Italics mine.

12. Yigal Allon, *The Making of Israel's Army*, p. 13.

13. Maimon, *Women Build a Land*, p. 157.

14. Margaret Larkin, *The Hand of Mordechai* (London: Victor Gollancz, 1968), p. 80. This book, a biography of the kibbutz Yad Mordechai, is based on documents and on the author's interviews with fifty-five men and women veterans of the War of Independence who were members of that kibbutz. The author's field work took place during 1959–1960 and provides some insight into the military roles which women played during the War of Independence. Although her research was conducted approximately ten years after that war, during which time many myths could have become established, her account is similar to that provided by other sources, including interviews which I have conducted. An Israeli official whom I interviewed who lived on Yad Mordechai during this period also confirmed the accuracy of her account. See also Lesley Hazleton, *Israeli Women* (New York: Simon and Schuster, 1977), p. 20, for discussion of women's military roles prior to statehood.

15. Tiger and Shepher, *Women in the Kibbutz*, pp. 184–85. Of special use to my research was their documentation of women's roles in the *Hagana* and *Palmach*, citing the works edited by Slutsky, *Sefer Toldot Ha-Haganah* (1972) and Gilad and Meged, *Sefer Ha-Palmach* (1954).

16. Larkin, *The Hand of Mordechai*, p. 79.

17. "The Foundations of the Hagana," (Haganah Archives), drawn up in 1941 and reproduced in Allon, *The Making of Israel's Army*, pp. 117–18, states: "The Hagana is open to all Jews prepared and able to fulfill the duties of national defense. Membership in the Hagana, while both an obligation and a privilege for every Jewish man and woman is based upon the free and voluntary choice of the individual."

18. Maimon, *Women Build a Land*, p. 157.

19. Maimon, *Women Build a Land*, p. 219.

20. Shelford Bidwell, *The Women's Royal Army Corps* (London: Leo Cooper, Ltd., 1977), pp. 96–100.

21. Zeev Schiff, *A History of the Israeli Army (1870–1914)* (San Francisco:

Straight Arrow, 1974), p. 24; Netanel Lorch, *Israel's War of Independence 1947–1949* (Hartford, Conn.: Hartmore House, 1961, 1968), p. 30. While no mention is made by the various sources stating the actual number of women in the Hagana in fall 1947, one estimate is that 15 percent of the fully mobilized group were women. See Harry Sacher, *Israel: the Establishment of a State* (London: Weidenfeld, 1952), p. 271; *Jerusalem Post*, September 25, 1978 (considered by Israeli officials to be a reliable source).

22. Nancy Goldman, ed., *Female Soldiers: Combatants or Noncombatants* (Westport, Conn.: Greenwood, 1982) will include information on the percentage of women in irregular military groups in recent wars.

23. Netanel Lorch, *Israel's War of Independence 1947–1949*, p. 30.

24. Slutsky, 1972, cited in Tiger and Shepher, *Women in the Kibbutz*, pp. 185–86.

25. Both quotations from Yigal Allon, *The Shield of David: The Story of Israel's Armed Forces* (London: Weidenfeld and Nicholson, 1970), pp. 129, 128. In this volume Allon mentions women's roles only on these two pages. Allon served in that unit as a recruit, becoming its commander during the War of Independence.

26. Edward Luttwak and Don Horowitz, *The Israeli Army* (London: Allen Lane, 1975), p. 40. This history of the IDF from 1904 through the October War of 1973 documents women's contributions during this period, including their role in the Palmach, Irgun and Stern Gang. The authors include extensive references to archival sources in Israel.

27. Maimon, *Women Build a Land*, p. 218. Goldman's interview with a commander of an Irgun women's unit substantiated Maimon and the fact that women participated in all activities with men except combat missions.

28. Lorch, *Israel's War of Independence*, p. 35; Karen McKay, "Chen," *Army* (September 1978): 34. McKay's article includes quotations from her interviews with present officers of the Chen as well as with veterans of the War of Independence. These were particularly useful to me.

29. Geula Cohen, who was an anti-British revolutionary member of the Stern Gang, has written of her experience with this group from 1943–48. In her memoirs she described her primary job as a radio operator. She was put in jail for illegally possessing a radio transmitter, four revolvers, and forty-eight rounds of ammunition. She writes that her gun was less a weapon than the radio which she operated. From her memoirs it would seem that her role was that of a radio operator, not that of a combat soldier. Guela Cohen, *Woman of Violence, Memories of a Young Terrorist, 1943–1948* (New York: Holt, Rinehart and Winston, 1966), pp. 191, 120.

30. Allon, *The Making of Israel's Army*, p. 197.

31. Lorch, *The War of Independence*, p. 75.

32. Larkin, *The Hand of Mordechai*, p. 80; Maimon, *Women Build a Land*, p.

222, sums up women's main contribution in Jerusalem: "In those days the women's guard did a great deal for the city. Hundreds of women nursed the wounded in hospitals, feeding those who were incapable of lifting food to their mouths. Women in the Hagana rendered first aid while shells flew over their heads."

33. Allon, *The Making of Israel's Army*, p. 200; Lorch, *The War of Independence*, p. 75; and Dan Kurzman, *Genesis 1948: The First Arab-Israeli War* (New York: World Publishing Co.), pp. 167–68, 384, 97. Although his book is an historical novel, Kurzman states accuracy as his objective and indicates that he has used a wide variety of primary sources including personal interviews with many of those involved in the war. These incidents about which he writes do depict situations referred to in the histories of Allon and Lorch. I believe it is a fairly accurate account.

34. Lorch, *The War of Independence*, p. 59.

35. Sacher, *Israel*, p. 271; Luttwak and Horowitz, *The Israeli Army*, p. 23; Tiger and Shepher, *Women in the Kibbutz*, p. 186; Maimon, *Women Build a Land*, p. 217; Schiff, *A History of the Israeli Army*, p. 121. The latter book, a semiofficial history, includes a chapter, "Women in the Israeli Defense Forces." One section of this chapter, "Fighting Women in History," provides a useful, although brief, overview of the subject.

36. McKay, "Chen," p. 35. It should be noted that covert activities, such as smuggling, are roles for which women have often been utilzied in wartime.

37. As revealed to Anne Bloom (a research psychologist studying women in the IDF) in her interviews and confirmed by Goldman's interviews. Also see McKay, "Chen," p. 39.

38. Lorch, *The War of Independence*, p. 75. The fear of rape by the Arabs was prevalent in the "civilian" as well as in the military sector and was discussed and emphasized in many interviews which I conducted.

39. Lorch, p. 59; Kurzman, *Genesis 1948*, p. 65.

40. Nancy Goldman and Richard Stites, "The Utilization of Women in Combat in the Armed Forces of Great Britain, World War I through 1980." Mimeographed. Chicago, 1980.

41. CHEN is the Hebrew acronym for women's corps. In "*Chen*," *the Women's Corps*, an official pamphlet issued by the IDF spokesman, 1977, underlined and capitalized at the top of the first page is "'*CHEN*' *TRANSLATES* '*CHARM*'."

42. *Statistical Abstract of Israel, 1968*, p. 9. American University, Washington, D.C., *Area Handbook for Israel* (Washington, D.C.: U.S. Government Printing Office, 1970), p. 61.

43. Israel Defense Forces, "The Women's Corps," in *Features of Israel*, published by the IDF (no date), p. 74.

44. *Features of Israel*, p. 72. See also IDF, *Chen*, p. 2.

45. Verna J. Dickerson, "The Role of Women in the Defense Force of Israel," Individual Research Project, U.S. Army War College, 1974 (Alexandria, Va.: Defense Documentation Center), p. 55. This study was one of the first on this subject. It is an excellent study focusing on women in the IDF. The material taken from her interviews with Chen officials was particularly useful here.

46. Col. Dahlia Raz, "The Future of Women in the Armed Services," Report of a seminar given at Royal United Service Institute on June 23, 1977, p. 3.

47. Lorch, *War of Independence*, p. 75.

48. Quoted in Tiger and Shepher, *Women in the Kibbutz*, p. 204.

49. Cecile Landrum, "The Israeli Fighting Women: Myths and Facts," *Air University Review*, (December 1978): 70.

50. Sagan-Aluf Shaul Ramati, "The Israel Defense Forces," *Israel Today*, no. 4 (Tel Aviv: "Israel Digest," December 1966), p. 9.

51. Landrum, "Israeli Fighting Women," p. 71.

52. Tiger and Shepher, *Women in the Kibbutz*, p. 190.

53. Schiff, *History of the Israeli Army*, p. 121. The use of women pilots in 1967 was parallel to that of WASPs by the United States in World War II—they were not even considered to be part of the military.

54. S.L.A. Marshall, "Were Girls in Combat?" *Army-Navy-Air Force Register* 80 (December 20, 1958).

55. Schiff, *History of the Israeli Army*, p. 119.

56. "Women's Lib Wins a War," *To the Point*, June 23, 1978, p. 16. It has been reported to Goldman by an Israeli official that this experiment has not been a success since women have not sought shipboard roles.

57. Landrum, "Israeli Fighting Women," p. 77.

58. Landrum, "Israeli Fighting Women," p. 76.

59. Cecile Landrum, "After Action Report, Trip to Israeli Air Force, Oct. 25–31, 1979," Attachment 3.

60. Ruth Cale, "Women Soldiers and Jewish Orthodoxy," *Baltimore Sun*, July 4, 1978. An Israeli journalist describes this situation and quotes the chief of staff of the Israeli Army: "By not drafting women the precarious manpower situation will deteriorate further." According to an article in *Time* magazine, July 24, 1978, even before the law was passed, there was a 9 percent rise in exemptions and a report by the Defense Ministry predicted that 30 percent of the women due to be drafted in 1978 would claim religious exemptions as compared with the previous average of about 18 percent.

61. Hazleton, *Israeli Women*, p. 169.

62. Landrum, "The Israeli Fighting Women," p. 70; McKay, "Chen," p. 36; Dickerson, "The Role of Women in the Defense Force of Israel," p. 13; Schiff, *History of the Israeli Army*, p. 122.

63. The military roles played by Israeli women, especially during the War of Independence, are in many respects parallel to those filled by women on the American frontier and during the American Revolution. See Linda Grant DePauw, "Women in the American Revolution," *Armed Forces and Society* (Winter 1981).

64. See Nancy Goldman, "The Utilization of Women in the Armed Forces of Industrialized Nations," *Sociological Symposium* (Spring 1977). Also Goldman and Stites, "The Utilization of Women in Combat."

65. During World War II, the government of Great Britain insisted on defining as noncombatant the roles of women in anti-aircraft units, although these women served in mixed-sex units and did everything except fire the guns (Goldman and Stites, "The Utilization of Women in Combat"). Several thousand American women soldiers received combat pay during the Vietnam War, and today in Korea, U.S. women soldiers are stationed within two miles of the DMZ. Although their jobs are noncombat ones, a war between North and South Korea would almost certainly involve them in combat.

# Bibliography
## Scholarly Writings of Morris Janowitz on Armed Forces and Society

prepared by MICHEL L. MARTIN

The present bibliography is certainly not exhaustive. It excludes book reviews, articles published in the popular and non-scientific press, and most unpublished papers. Moreover, this list presents only the original publications—reprints and republications being somewhat numerous—and ignores translations into other languages. This being said, the following collection, which is arranged chronologically, is thought to be fairly representative of Morris Janowitz's contributions to the field of military studies.

"Trends in Wehrmacht Morale," with M. I. Gurfein, *Political Opinion Quarterly* 10 (Spring 1946): 78–84.

"Cohesion and Disintegration in the Wehrmacht in World War II," with Edward Shils, *Political Opinion Quarterly* 12 (Summer 1948): 280–315.

*The Dynamics of Prejudice: A Psychological and Sociological Study of Veterans.* With Bruno Bettleheim. New York: Harper and Row, 1950.

"The Professional Soldier and Political Power" Mimeographed, University of Michigan, Institute of Public Administration, 1953.

"Military Elites and the Study of War," *Journal of Conflict Resolution* 1 (March 1957): 9–18.

"Soldier, Scholars, Liberals," *The Antioch Review* 17 (September 1957): 394–400.

Editor, *A Psychological Warfare Casebook.* With W. E. Daugherty. Baltimore: Johns Hopkins University Press, 1958.

"Changing Patterns of Organizational Authority: The Military Establishment," *Administrative Science Quarterly* 3 (March 1959): 474–79.

*Sociology and the Military Establishment.* New York: Russell Sage Foundation, 1959; revised edition, with Roger W. Little, 1965; third edition, Sage Publications, 1974.

"The Ineffective Soldier: A Review Article," *Administrative Science Quarterly* 5 (September 1960): 296–303.

*The Professional Soldier: A Social and Political Portrait.* New York: Free Press, 1960; expanded edition, 1971; third edition, 1975.

*A Study of the Military Retired Pay System and Certain Related Subjects: A Report to the Committee on Armed Services* (U.S. Senate). Washington, D.C.: Government Printing Office, 1961.

"Military Organization and Disorganization," in *Contemporary Social Problems,* edited by R. K. Merton and R. A. Nisbet, pp. 515–52. New York: Harcourt, Brace and World, 1961.

"The Military in American Society," *Items* (December 1963): 45–47.

"The Military in the Political Development of New Nations," *Bulletin of Atomic Scientists* 20 (1964): 6–10.

*The Military in the Political Development of New Nations.* Chicago: University of Chicago Press, 1964.

"Organizing Multiple Goals: War Making and Arms Control," in *The New Military: Changing Patterns of Organization,* edited by Morris Janowitz, pp. 11–31. New York: Russell Sage Foundation, 1964.

Editor, *The New Military: Changing Patterns of Organization.* New York: Russell Sage Foundation, 1964; W. W. Norton, 1969.

"Armed Forces in Western Europe: Uniformity and Diversity," *Archives européennes de Sociologie* 6 (1965): 225–37.

"The Logic of National Service," in *The Draft: A Handbook of Facts and Alternatives,* edited by S. Tax, pp. 73–90. Chicago: University of Chicago Press, 1967.

"American Democracy and Military Service," *Transaction* 4 (March 1967): 5–11 and 57–59.

"Armed Forces and Society: A World Perspective," in *Armed Forces and Society: Sociological Essays*, edited by J. A. A. van Doorn, pp. 15–38. The Hague: Mouton, 1968.

"International Perspective on Militarism," *The American Sociologist* 4 (February 1968): 12–16.

Introduction to *Communist Soldiers in the Korean Conflict: Mass Behavior in Battle and Captivity* by William C. Bradburn. Chicago: University of Chicago Press, 1968.

*Social Control of Escalated Riots.* Chicago: University of Chicago Press, 1968.

"Sociological Research on Arms Control," *The American Sociologist* 6 (June 1971): 23–30.

"The Evolution of Civilian Surveillance by the Armed Forces," *The American Sociologist* 6 (August 1971): 254–56.

"Youth and National Service," Introduction as guest editor to the special issue on national service options of *Teachers College, Record* 73 (September 1971).

"National Service: A Third Alternative?" *Teachers College, Record* 73 (September 1971): 13–25.

Introduction to *El Militar de Carrera en España: Estudio de Sociologia Militar* by Julio Busquets Bragulat. Barcelona: Ediciones Ariel, 1971.

"Basic Education and Youth Socialization in the Armed Forces," in *Handbook of Military Institutions*, edited by Roger W. Little, pp. 167–210. Beverly Hills: Sage Publications, 1971.

"Military Organization," in *Handbook of Military Institutions*, edited by Roger W. Little, pp. 13–52. Beverly Hills: Sage Publications, 1971.

"The Emergent Military," in *Public Opinion and the Military Establishment*, edited by Charles C. Moskos, pp. 255–70. Beverly Hills: Sage Publications, 1971.

Editor, *On Military Ideology*. With Jacques van Doorn. Rotterdam: Erasmus University Press, 1971.

Editor, *On Military Intervention*. With Jacques van Doorn. Rotterdam: Erasmus University Press, 1971.

"Comparative Analysis of Middle Eastern Military Institutions," in *On Military Intervention*, edited by Morris Janowitz and Jacques van Doorn, pp. 301–34. Rotterdam: Erasmus University Press, 1971.

"The Volunteer Armed Forces and Military Purpose," *Foreign Affairs* 50 (April 1972): 428–43.

"Toward an All-Volunteer Military," *Public Interest* 27 (Spring 1972): 104–17.

"Strategic Dimensions of an All-Volunteer Force," in *The Industrial Military Complex: A Reassessment*, edited by Sam Sarkesian, pp. 127–66. Beverly Hills: Sage Publications, 1972.

"The U.S. Forces and the Zero Draft," *Adelphi Papers* 94 (January 1973).

"Toward a Redefinition of Military Strategy in International Relations," *World Politics* 26 (July 1974): 473–508.

"Racial Composition in the All-Volunteer Force: Policy Alternatives," with Charles C. Moskos, *Armed Forces and Society* 1 (Fall 1974): 109–23.

"Stabilizing Military Systems: An Emerging Strategic Concept," *Military Review* 55 (June 1975): 3–10.

"The All-Volunteer Force as a Socio-Political Problem," *Social Problems* 23 (October 1975): 433–49.

Foreword to *L'Armée et la société en Afrique: essai de synthèse et d'investigation bibliographique* by Michel L. Martin. Bordeaux: Centre d'Etude d'Afrique noire, 1975.

*Military Conflict: Essays in the Institutional Analysis of War and Peace.* Beverly Hills: Sage Publications, 1975.

"Military Institutions and Citizenship in Western Societies," in *The Military and the Problem of Legitimacy*, edited by Gwyn Harries-Jenkins and Jacques van Doorn, pp. 77–92. Beverly Hills: Sage Publications, 1975.

Comment, with Charles C. Moskos, to "Race and the All-Volunteer System: A Reply to Janowitz and Moskos," *Armed Forces and Society* 2 (Spring 1976): 433–34.

Foreword to *Le système militaire des Etats-Unis: bilan et perspectives*, edited L. Mandeville. Paris: Editions Delarge, 1976.

"From Institutional to Occupational: The Need for Conceptual Continuity," *Armed Forces and Society* 4 (Fall 1977): 51–54.

"Beyond Deterrence: Alternative Conceptual Dimensions," in *The Limits of Military Intervention*, edited by Ellen P. Stern, pp. 369–89. Beverly Hills: Sage Publications, 1977.

"The Limits of Military Intervention: A Propositional Inventory," with Ellen P. Stern, *Military Review* 58 (March 1978): 11–21.

Foreword to *The Changing World of the American Military*, edited by Franklin D. Margiotta. Boulder: Westview Press, 1978.

"Military Participation and Total War," in *The Last Half-Century: Societal Change and Politics in America*, pp. 164–217. Chicago: University of Chicago Press, 1978.

Foreword to *World Armies* by John Keegan. New York: Facts on File, Inc., 1979.

Foreword to "Civil-Military Relations in the Federal Republic of Germany," edited by Ralf Zoll. *Armed Forces and Society* 5 (Summer 1979). Special issue.

"The Citizen-Soldier and National Service," *Air University Review* 31 (November–December 1979): 2–16.

"Five Years of the All-Volunteer Force: 1973–1978," with Charles C. Moskos *Armed Forces and Society* 5 (Winter 1979): 171–218.

"On the Current State of the Sociology of the Military Institution," *Sozialwissenschaftliches Institut der Bundeswehr Berichte* 17 (1979): 9–25.

"Les conditions de la survie d'Israel," in *Annuaire de l'Afrique et du Moyen-Orient: les armées et la défense*, edited by Michel L. Martin, pp. 101–106. Paris: Editions Jeune Afrique, 1980.

Foreword to *Warriors to Managers: The French Military Establishment since 1945* by Michel L. Martin. Chapel Hill: University of North Carolina Press, 1981.

Editor, *Civil-Military Relations: Regional Perspectives*. Beverly Hills: Sage Publications, 1981.

"Patriotism and the U.S. All-Volunteer Military," *Air University Review* 33 (January–February 1982): 31–39.

Foreword to "Defense and Military Institutions in Contemporary France," edited by Michel L. Martin. *Armed Forces and Society* 8 (Winter 1982). Special issue.

"Consequences of Social Science Research on the U.S. Military," *Armed Forces and Society* 8 (Summer 1982): 507–24.

Editor, *The Political Education of Soldiers*. Beverly Hills: Sage Publications, 1983.

"Civil Consciousness and Military Performance," in *The Political Education of Soldiers*, edited by Morris Janowitz. Beverly Hills: Sage Publications, 1983.

*The Reconstruction of Patriotism: Education for Civic Consciousness*. Chicago: University of Chicago Press, 1983.

# Index